TRICKS OF THE LIGHT

TRICKS OF THE LIGHT

ESSAYS ON ART AND SPECTACLE

Jonathan Crary

ZONE BOOKS · NEW YORK

2023

ZONE BOOKS
633 Vanderbilt Street
Brooklyn, NY 11218

Printed in the United States of America.

Distributed by Princeton University Press,
Princeton, New Jersey, and Woodstock, United Kingdom

Library of Congress Cataloging-in-Publication Data
Names: Crary, Jonathan, author.
Title: Tricks of the light : essays on art and spectacle / Jonathan Crary.
Description: New York : Zone Books, 2023. | Includes bibliographical references and index. | Summary: "This book features essays on modern and contemporary art and media systems" —Provided by publisher.
Identifiers: LCCN 2022053767 (print) | LCCN 2022053768 (ebook) | ISBN 9781942130857 (hardcover) | ISBN 9781942130864 (ebook)
Subjects: LCSH: Arts and society—History—20th century. | Arts and society—History—21st century.
Classification: LCC NX180.S6 C72 2023 (print) | LCC NX180.S6 (ebook) | DDC 709.04—dc23/eng/20230324
LC record available at https://lccn.loc.gov/2022053767
LC ebook record available at https://lccn.loc.gov/2022053768

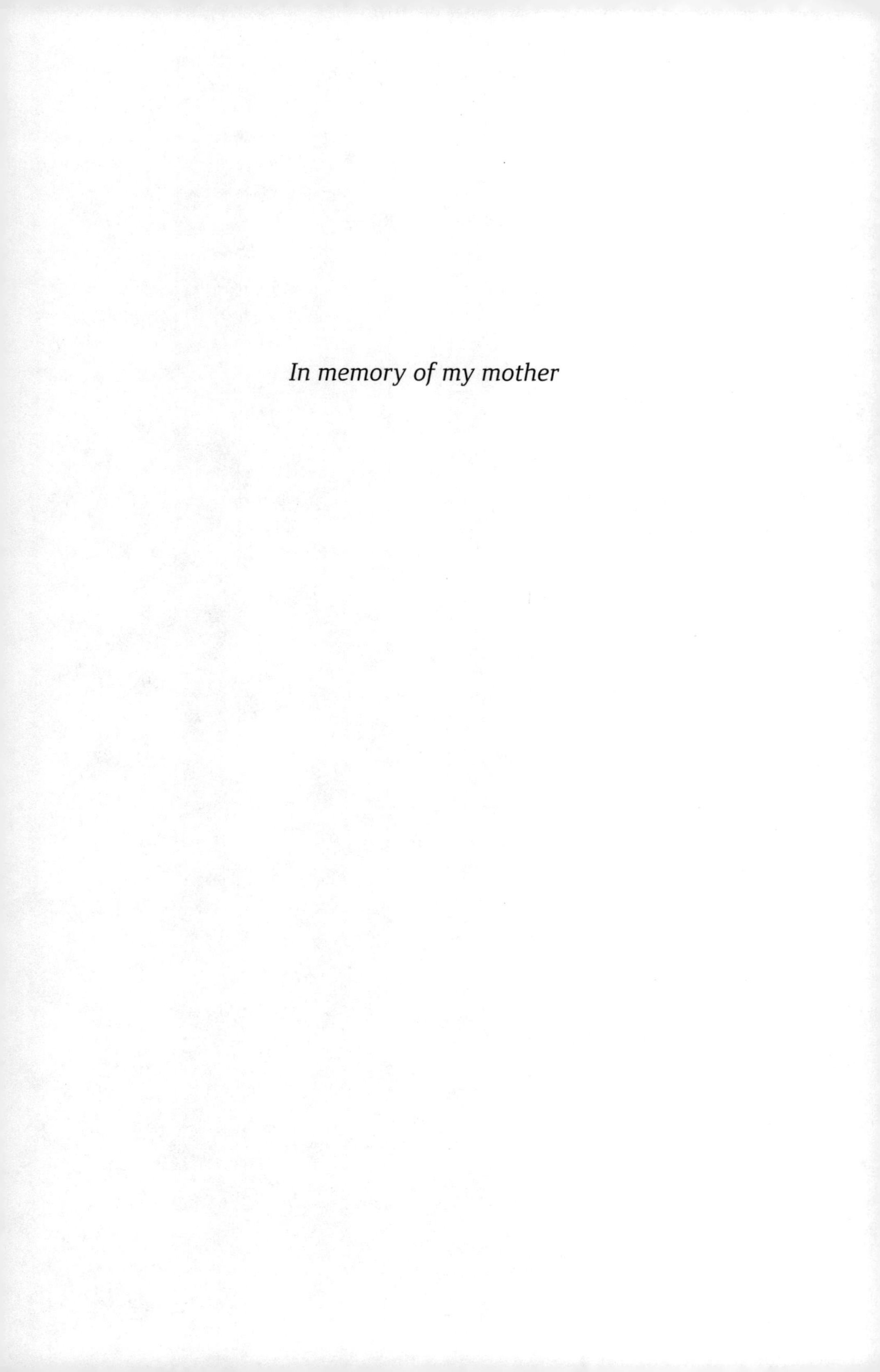

In memory of my mother

CONTENTS

Preface

In this volume I have brought together a selection of twenty-five essays to supplement my book-length publications on nineteenth-century visual culture and on late capitalism and technology. Written over several decades, these reflections and speculative analyses mark out a path through many of the themes and objects that have nourished and shaped my thinking. I've included several expansive texts on questions of spectacle, mass culture, and the modernization of perception. In them I examine reconfigurations of twentieth-century media systems for the management of attention, the imposition of social separation, and the maintenance of political docility. Interspersed with these are a larger number of more focused studies on individual artists, writers, and filmmakers. Their works are intertwined with the historical developments discussed in the former but pose divergent or dissonant models of shared experience and visuality. My title, *Tricks of the Light*, is at least partly a shorthand for all the "techniques of the observer" that have tethered us to a reified world of increasingly dematerialized commodities. But it also stands for the visionary projects of artists that challenge or elude the many phantasmagoric spheres of engineered appearances.

At least five of the essays here directly address the cultural and political problem of television and its obdurate, mutating persistence in the screencentric world of the digital twenty-first century. My discussions of Lang, Cronenberg, Godard, Kubrick, Bender, Virilio, and Kentridge explore a range of overlapping issues, often related to the omnipresence of the televisual image. At the same time, I have included texts on artists who have crafted disparate modes of visuality that bypass the sensory monotony of electroluminescence. Riley, Evans, Irwin, Barth, and Flavin all stake out their own counterpractices of chromaticism, opticality and luminosity that disrupt the habituation and commodification of looking. Another group of essays looks at work by Ruscha, Antin, Ballard, Koolhaas, Fend, and Oppenheim that engages the derealization and dereliction of urban space or that undertakes political and aesthetic interventions on physical territories.

In spite of the threads of coherence I've retrospectively noted here, these essays are, in many cases, the result of fortuitous occasions and unplanned encounters. My own intellectual interests and inclinations repeatedly were enlarged or reoriented in response to innovative artwork, new friendships, and unfamiliar environments. The book's contents are also traces of my meandering passage through an estranging time of political and social transformations whose catastrophic consequences now surround us.

Allan Kaprow's "Activities"

Looking back on the early Happenings, Allan Kaprow has expressed dissatisfaction with a notable feature of those works: the presence of an audience. Although there was often audience involvement in them, a conventional theatrical division still prevailed between performer and nonperformer. From the early 1960s on, he sought to phase out the audience altogether and to achieve a more complete integration of his performances with the environment in which they were done. Beginning with the Happenings, his work was part of a movement that attempted to transform fundamentally the conditions under which art was experienced. He chose to characterize the new work as "intermedia" instead of multimedia, suggesting an art that hovered outside of previously defined boundaries and that fluctuated between art and the world. In both his writing and his art activity Kaprow has consistently explored the perimeters that delimit art from life. His position has never been anti-art, but it has become increasingly disengaged from an exclusively art-oriented framework. Psychology, sociology, and philosophy are no less important to him than art and aesthetics. But he does not consider these to be separate disciplines, and his recent work is often an interpenetration of them all.

In the mid-1960s Kaprow began to tone down the scale of his Happenings in terms of the number of participants and the scope of his imagery. By 1967 his work had assumed a distinctly new form, and he used the word "Happening" less frequently to describe his activity. He became preoccupied with the problem of work as a collective social endeavor, and his performances from 1967 to 1971 consisted of groups of people engaged in various kinds of physical labor. He called them "Work Routines." In particular, he was interested in the area of overlap between work and play, and, whether it was building a road or erecting a wall, he questioned and blurred the differences between labor and recreation. By concentrating on the organizational aspects of his Routines, coordinating the operation of a social unit, he hoped to transform the teamwork required for work into a teamwork of play. Efficiency was discarded as a goal of organization, and real work became quasi-work. Also, the contingent and nonutilitarian nature of the tasks performed was important (e.g., a brick wall joined together with bread and jam instead of cement). The Routines seemed to contain a key transgression of the opposition of those primordial categories, work and play—work representing the stable order of socialized existence and play as something disruptive of that order, which, from earliest times, was generally limited to carnival and feast days and later to holidays. Kaprow's current practice suggests that, in an increasingly technological society, this opposition has lost much of its force and that our conception of leisure time should be radically reevaluated.

Around 1971 another shift in his work became evident. He began to focus on relationships between individuals instead of on people functioning together as units. It was a turn from the observation of large group movement to smaller and more interiorized studies. (It can be assumed that this reorientation corresponded to the general social quietism that emerged in the wake of the 1960s.) Since 1971 Kaprow has done between thirty and forty related performances. The core of each piece is his set of written directions (or script). The procedure for executing the works begins with a gathering of a preselected group of people, usually a day before the actual performance, in order to distribute the directions and possibly explain them. The next day the participants split up into groups of two, occasionally three, which each perform the same script. In conclusion the whole group reassembles to discuss the event and individual experiences. This three-part structure is common to all the individual pieces.

Kaprow calls them "Activities" to distinguish them qualitatively from Happenings. Intrinsic to his conception of them are the absence of an audience of any kind, that it is carried out in a physical environment without art world or institutional associations, and that there be no documentation of the event. Each Activity has been performed only once, although there

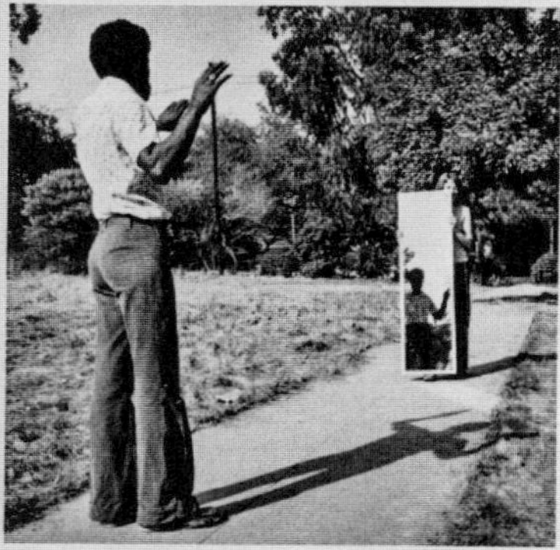

1

standing somewhere
facing a friend holding a large mirror

trying to catch one's reflection

signalling to tilt the mirror variously
until the reflection is caught

both moving apart a few steps
repeating process

moving apart again and again
repeating process
until it's no longer possible
to see oneself

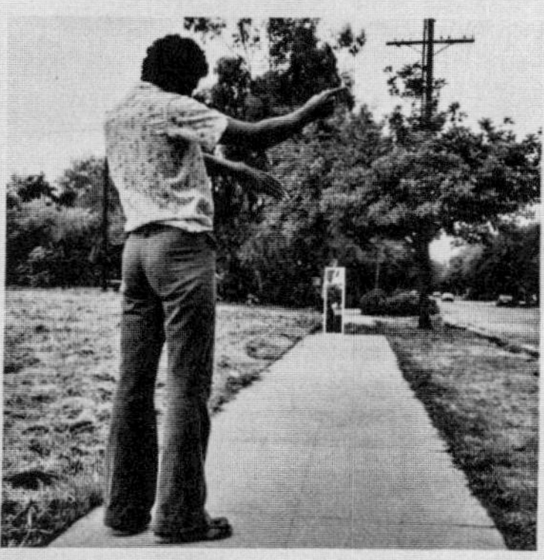

Allan Kaprow, *Routine*, 1973, activity book.

is no major reason why they couldn't or shouldn't be repeated. The scripts of many of the Activities have been released in book form with accompanying photographs of a simulated enactment of the work. He insists that this procedure does not document the piece, that the books illustrate in the manner of an instruction manual. In a recent article Kaprow expressed wariness about the documentation of performance art in general.[1] He believes that photographs and texts in a gallery shift the focus from the original event to themselves, thereby undermining the essential priority of the performance. His books, however, do not seem to completely avoid this "artification" of the work.

One of the earlier Activities was called *Time Pieces*. Participants were equipped with cassette recorders and divided into pairs. They were directed by the script to follow an intricate pattern of taping themselves counting aloud the rates of their breathing and pulse, first of one's own body and then that of the other. It also involved the physical exchange of breath, from mouth to mouth and by means of a plastic bag. As a body-consciousness piece, it seems relatively straightforward, but Kaprow made the intersubjectivity in the work of primary importance. It concentrated one's attention on bodily processes which are almost always unconscious, yet it did so by mirroring the identical processes in another person. If the work, then, became a meditation on mortality, it was a shared meditation, a kind of communal apprehension of human temporality. It should also be noted that the script of *Time Pieces* can be read as the score of a musical composition, formed in distinct movements, in which the sound of breathing and counting are arranged in an unusual theme and variation.

Another Activity, *Routine* from 1973, was also concerned with how the mechanics of self-perception are lodged in human relationships. Part of this piece involved the use of large mirrors: two people face each other, one holds a mirror, and the other gestures how the mirror should be tilted in order to catch his or her reflection. Each time a reflection is caught the pair moves several steps further apart, and the process continues until it becomes impossible to see oneself in the mirror. This procedure formed one section of five in the piece; the other four also called for some kind of echoing or reflecting of one's words or gestures through the use of mirrors or over the telephone. The work is structured very precisely, with a formal rhyming of its sections, but important elements of the performance are determined by decisions of the participants, such as what words and gestures are to be used and, significantly, how long the Activity is to last.

Kaprow here works with an interplay of verbal and visual imagery which relates back to aspects of his Happenings. For example, he toys with linguistic phenomena of everyday speech (i.e., "he echoed what I had said" or "I saw myself reflected in her") and directs the participants to enact literally this usage. In another Activity, *On Time*, he incorporated ice and boiling water into the work to explore what it means to say that someone is a warm or a cold person. Kaprow does not seem to be advancing any specific theory of language, but he is setting up a context in which the participants can examine what degree of overlap there is between the metaphorical and the propositional meanings of the same statement.

The Activities gradually became more complex, both structurally and psychologically. Scripts were written for three people instead of two, and alternations of roles within them were introduced. *Take-Off*, performed in Genoa in 1974, was important in this development. Units of three people enact the script. It is organized around the transmission of one person's statement that he or she has performed a certain action (such as "I am undressing") along with a request that the recipient of the message, who is in a different location, perform the same action. The communication is affected by an intermediary who documents the action with a Polaroid camera and tape records the statement and request. The go-between is to return to the first person with the same kind of audiovisual evidence to show that the second person has carried out the request. The catch is that the piece has the opportunity for deception built into it. It calls not only for a photograph of the action completed by the first person but also for a staged photograph to simulate a different action that never occurred. The go-between, who is in possession of a "true" photograph and a "false" one, may present only one of them to the third person; that is, he or she may choose whether to corroborate or contradict the taped statement with visual evidence. The third person must decide whether both the others are being truthful, or whether one or both are lying.

The Activity is in three identical parts, allowing the participants to experience each of the three roles, and each time new systems of trust and manipulation develop. In addition to the general problem relating to the "truth" of documentary materials, Kaprow is especially interested in the

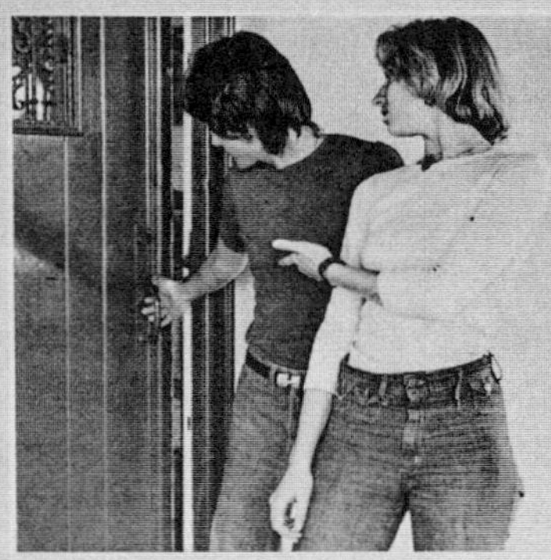

1 A and B
passing backwards
through a doorway
one before the other

the other, saying you're first

passing through again
moving in reverse
the first, saying thank me
being thanked

locating four more doors
repeating routine

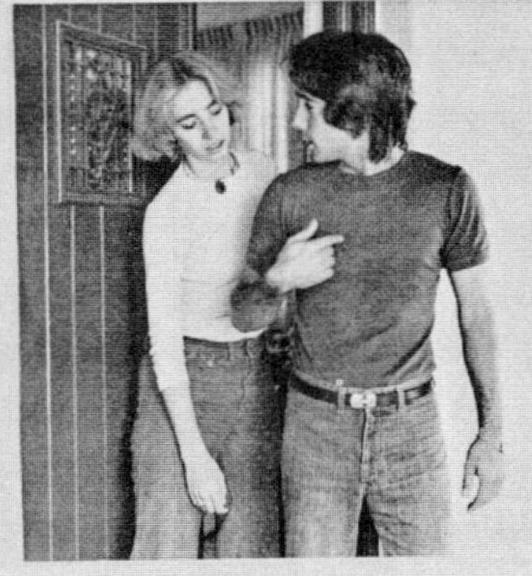

Allan Kaprow, *Maneuvers*, 1976, activity book.

position of the go-between and the degree of confidence he or she wins from the others. Any trust or betrayal that occurs does so according to a logic and necessity distinct from real life. Decisions made by the participants are uniquely arbitrary, emptied of the usual kind of consequences, and the formal patterns of the behavior become discernible. Kaprow writes, "The Take-Off lies in the fact that the whole activity is a grand collusion in which each of the participants knows the scheme from the start and knows that the others know."

Another more complicated Activity was *Satisfaction*, done in April 1976. The core of the script calls for one person to demand specified responses from another, that is, to receive "satisfaction." But in order to be praised, fed, kissed, comforted, he or she must demonstrate to the other person exactly how the satisfaction is to be given. So whatever is received in the way of satisfaction must first be given as a means of describing what is wanted. Once the request is made by means of demonstration, the other person has the option of refusing to comply with it. The piece is further complicated by the entrance of another pair who have also carried out the same preceding routine. The second couple, as a team, proceeds to direct one member of the first pair to "satisfy" (praise, feed, kiss, comfort, etc.) his or her partner, but the second couple must demonstrate between themselves how this is to be accomplished. Again the participants are provided with the option of not complying.

It is difficult to summarize briefly any of Kaprow's recent pieces. The unfolding of the work is dependent on the choices, agreements, and refusals of the performers, and the possible permutations of the scripts are immense. Kaprow once said in an interview that the scripts "don't contain anything; it's what they unleash that interests me.... They contain only the system of a movement which sets off a mechanism, a system to make something happen. They are a potential waiting for what is going to happen, that's all. All the rest is done by the others, by the participants."[2] Kaprow has clearly concentrated on the unpredictable possibilities of his scripts. (The word "script" is an inadequate characterization for they often resemble scores, dance notation, or even poetry.) Some features are rigidly prefixed: groupings and combinations of performers, certain words and exchanges. On the other hand, crucial choices which will govern the development of an individual performance are left to the participants. Duration, in particular, is an area over which he exercises little control. He has been critical of performance art that has been shaped to conform to conventional audience expectations of appropriate length. Some of his Activities are composed so that the obstinacy or enthusiasm of even one participant can extend the work indefinitely. Performance time, for Kaprow, should correspond to our experience of time in real life rather than in the theater. But his concept of duration is also like time in a chess game, whose length is determined by a combination of rules and free choices. The moves which he leaves open to his performers are countered by the moves he has written into his scripts.

Many of the Activities, including *Take-Off* and *Satisfaction*, investigate how various kinds of information are exchanged between individuals. Specific pieces will study single or combinations of sign systems. *Comfort Zones*, performed in Spain in 1975, examined the language of eye contact and territorial space by directing the participants to transgress conventional standards of physical distance and length of eye contact. *Maneuvers*, done this year in Naples, studied, in a kind of parody, the exchange that occurs when two people approach a doorway at the same time and each defers to the other. In a preface to this piece, Kaprow wrote, "Within the forms of polite behavior there is enough room to transmit numbers of complex messages." He is deeply concerned with the semiotic content of ordinary human encounters in which gesture, distance, hesitations become carriers of meaning as much as or more so than spoken language, and how secondary signs are fused onto primary ones to constitute an irreducible complexity of signification.

Kaprow has used the analogy of "research" to describe his work and has indicated that it sometimes comes close to being social-psychology. Certain features of his procedures have the semblance of research: for each performance he is careful to have at least three or four units of people perform the same script so that the different experiences of each group may be compared. He is also conscious of both the cultural environment where the performances take place and the backgrounds of his participants. This means that he has made an effort to work in many different nations and parts of this country and tries to assemble divergent groups of performers, although it has been difficult for him to get people who are free of associations with the art world, the social sciences, and universities. But his work does not take the form of scientific inquiry and explanation. He is not interested in the kind of results yielded by detached observation of social phenomena; his Activities are not formulated with any preconceived hypothesis about the nature of what he is investigating, for which he is seeking experimental confirmation. Rather, he is after the commonsense knowledge gained from direct engagement in social encounters. The work becomes research in terms of the information acquired by each individual participant (of whom Kaprow is always one). Self-knowledge, then, is an important "practical yield."

Kaprow's art has always been highly formal. Many people are unaware how carefully composed his Happenings were. But if his work is formal, it is because "form is a character of mind.... The structure of our cerebral cortex and all our biological functions permit us only patterned responses and thoughts of one kind or another."[3] The organization of his Activities is tied, in part, to his familiarity with contemporary music, and his study with John Cage is of significance in this respect. Most of Kaprow's pieces are composed according to self-imposed regulations of groupings and regroupings with varying degrees of indeterminacy set into them. Although his work has identifiable and often sophisticated aesthetic form, it's of secondary importance to him. The aesthetic attitude, which isolates aesthetic features from non-aesthetic ones, is now alien to him. Accidents, embarrassments, misunderstandings—developments that are flaws in an aesthetic sense—are frequently part of his performances, and he considers such disruptions fortuitous and vital to their success.

If Cage's formalism was intended to "imitate nature in her manner of operation," Kaprow's could be said to imitate social processes in their manner of operation. As with all successful mimetic art, Kapow uses techniques of defamiliarization, and these are central to his work. His Activities are like fictions about the substance of everyday life in which language and gesture are rearranged, recombined, and thus made strange. The alternation of roles, the use of tape recorders and mirrors, the repetition and ritualizing of certain actions, all work to break down our habitualized perception of the most basic kinds of social exchange. Henri Lefebvre wrote that everyday life was modernity's unconscious and Kaprow's Activities seem designed to rouse their participants into consciousness by decomposing and recomposing the fabric of that life. Put another way, they are sensitizing devices. Despite superficial similarities, however, they are unlike sensitivity groups and certain psychological testing methods which are usually highly obvious in form, specifically goal-orientated, and intrinsically dependent on the presence of a leader or authoritarian figure. What also distinguishes Kaprow's work is its inherent unpredictability and its implied assertion that paradox and ambiguity will always be at the heart of any social interaction.

Although his activity reverberates with social and political implications, Kaprow disowns the roles of activist or theoretician. His relationship to politics is tempered with irony, characterized perhaps by a recent observation that "for every political solution there are at least ten new problems." Nonetheless, he is preoccupied with possible practical applications of the ideas behind his work, and, in the past, has been closely involved in teacher education and experimented with Happening-type situations as a means of transforming learning experience. Now he is hopeful that the Activities or related forms might fulfill a larger social purpose in the future. The current work is political on a small interpersonal level, and one of his toughest problems is how to transfer gains made in personal politics to the level of community politics. Kaprow offers no easy answers.

His inflexible opposition to spectators or audiences is linked to an underlying social critique. He appears aware of the increasing technical capacities of commercial and financial institutions to dominate the material conditions of our lives so that existence becomes spectacular (in the sense of looking on or watching) and that life itself, let alone art, becomes a show to be contemplated passively. His Activities work to subvert this kind of passivity, unlike much other performance art. The kind of self-awareness and introspection he hopes to cultivate is possible only in an interactional situation where there is reciprocal exchange and reflection on a basis of equality. Some performance art has tended to perpetuate the mystique of the artist whose aura of singularity is amplified by the performance event, excluding the possibility of dialogue and intersubjectivity. Kaprow is intent on breaking down this distance of artist from the world, insisting that there is no danger of contamination. Throughout his career he has persistently challenged "rectangular" thinking which inevitably puts frames around objects, roles, and experiences instead of apprehending them as part of a wider context. There are no sharply defined boundaries for Kaprow, who once wrote that "as the identity of 'art' becomes uncertain, the artist can no longer take refuge in its superiority to life, as he was once accustomed to do. This is when, suddenly, decisions regarding human values become imperative."[4]

1. Allan Kaprow, "Non-Theatrical Performance," *Artforum*, May 1976, pp. 45–51.
2. Mirella Bandini, "Allan Kaprow," *Data*, June 1975, p. 66.
3. Allan Kaprow, "The Shade of the Art Environment," *Artforum*, Summer 1968, pp. 32–33. This is Kaprow's response to Robert Morris's "Anti-Form" essay from the same year.
4. Quoted in Barbara Rose and Irving Sandler, "Sensibility of the Sixties," *Art in America*, January 1967, p. 45.

Originally published in *Arts Magazine*, September 1976.

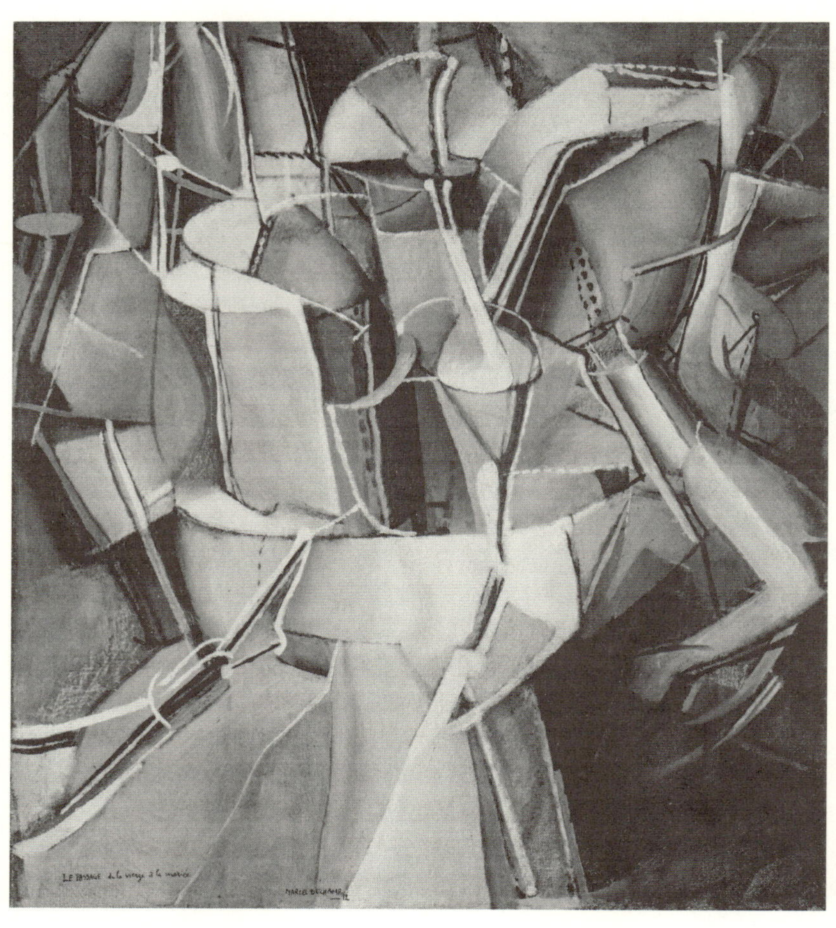

Marcel Duchamp, *The Passage from Virgin to Bride*, 1912.

Marcel Duchamp's *The Passage from Virgin to Bride*

> Eroticism is an experience that we cannot assess from the outside like an object. Poetry leads to the same place as all forms of eroticism, to the blurring and fusion of separate objects. —GEORGES BATAILLE

In the summer of 1912 Marcel Duchamp traveled to Germany to spend what were to be several of the most important months of his career. "My stay in Munich," he recalled many years later, "was the scene of my complete liberation, when I established the general plan of a large-scale work which would occupy me for a long time…"[1] It was the commencement of work on *The Large Glass*, but also the culmination of his activity as a painter. Because that summer was an interval of transition for Duchamp, the paintings produced then, particularly *The Passage from Virgin to Bride*, have been considered primarily in terms of the major work that was in preparation, and consequently, some of their essential qualities have been overlooked.

Most accounts of his art from 1911 to 1912 have sought and, predictably, found patterns of a step-by-step development among his works that lead inevitably to *The Large Glass*, and thus the art of July–August 1912 has often been seen as an intended prelude to what was to follow. Art history has trained us to search for continuities, and it is convenient to emphasize the relationship between certain visual forms present in several of his paintings and *The Large Glass*. These connections are not unimportant, but we miss something central in Duchamp's art if we do not also see it as discontinuous, as standing outside of a comprehensible evolution; we must identify the breaks, the nonrelations between works as well.[2] If we view *The Large Glass* as mainly the outcome of an intelligible process that begins with *Coffee Mill* in 1911, as a point on the same linear sequence and part of the same discourse, we fail to see it as the rupture with his previous work which, in many ways, it is. Similarly, we misunderstand his paintings of 1912 if we do not first question them for themselves, to learn how they each work on their own, without being made part of a progression that leads to another work. Because its title relates thematically to works which both follow and precede it, *The Passage from Virgin to Bride* is usually inserted into a series, unified by an assumed association of iconographic material, without a recognition of how, as a painting, it functions very differently from anything else he had done.

Roland Barthes has suggested that every major writer produces at some time an *oeuvre-limite*, literally a frontier or boundary work in which his powers are exhibited at their limit, extended to a pinnacle of creative possibilities.[3] If we could appropriate this term for the study of painting, it would be fair to say that *The Passage from Virgin to Bride* is, for Duchamp the painter, his *oeuvre-limite*. What initially distinguishes it is the absence of any recognizable or identifiable forms. We cannot locate right off a virgin or a bride as we can a young man on a train, a nude on a stairway, or a king and a queen in his other paintings. There is nothing here we can "name." At the same time there is no logical code, no ordering principle by which we can decipher the painted surface.

For all his later comments about "retinal" art, the strengths of this painting depend on those qualities which he subsequently disdained. Our experience of the work begins with its optical subtleties, its glowing seductive color, how it leads us over and through forms that unfold, vanish, and reappear only to turn themselves inside out. Volumes suddenly become voids, planes modulate into lines, and lines disintegrate into dots. Distinctions between figure and ground, between surface and depth, are impossible to make. Shapes at the bottom left of the canvas appear flat, at the bottom right we seem to look into a shadowy, undetermined depth; other forms have no relation at all to these spatial indications. In its intrinsic irrationality and its subversion of *l'esprit géométrique*, Duchamp's visual syntax is proto-Dada, but it also displays a highly sophisticated understanding of the paradoxes of conventional spatial notation.

The question of the work's readability is important: how do we engage

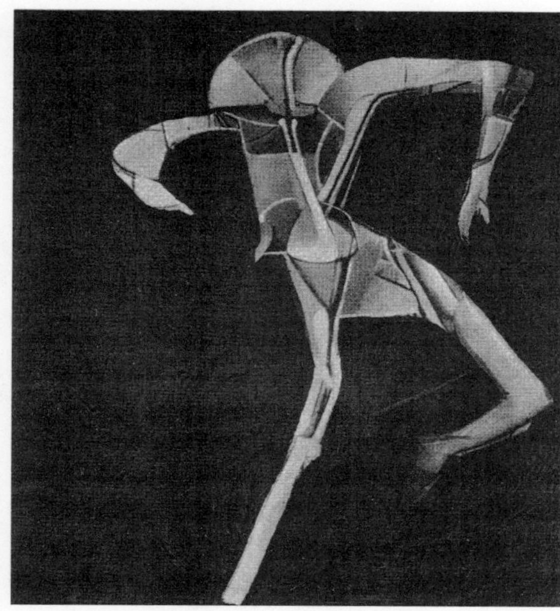

The Passage from Virgin to Bride, author's diagram.

such apparent confusion? It would be misleading to call *The Passage* an abstract painting. Duchamp resisted these characterizations, believing that such work came too close to being decorative art. Because of his increasing preoccupation with linguistic problems, he may have been unwilling to abandon some kind of commonly shared vocabulary of visual signs. While nothing is described explicitly in the work, there are forms that trigger a near subliminal recognition: shapes that suggest limbs, mannequin-like armature, parts of cylinders, a section of pipe, hints of human skin, membranes, and organs. These are his signs, and he carries this vocabulary right to the line where representation becomes allusion.

Because of the title, we begin to look for human forms lodged in the turmoil of the painting and to refashion the fragmented surface into the figures of a virgin or a bride. One imprecise configuration modified my experience of the work for several years. It is an attenuated image of a body in a sprawled out pose, not unlike the disposition of the model in the *Étant donnés*. What I read as the left leg twitches in apparent movement; the head is a semicircle, like a fan or seashell, a line of dots around its periphery denoting a faint fluttering.[4] Nonetheless, I believe that such a reformation and stabilizing of "content" distorts the essential nature of the painting. It imposes something concrete and fixed onto a work that simply does not support such a reading. Any attempt to anthropomorphize the work entails a denial, not only of other equally credible readings, but of the actual visual data presented. My figure, and many others, take shape only by violating a reading of the optical information on the surface and forcing onto it a gestalt, which is more a phantasmic production of my own mind than of the painting.

Lawrence D. Steefel, in an extensive study of *The Passage*, proposes that he has discovered a hidden double imagery in the depths of the work consisting of "a group of curiously grotesque figures."[5] He has identified "a robot-like voyeur," "a hieratic figure," and "a looming mask" and reconstructs a drama enacted among them, which he believes has important links to other works by Duchamp. The images that he purports to see, however, seem no more pivotal to the painting than mine, or anyone else's. Iconographic studies of Duchamp's art are inherently inadequate; rarely do we feel they have taken us closer to the core of his work. Some become fictions in themselves, exercises in interpretive virtuosity, self-enclosed and circular. It's notable that all the supposed decipherments of Duchamp are able to generate proof of their own validity, yet none is able to convincingly claim priority. The specific content of his art is not irrelevant, but we ought to acknowledge how self-consciously private much of it is. Something may be gained, then, by provisionally bracketing questions of iconography and meanings in order to examine the mechanisms at work beneath any content.

Like the poetry of Mallarmé, *The Passage* is an interlacing of mutually resonant effects and relationships, none of which has precedence over any other. This is a key link between Mallarmé and Duchamp: there is no favored single reading of a work. David Antin, in an essay on Duchamp and language, writes, "If any reading were so plausible that it annihilated the other plausible readings associated with the work, the work would break down."[6] Rather, there are myriad significances, affinities, and associations. Any part of the work can be read in multiple ways, recalling Duchamp's comment about "the fact that any form is the perspective of another form according to a certain vanishing point and a certain

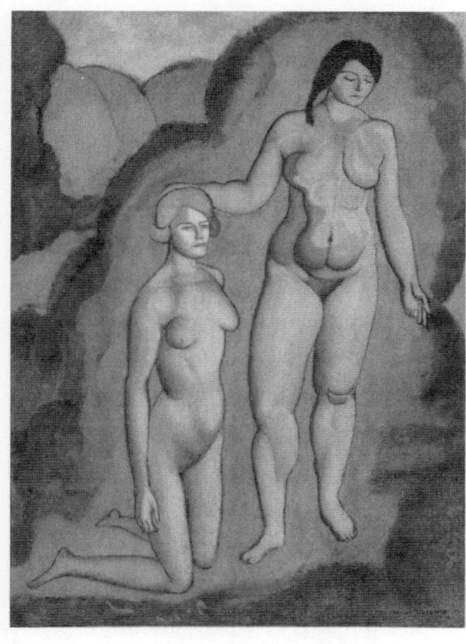

Marcel Duchamp,
The Thicket, 1910–11.

distance."[7] Much later, in his lecture "The Creative Act," Duchamp implied that the number of possible interpretations of a given work is limited only by the number of spectators.[8] The means by which a painting left itself open to so many possible explications becomes more important than any one interpretation. He described how an earlier painting, *The Thicket* (1910–11), "evoked for me the possibility to invent a theme for it afterwards."[9] There could be anecdotes or narratives connected with it, he indicated, but they would be of the spectator's making. A work, in this sense, can be created anew with each fresh viewing. Writing about Mallarmé, Marcel Raymond could almost be describing *The Passage*: "Mallarmé's poetics implies the continuous disregard of facts and objects, in favor of the allusion.... The images will slip in obliquely, they will remain undeveloped, implied in one another, they will suddenly flutter by, flashing a bit of color, a spark. A complex syntax will trace almost in visible relations between the words, *and these relations will remain in a sense virtual, up to the moment when the reader perceives them*."[10] The aesthetic principle of obscurity, derived from Hugo and Baudelaire, is brought to a new level of refinement by Mallarmé and, in this painting, by Duchamp. The avoidance of any precise references only intensifies and expands the possibilities that the work can invoke. Mallarmé intimated how this happens in his prose poem "Le nénuphar blanc." The poet is obsessed with a woman he lives near but has never seen. One day he has the opportunity to meet her but backs away from it, fearful that to actually see her face would irrevocably diminish the splendor of his imagined images of her: "So vague an idea is sufficient: and will not transgress the delight marked by generality which permits and commands the exclusion of all faces, to the point where the revelation of one (do not incline it, established beyond doubt, over the stealthy threshold where I reign) would banish my emotion, with which it has no connection."[11]

For Duchamp to show us anything specific would be to circumscribe our encounter with the painting and to reduce the scope of its effects. But, like Mallarmé, he is careful to construct a surface that is sensuous enough so that one is drawn into the deeper texture of the work, possibly to read beyond the initial allurement. No other painting by Duchamp approached this evasive obscurity. *The Bride*, painted soon afterward in August 1912, is quite different: there is a generally readable three-dimensional space, a distinct separation of figure and ground, and each element, although enigmatic, is clearly attached to others in static locations, which do not change from viewing to viewing.

Working in a historical context permeated with cubist and futurist ideas, Duchamp in *The Passage* kept his distance from them. When his detractors label him a second-rate painter, they usually imply that he failed to adequately assimilate cubist theory, not studying his work carefully enough to see he was doing something else. Cubism may have shown him means by which the object could be dismantled but, because it was about the description of static forms and the space around them, he moved away from it. "Cubism," he told Pierre Cabanne, "interested me only for a few months, in 1911."[12] He distrusted its systemization and wanted to "detheorize" it. *Nude Descending a Staircase*, for instance, separated itself from cubism because it was a painting of what was not seen, of what could not be apprehended visually. Before he knew anything about futurism he was preoccupied with problems of movement in relation to physics, metaphysics, even pataphysics. Motion, for Duchamp, seems to have been something disquieting: it amplified an intuition of the loss of fixed and stable locations for the objects of consciousness.

It is difficult to measure how or if he was influenced by futurism. "The trajectory" was a key concept for the futurists, something which had already concerned Duchamp. They had expressed dissatisfaction with Marey's chronophotography because it displayed only a linear succession of static positions. What Duchamp may have liked about the futurists was their desire to create the sensation of movement, to describe a reality that was always vibrating and in motion, which could not be shown as stable and whole.[13] They claimed that states of mind were most important in painting and that intoxication was a goal of their art. But, in spite of their theories, their "laws of interior mathematics" and "force lines," they never quite achieved these aims. The diagrammatic aspects of their art, with few exceptions, didn't really disappear. If *The Passage* is linked to futurism at all, it would be more to some of their aspirations than their material achievements, to the desire to paint the affective qualities of an event. Boccioni, for example, wrote that painting should be "an emotive environment which creates sensation and completely involves the viewer."[14]

This is not far from what Duchamp accomplishes in *The Passage*. He describes experience from the interior, without reference to any detached point of view or to any spatial coordinates. Because the painting concerns interior experience, its temporal dimension is particularly important. The idea of the trajectory and the temporality it presupposed have been abandoned. Instead he shows us an event with no past and no future, without continuity or linear form; it is a present without shape or solidity. This is the time of the mythological figure of Aion, radically unlike the extensive and divisible time of Chronos. For Gilles Deleuze, Aion denotes an instantaneity, a chaos, an immeasurable state of pure intensity.[15] We see something like this in *The Passage*: a convulsive time in which logic breaks down and in which the individual dissolves, no longer a separate or independent body. Distinctions between subject and object, between causes and effects, become meaningless. Eroticism, Duchamp's "pre-eminent example" of the fourth dimension, is nonsignifying, affective, and it deterritorializes anything stable and unified.[16] The event in the painting is like the image of falling in Mallarmé: a vertiginous suspension from our normal experience of time and consciousness. We can see *The Passage* as a doing, a becoming that has no subject, as in Nietzsche's famous section in *The Genealogy of Morals*: "There is no 'being' behind the doing, acting, becoming; the doer has simply been added to the deed by the imagination—the doing is everything."[17] A paradox of the work, though, is that we always experience it in an extensive state, and we inevitably attempt, as I did, to totalize it, to reconstitute a subject. But we can do so only by falsifying what is there.

Duchamp chose his titles with great care, and in this case, it may give some indication of how the work functions. Unlike those of most of his other paintings, this title describes an action, an activity, rather than persons or objects. While words like virgin and bride denote discrete, whole, and delimited entities, passage describes something open, in process, and dynamic. In this sense the painting is about a category of experience independent of enclosed and unitary concepts in the title. On another semantic level, "bride" designates a state of marriage, itself an enclosure in which the individual is territorialized and binaries maintained. In this context, "passage" would indicate a "bachelor" state, an unconstrained flux in which the trap of conjugality is evaded. Even if one should take "passage" to mean the anatomical passage that physically separates a virgin from a bride, it still points, because of the syntax of the title, to something in process and intensive: eroticism itself. But if the activity in the painting occurs outside the limits of totalizing concepts, the title ironically implies the finite duration of such an event, even though the notion of duration has no meaning while it is happening.

With *The Passage*, Duchamp advanced his transformation of the role of the spectator, which would be fully realized in *The Large Glass*. More than in any of his other paintings, the audience becomes a key agent in the creation of the work. Cubism defined a different role, and despite whatever difficulty the viewer might have in deciphering the image, everyone ultimately is led to the same reading in an essentially closed work. For all the complication in Picasso's *Ma Jolie* (1912), there is still only one privileged reading of it. The subject is fractured and disguised, but is still there, central, like an icon, beneath a grid ordered by quasi-intelligible principles. It announces the presence of something whole and unified amid its fragmentation. Probably the most important feature of *The Passage* is its openness. It has no subject and no center, only a sense of their absence. Instead, within a framed and limited space, we have an active field of potentially unlimited relationships, of floating elements, which resist being inserted into a structural logic. It is a "field of freeplay," where oppositions are not contradictions and where any form is free of any necessary relation to any other."[18] *The Green Box*, an integral part of *The Large Glass*, epitomizes this idea of freeplay: Duchamp placed his notes loose, in random order, in a box so that *the Glass* would be experienced through a process of reworking and recoding them. Here again is an enclosure that contains an infinite number of possible orderings and substitutions.[19] The artwork becomes an activity, and, as in *The Passage*, the viewer is implicated in a process of producing meanings.

Operating in *The Passage*, then, is a system whose components are linked by the very absence of any natural or logical tie between them, and there is no antecedent totality to which they belonged. The painting is built out of layers of simultaneously existing structures in which a given element of one can play a different but equally important role in another.[20] As in the late poems of Mallarmé, we can always enter it afresh to find new relationships and abandon old ones. Perhaps we can go further than saying there is no one correct reading. Deleuze seems to be close to identifying some of Duchamp's ambitions, when he writes: "The modern work of art is anything it may seem; it is even its very property of being whatever we like, from the moment it works.... It depends solely on its functioning, which in turn depends on its separate parts. The modern work of art has no problem of meaning, it has only a problem of use."[21]

The Passage, though not Duchamp's last painting, has something about it of a conclusive, private achievement in this medium. He finished it during the summer in which problems of language assumed a central position in his art, and much as the painting can anticipate what was to follow, it also looks backward, almost as a summing up of his work before this major turning point. Done at age twenty-five, it is the brilliant work of his youth, and I think we miss something in it if we do not see its dark rapture. Like his mythic paintings of 1910–11, such as *Paradise*, *Baptism*, and *The Thicket*, it is an effort to recover a lost experience of carnal or spiritual initiation. The tumult of *The Passage* is the other side of those earlier meditative and spellbound images. They were suffused with a prelinguistic silence. In *The Passage* he creates the rending, the cry of a moment, as in ecstasy or pain, when language falters and breaks down.

In one of Mallarmé's most perfect achievements, his poem "Autre éventail," the soft movement of a fan in a woman's hand, like an erotic undulation, is able to contort space and condense time.[22] Consciousness becomes "a savage paradise," where desire, detached from any object, soars in "pure pathless delight," in "space shivering like a vast kiss." The fan, unfolded and in motion, is a blossoming, a flowering; it is a limitless becoming, like the act of producing poetry itself. But at the close of the poem, a simple gesture folds the fan into a rigid, motionless scepter. It becomes a "white closed flight." Duchamp's painting functions much like Mallarmé's fan. As viewers, we can either let the work remain open, fugitive, and virtual or close it into a fixed and stable object. Only by keeping the painting in flux, through our own active participation, do we encounter its phosphorescent delirium.

1. Anne d'Harnoncourt and Kynaston McShine, eds., *Marcel Duchamp* (New York: Museum of Modern Art, 1973), p. 263.
2. Pierre Cabanne, *Dialogues with Marcel Duchamp* (New York: Thames & Hudson, 1971), p. 38. Duchamp says, "In *The Bride*, in *The Glass*, I tried constantly to find something which would not recall what had happened before. I have had an obsession about not using the same things.... It was a constant battle to make an exact and complete break."
3. Roland Barthes, *Essais critiques* (Paris: Éditions du Seuil, 1964), p. 90. "Qu'il existe dans la production des très grands écrivains, une *oeuvre-limite*, une oeuvre singulière, presque gênante, dans laquelle ils déposent à la fois le secret et la caricature de leur création...ou se mêlent d'une façon rare le positif et le négatif d'un créateur."
4. Several of Max Ernst's works of the early 1920s echo this fan-head. See *Woman, Old Man, and Flower II* (1923), Museum of Modern Art, New York, and *The Chinese Nightingale* (1920), D. Genon-Catalot collection, Paris.
5. Lawrence D. Steefel Jr., "The Art of Marcel Duchamp: Dimension and Development in *Le Passage de la Vierge a la Mariée*," *Art Journal* 22, no. 2 (Winter 1962–63), pp. 72–79. Reprinted in Joseph Masheck, ed., *Marcel Duchamp in Perspective* (New York: Prentice-Hall, 1975).
6. David Antin, "Duchamp and Language," in d'Harnoncourt and McShine, *Marcel*

Duchamp, pp. 100–15.

7. Marcel Duchamp, *Notes and Projects for* The Large Glass, ed. Arturo Schwarz (New York: Thames & Hudson, 1969), p. 108.
8 Marcel Duchamp, "The Creative Act," in *The New Art: A Critical Anthology*, ed. Gregory Battcock (New York: Dutton, 1973), pp. 46–48.
9 D'Harnoncourt and McShine, *Marcel Duchamp*, p. 249.
10. Marcel Raymond, *From Baudelaire to Surrealism* (London: Methuen, 1970), p. 21. Emphasis added.
11. *Mallarmé*, trans. Anthony Hartley (Harmondsworth, UK: Penguin Books, 1965), p. 148.
12. Cabanne, *Dialogues with Marcel Duchamp*, p. 38.
13. Anton Giulio Bragaglia, "Futurist Photodynamism," in *Futurist Manifestos*, ed. Umbro Apollonio (New York: Viking, 1973), p. 43.
14. Umberto Boccioni, "Futurist Painting and Sculpture, 1914," ibid., p. 177.
15. Gilles Deleuze, *Logique du sens* (Paris: Éditions de Minuit, 1969), pp. 74–82 and 190–97.
16. Robert Lebel, *Marcel Duchamp* (New York: Grove Press, 1959), p. 28.
17. Friedrich Nietzsche, *The Birth of Tragedy and The Genealogy of Morals*, trans. Francis Golffing (New York: Doubleday, 1956), pp. 178–79.
18. See Jacques Derrida, "Structure, Sign, and Play in the Discourse of the Human Sciences," in Edward Macksey and Euginio Donato, eds., *The Structuralist Controversy: The Languages of Criticism and the Sciences of Man* (Baltimore, MD: Johns Hopkins University Press, 1970), p. 260.
19. Because of Duchamp's insistence on the random order of the notes, the efforts of Arturo Schwarz, their editor, to arrange them chronologically seem ironically misplaced, including the hiring of a graphologist to date Duchamp's handwriting.
20. See Gilles Deleuze and Félix Guattari, *L'anti-Oedipe: Capitalisme et schizophrénie:* (Paris: Éditions de Minuit, 1972), pp. 476–77. The authors outline this idea of randomly related simultaneous structures in the context of Jean Tinguely's work.
21. Gilles Deleuze, *Proust and Signs* (New York: George Braziller, 1972), pp. 128–29.
22. *Mallarmé*, p. 66.

Originally published in *Arts Magazine*, January 1977.

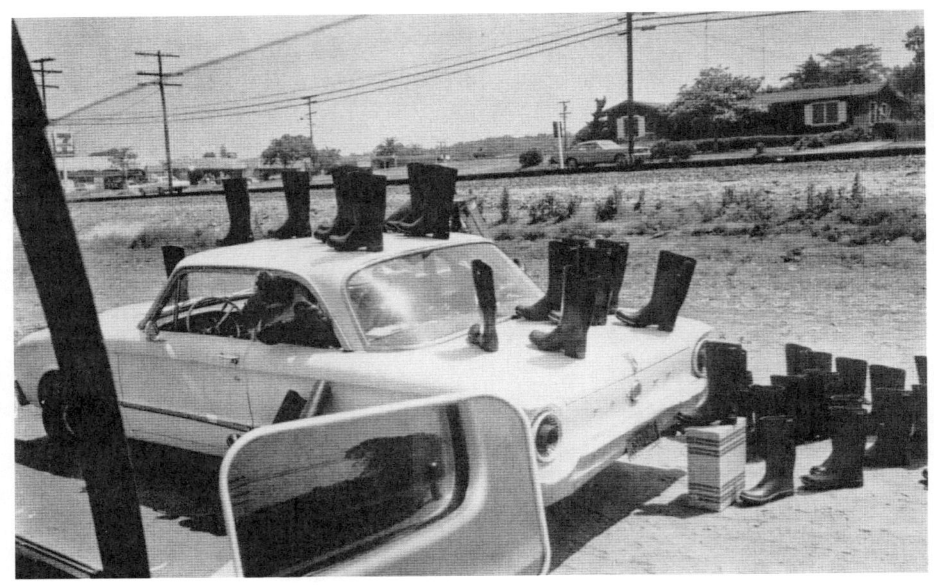

Eleanor Antin, from *100 Boots*, 1971–73.

Eleanor Antin's Nomadic Itineraries

Eleanor Antin's art resists efforts to analyze it or position it within the terminology now popular in contemporary art writing. An attempt to articulate a structure common to her different activities would be either unsuccessful or inconsequential. Nor would it be necessarily helpful to associate Antin with other current art until we see what her work is, what its *own* shapes are. And finally, we should not approach it as a stratification of layers from which we must disentangle meanings. The diverse and broken surfaces of her art are not concealing or displacing meanings which are to be recovered. Rather, the multiplicity and discontinuity are what is really there, to be experienced for itself, for its affects, and not to be interpreted. What we want to know, to sense about her projects, is what they do, how they operate as agencies, as instruments.

Antin once indicated that her work *100 Boots* (1971-73) has affinities with the form of the picaresque novel, and it may be worthwhile to consider this acknowledgment. The picaresque is distinguished by its episodic organization, by the virtual nonrelation between its internal units; it is an accumulation of episodes without necessary structural links between them. Behind the superficial appearance of a conventional fictional development there is actually a piling up of essentially discontinuous, often interchangeable events which are bound together only by the loosest narrative or temporal logic. Like such novels, *100 Boots* is nomadic; it is perpetually in transit, following an erratic, fragmented itinerary over an ambiguously defined terrain, both in its narrative and its distribution through the postal system. The breaks between the various appearances of the boots are more prominent than any continuity, and this lack of an intelligible narrative gives the work an improvisational character; the chosen form does not dictate an *a priori* hierarchy or restriction of narrative possibilities; and each photograph of the boots has the same value as any other. (Antin's caricature of the picaresque wryly conforms to the traditional conclusion of such novels, in which a roguish, footloose hero is reassimilated into the stable, static norms of the society he or she initially deserted: her piece ends with the boots entering the Museum of Modern Art.)

Since 1972 her autobiographical projects seem to depend on a similar kind of nomadism. Over and above the individual personalities she assumes is the act of passage to and from them. Crucial for her is a psychological vagrancy, an ability to wander from one identity to another, not only from work to work, but often within a given performance in which she will take on many identities. The internal elaboration of a specific personality, the Nurse, Ballerina, King, Movie Star, or ancillary characters, then, should not distract us from examining the means of flowing in and out of different selves, of effecting a continuing self-transformation. Autobiography, for her, is a mobile, in-process act of narrating; the prefix *auto-* literally denotes a self-propelling biography. She cuts herself loose from the fabric of her past and establishes autobiography as an activity, something to be lived, to be made and remade. In this way she becomes a shifting collage of multiple selves, a palimpsest on whom remain the inscriptions of all her roles. Her art is a machine, an apparatus for crossing boundaries, for breaking down frames. She produces new limits and territories only to then dissolve them.

Some of her earlier projects, like *California Lives* (1970) and *Eight Portraits of New York Women* (1970), were marked by their effacement of the subject, by the way its absence became a disquieting, palpable component of space. These works cannot be described adequately as object portraits; they don't set up an emblematic equivalence between material object and personality as did, say, Francis Picabia's *Ici, c'est ici Stieglitz* (1915). Instead, her objects and commodities circle ambivalently around a missing presence, a lost center, to which they have no direct link. With *Carving* (1972), however, the subject reenters her work. Although this project does draw our attention to what is not there, to the spaces and time between

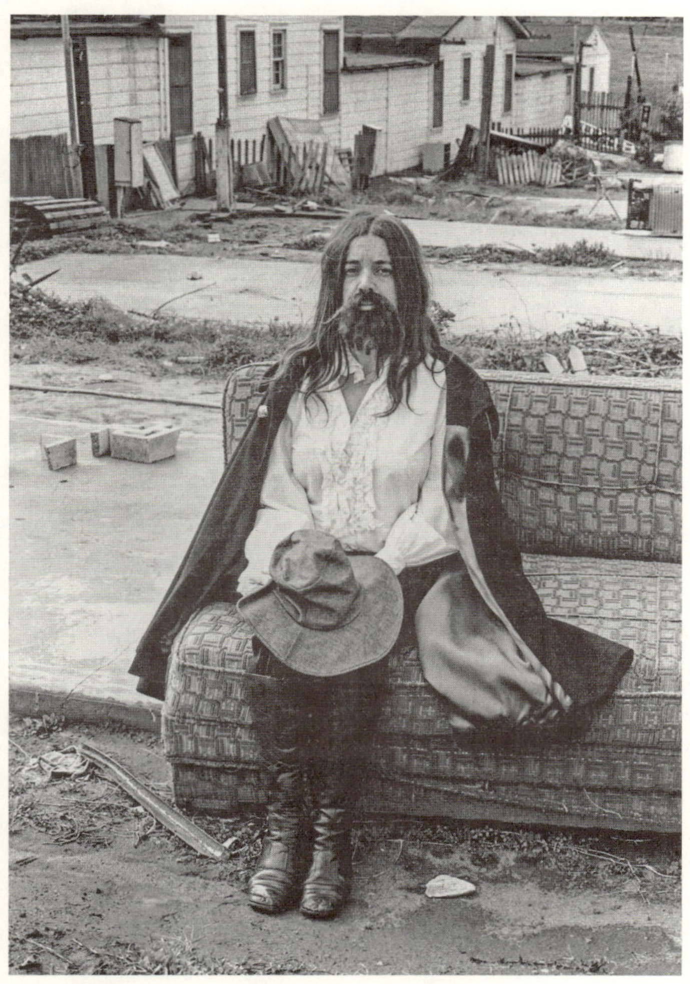

Eleanor Antin, from *The King of Solana Beach*, 1974.

what is shown, Antin is more preoccupied here with the transformation of the subject than with its absence. And *Carving*, with its careful monitoring of changes in her physical self, seems to lead directly into works in which her identity is transformed. In spite of its apparently objective documentation, it insists on a subject that is undergoing constant modification. And that cannot be fully observed or assessed. In her videotape *The King* (1972) in which Antin methodically transforms herself into a king, or in *Representational Painting* (1972) where another transformation with makeup occurs, there is no point at which she suddenly stops being Eleanor Antin. What she becomes is already part of her, and she never ceases to be what she is to begin with. There are no borders, no precise contours, no center. She is the autobiographer of a subject-in-process.

Earlier artists have been preoccupied with the experience of self-transformation. Some of the surrealists had aspirations that seem similar to Antin's. We can remember how Robert Desnos, in his trances, would become "the leader of a religion, the founder of a city, the tribune of a people in revolt."[1] Dreams and dreamlike states offered the possibility of a delirious flight from the self, of what Artaud, while still sympathetic to the movement, called "that magnificent power of escape."[2] But unlike the surrealists, Antin does not make distinctions between waking and daydreaming, between hallucination and everyday perception. André Breton, in his novel *Nadja* (1928), sketched the outline of a figure who also refused to make such distinctions and who perhaps has more interesting links with Antin than most of the real-life surrealists. Nadja was characterized by her independence from any conceptual or social containment, her freedom from rational thought and logic, and her resistance to any kind of territorialization. She moved in a floating schizo state, which both fascinated and disturbed Breton. She was an image of possibilities which intrigued surrealism but which it inherently rejected; Breton ultimately could only objectify Nadja in an idealization of madness.

One earlier figure immersed himself unconditionally in a major enterprise of self-transformation: Alfred Jarry, whom I have mentioned previously in connection with Antin. He made one of the most audacious attempts to transform himself into an invented personality. Jarry's life was a near-complete convergence with a fictional role of his own making; he sought to merge his life with his text, and his text became closer to life.

Ubu, the multifaceted creation who obsessed him throughout his life, was his machine for overthrowing the constraints of his own individuality, for attempting to unify life and desire. At the forefront of Jarry's thought was his refusal of the idea of contradiction. For him, no state of being ever excluded its opposite. This is a major affinity between Jarry and Dada, the Dada of Tristan Tzara's 1918 manifesto in which logic and dialectics were abolished. Unlike the surrealists, Jarry and Dada reveled in the play of contradictions, of multiplicities, the subversion of all systems and doctrines. Antin's work, if we look at it art historically, does descend in part from a Dada sensibility. In *Angel of Mercy* (1977) the point is not that she has tried to change herself completely into someone else but that she is simultaneously both Eleanor Antin and a nurse in the Crimean War. We need not make an either/or choice about who she is. For there is no order or logic that determines the substance of the work. There is no sequence, no connection between one identity and another, no unifying psychology. The only fact they have in common, and at the same time their finest justification, is that she chose them. The impossibility, the contradictoriness of her project is what sustains it, what gives it force.

Angel of Mercy orchestrates a polyphony that occurred on a smaller scale in earlier Antin works such as *Adventures of a Nurse* (1976). *Angel* is built out of a plurality of voices and consciousnesses. She achieves a kind of carnivalization of reality, the term used by the postformalist critic Mikhail Bakhtin in his study of Dostoevsky. It describes the freeplay, the unmotivated interaction of an accumulation of different minds and voices; it entails a rejection of stylistic unity and becomes a loosely controlled disorder in which we hear the contending speech of characters, conversing with their opposites. Bakhtin writes: "In *Crime and Punishment* everything approaches its own borders, everything is prepared to become its own opposite, although not in an abstract dialectical sense.... There is nothing in the novel which could become stabilized, nothing which could enter into the normal course of biographical time and develop in it. Everything requires change and rebirth. Everything is depicted in the moment of an uncompleted transition."[3] And in *Angel of Mercy* there is a piling up of unfinalized characters, each one an ideology, a partial point of view. All these fragmentary voices, though, cannot be added up into a comprehensible whole. In spite of the appearance of an enclosed narrative, we are

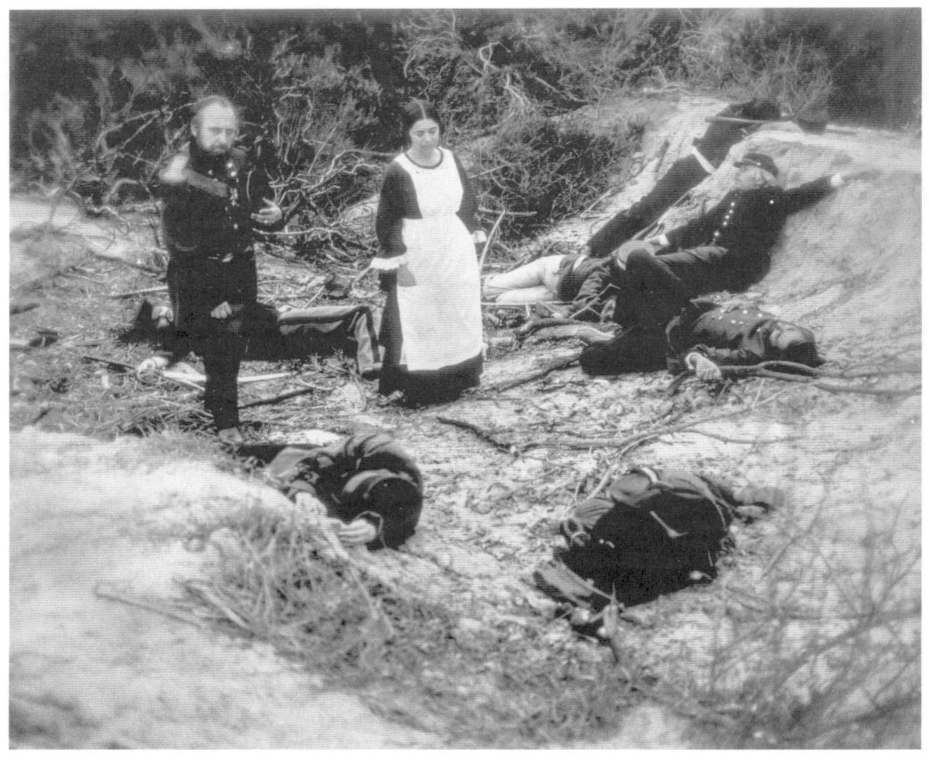

Eleanor Antin, *In the Trenches before Sebastopol,* from *The Angel of Mercy*, 1977.

left with an essential absence of a coherent set of connections between the constantly shifting identities that she assumes.

The linguistic operation that Antin undertakes is complex and difficult to adequately assess. During her performance her speech is simultaneously that of Eleanor Antin, of the Nurse, and of each of the other characters she momentarily becomes. So at all times she is double-voiced and is often multivoiced, and this vocal overlapping is central to the work. Although its strict oral reality is a soliloquy, *Angel of Mercy* is fundamentally dialogical. (And soliloquy is often a dialogue with oneself.) As a dialogical work her performance is constituted by the spoken intercourse between people. The Nurse emerges as real through the encounter of her voice with other voices. Again Bakhtin: "Carnivalization makes possible the creation of an open structure and allows people's social interaction to be carried over into the sphere of the spirit and the intellect, which had always been primarily the sphere of a single, unified monological consciousness whose development took place within its own limits. The carnival attitude overcomes... both epistemological and ethical solipsism."[4]

Much could be said about the organization of her installation, consisting of both the painted figures and photographs. It presents a conundrum of formal and semantic problems, some worth pursuing more than others. Unlike her performance the photographs seem to insist on the facticity of her life as a nurse in the Crimean War. As documents they are a kind of irrefutable evidence that she was there. But I think we misread these images if we assume their purpose is to persuade us of their veracity, for they seem to operate in a distinctly ironic mode. Irony describes a statement that denotes the opposite of what it appears to affirm. According to Hayden White, "it presupposes the occupation of a 'realistic' perspective on reality, from which a non-figurative representation of the world of experience might be provided."[5] At face value her photographs are a kind of visual counterpart to a nineteenth-century historical novel: they depict well-delineated characters, social types, located in space and at a determinable point in history. But at the same time they participate in some of the main currents of Antin's enterprise: an essential ahistoricism, a simultaneity of events, and the interchangeability of characters. Her whole endeavor of simulating an historical moment demands that the photographs be seen as images of people who are both themselves and not themselves, both there and somewhere else; they function like optical illusions which oscillate back and forth between their possible readings. Like her performance, the pictures are detached from a past or a future, and they demonstrate the futility of attempting to situate human experience in an objective historical chronology.

There is a principle of interchangeability at work in a number of Antin's pieces, an economy of exchange in which substitutions and displacements of individual elements can occur independently of the system which they constitute. The Nurse, the Ballerina, the Movie Star, and the King, in their uses, in what she does with them, all have basically the same value. Like the words and images in her *Proposal for a Film Festival* (1971), the consumer goods in *California Lives*, or the microscope slides in *Blood of a Poet* (1965–68), the material content, the specific personalities, are subordinate to the relation of that content to systems of consumption and circulation. It is as if Antin had gone shopping in a department store of the mind and, out of a multitude of possibilities, picked out the identities that she did. The content of other art seems similarly positioned, for example, Ed Ruscha's gas stations and parking lots, some Pop Art and even Photo Realism, where what is at issue is not repetition but exchangeability.

Obviously, such art is tied into what is unfolding socially. In Southern California, in America, under capitalism everywhere is a system in which not only commodities but also lifestyles, ideologies, languages, images are de-culturized and assimilated into unregulated, unfathomable networks where they circulate solely according to their exchangeability, their marketability. But a system in which everything is reduced to an exchange value becomes like a card game in which all the cards are wild; it begins to go out of control, barely perceptibly. And Antin carries these consequences to an extreme, paradoxically going outside of the network, subverting it. Capitalism can let everything flow chaotically except for one thing: the individual. It depends on the territorialized, enclosed individual not only for its efficient functioning but for its survival. What Antin does is to break down the idea of the individual, and she dissolves the limits and structures by which it is defined. Along with a number of other contemporary artists, she unmasks the individual as a fiction, an ideology, an imaginary product. If to be human means being a stable, unitary, rational entity, Antin is specifically anti-humanist. The poet Blaise Cendrars wrote, "Artists are, before anything else, those who struggle to become non-human."

She is working toward a new polymorphism, toward an interpenetration of life and desire. And the experience of her work, like other post-modern art, calls for a conceptualizing of reality, not in the form of a three-dimensional theatrical space, the interior of a cube where discrete events occur sequentially, but more like a Möbius strip.[6] A surface where distinctions between external and internal vanish, where locations and movements are relativized, where consciousness and unconsciousness come together, where the past and memory lose any privileged status, where dualistic structures collapse. These are the conditions within which her art works and flows. A character in one of her videotapes was a drifter who spent their life traversing the United States by hopping freight trains. Antin is not unlike him: nomadic, with an improvised itinerary and always a multiplicity of destinations.

1. Maurice Nadeau, *The History of Surrealism*, trans. Richard Howard (New York: Macmillan, 1965), p. 84.
2. Antonin Artaud, *Selected Writings*, ed. Susan Sontag, trans. Helen Weaver (New York: Farrar Strauss Giroux, 1976), p. 143.
3. Mikhail Bakhtin, *Problems of Dostoevsky's Poetics* (Ann Arbor: University of Michigan Press, 1973), pp. 139–40.
4. Ibid., pp. 148–49.
5. Hayden White, *Metahistory: This Historical Imagination of Nineteenth-Century Europe* (Baltimore, MD: Johns Hopkins University Press, 1973), p. 37.
6. See Jean-François Lyotard, *Économie libidinale* (Paris: Éditions de Minuit, 1973), pp. 11–14.

Originally published in the exhibition catalog for *Eleanor Antin: The Angel of Mercy*, La Jolla Museum of Contemporary Art, September 10 – October 23, 1977.

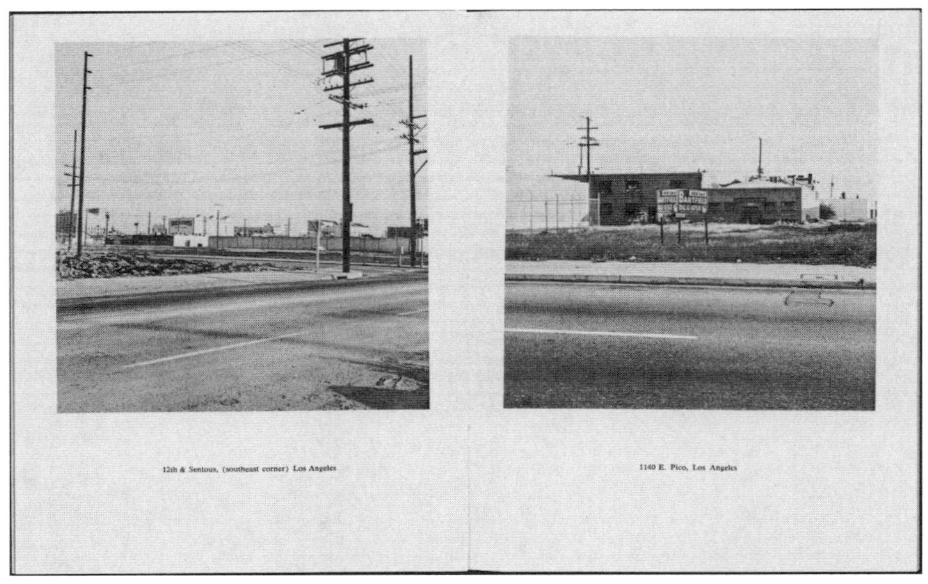

Ed Ruscha, *Real Estate Opportunities*, 1970: "12th & Sentous, (southeast corner) Los Angeles" and "1140 E. Pico, Los Angeles."

Ed Ruscha's *Real Estate Opportunities*

Ed Ruscha's books: enigmatic objects, first appearing in the early 1960s, predecessors of a recent wave of "artists' books." How do we confront his sleek, trim volumes and their repetitive sequences of mute, indifferent pages, their images of an impermeable and depopulated landscape? How do we read them, or are they readable at all? Rather than attempt to determine what features his books have in common, it may be valuable to examine one of them, not to generalize from it about Ruscha and his work but to see how it is formed, how it works, and what effects it produces.

Real Estate Opportunities (1970) consists of twenty-four pages, bound in a white paper cover with a glassine jacket; it has a title page with a date and author's name; there are twenty-five black-and-white reproductions of photographs, each of which shows an area of land and is identified by a street address. But before isolating any one or group of elements in the work, it is important to see the book as an object, as a whole unit. For unlike many artists currently producing books, Ruscha is highly aware of questions and problems intrinsic to books and is not using the format simply as a container for other ideas, writing, or projects. The images in *Real Estate Opportunities* are not contents that can be discussed separately as individual photographs, for by extracting a picture from the fabric of the total object it becomes a qualitatively different kind of sign. The images, individually and sequentially, are tied directly into a critique of books, how they function, how they are produced. Ruscha seems interested in two interrelated phenomena: the book as a manufactured product, a mass-produced commodity, and the book as a quantity of order, an instrument

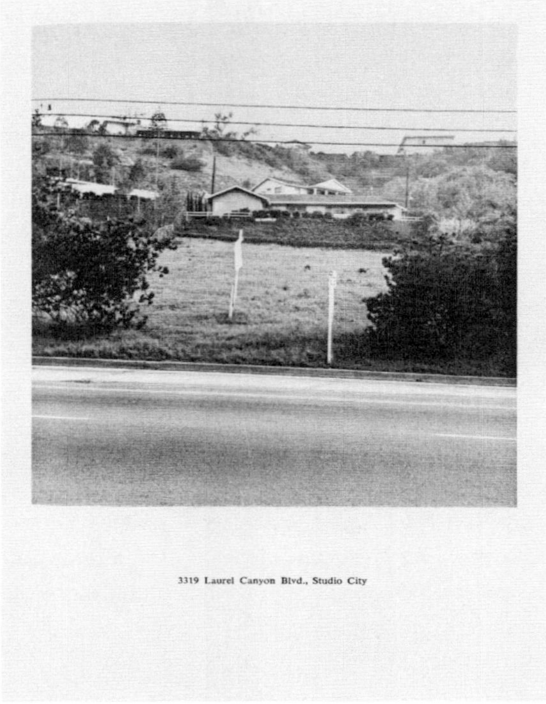

Ed Ruscha, *Real Estate Opportunities*, 1970: "3319 Laurel Canyon Blvd., Studio City."

of organization; and it may be unnecessary to recall that the printed book was the first mass-produced object and a key source of notions of repeatability, linearity, and uniformity.

Ruscha is not working with the book to invent new possibilities for it or to transcend its limits. If Mallarmé's unrealized *Le livre* stands at one extreme, an impossible work that was to be "an Orphic explanation of the world," a book like Ruscha's is at the other end, a work that explains nothing, that exists in fundamental co-identity with any other commodity. He cuts through to a set of its most essential features and reduces the book to a pure function of classification, of categorization, of regulating what would otherwise be an unstructured field of signs. By virtue of its format, in which elements can be arranged and compared, a book makes possible the establishment of concepts of resemblance and similitude. It is a system in which heterogeneous units can be aligned into series, into regularities

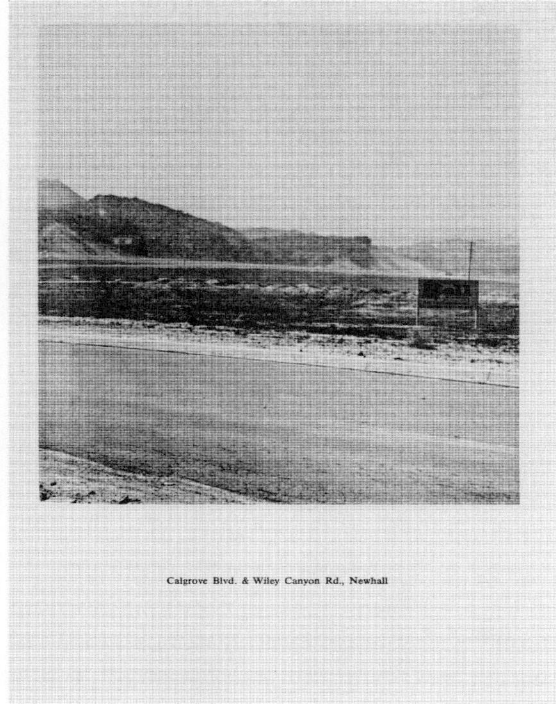

Ed Ruscha, *Real Estate Opportunities*, 1970: "Calgrove Blvd. & Wiley Canyon Rd., Newhall."

solely because of positions in a shared space where differences and distances between units are effaced.

Real Estate Opportunities is an inventory, a catalog whose principle of organization is similitude. The concept "land for sale" becomes a common denominator around which the work's apparent unity is founded. A chain of signs, constructed only on the basis of resemblance, sets up a continuous discourse from which not only difference is eliminated but also any hierarchy or chronology. The book works as a grid that systematizes a mass of signs, that orders them into a prescribed uniformity. There may be a beginning and an end in the book, but these no longer have meanings conventionally associated with them. We need no syntactic competence to read *Real Estate Opportunities*, for there is no syntax, no grammar. (It could be argued that the series of Los Angeles addresses or the rhythm of blank page to image supply the rudiments of narrative or grammatical structures, which he has elaborated in other books such as *A Few Palm Trees*, but here these are at most only minor, nonstrategic subcodes.) In one sense it is an object of complete coherence, an enunciation that is totally transparent, that conceals nothing, that is never ambiguous. A measure of redundancy, no matter how small, is necessary for any code to work, to be potentially comprehensible. But in *Real Estate Opportunities* there is a pure redundancy, a field that is fully coded, that seems to preclude the possibility of any deviation, modification, or dissonance. It affirms the prospect of absolute efficiency, predictability, a tautological perfection.

But we know there is more going on in Ruscha's work than the effects of a homogeneous and regulated space. The more we stay with it, the more it begins to fold silently in upon itself, unravel, and emit signals of a disorder covertly installed within it. We discover that a given arrangement or set of signs can produce a wholly different organization of reality, that the book is not formed in the same way that it actually functions. Its status as an apparatus of exclusion and invariance is subtly sabotaged by its own order of similitude. The principle of resemblance which organizes *Real Estate Opportunities* is not primarily visual or geographical. Superficially, the images appear to be similar—vacant areas of land, overgrown, adjacent to highways—but the crucial feature they all have in common is not visible: their exchange value, that they can be bought and sold. Something concrete (land) has been transformed into an abstract quantity (real estate), and all that finally supports each picture is the "For Sale" sign present in all of them, the index of their exchangeability.

And this is where the order of the book begins to break down, to go out of control. When the similitude determining a given formation is based solely on exchangeability, its underpinning is subject to collapse. When signs are as fluid as money, no regulating structure can hold things in static positions. The book may have been derived from a set of axioms like regularity, uniformity, similarity, but it has produced a volatile supplement, a surplus of code that exceeds what, in principle, is derivable from its axioms. It has been overcoded, through repetition and the elimination of syntax, and the chain begins to spill out in all directions. Signs take on a floating identity and become part of an immense activity of moving around, in which signs and commodities are equivalent.

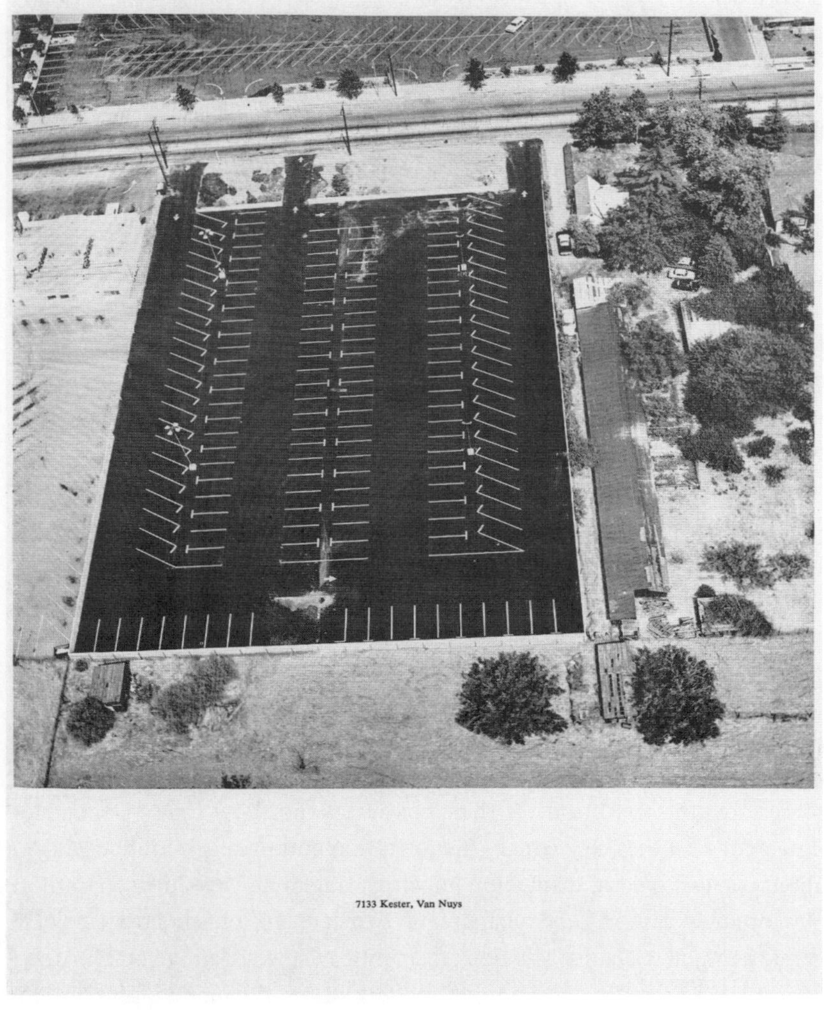

Ed Ruscha, *Thirty-Four Parking Lots*, 1967: "7133 Kester, Van Nuys."

Real Estate Opportunities works, in some ways, like a parking lot, a phenomenon Ruscha has examined elsewhere. Both are grids into which circulating elements are inserted, presenting an illusion of order and immobility, while the elements so contained are in fact constitutive of a larger, unknowably vast disorder. The parking lot, like the book, is a channeling device, a collecting point for units that move freely through a labyrinth of different networks. Two such networks appear in each of Ruscha's pictures, cutting across the image: roads and power lines. These are not metaphors but are material conduits on which signs and objects flow; they are arteries which canalize circulation without in any sense controlling them. If the parking lot is an illusory organization, the highway is a real disorganization. Like the telephone system, the highway system is an overlapping and interlocking of webs and strata so complex and untraceable that they cannot be described as structures. Instead, they are constituted as a great flowing, an undirected, ungoverned drifting of commodities, signs, bodies. And it is networks like these that Ruscha's book is plugged into.

What happens in *Real Estate Opportunities* does not reside in the horizontal coherence of elements but in how this order is overloaded, short-circuited, and how it intersects with a multiplicity of disorganizations. Ruscha operates in terms of categories, whether they are real estate, swimming pools, apartment buildings, or record albums, but he does so in order to dissolve the conditions of their possibility. For *Real Estate Opportunities* is not about a unity which categorization authorizes; it is about chaos, about a social field of dispersion on which fragments are shifting continually into new patterns and alliances, on which chains of signs traverse others, forming new chains. The book dismantles its own claim to stability and cohesiveness and becomes a random association of elements that are not categorizable, that are fundamentally deterritorialized. It describes a chaos that can be experienced only through an ideological mask of order. Precisely what is excluded from the work slips back in to disrupt it.

Ruscha's book *Every Building on Sunset Strip* (1966) operates in a related way. It presumes to represent Sunset Strip as a unified chain, as a perceivable whole. And at first glance this is what we seem to get: the signification of a continuous field, accomplished with a certain notational accuracy. But what begins to take over in our experience of it are the cuts, the breaks in the chain. Ruscha has assembled the work so that there is either overlapping or repetition where the individual images abut, occasionally enough repetition so that a single building appears twice in succession. Instead of being a unity the book is a series of disjunctions, a piling up of fragments that cannot be linked to form any spatial or temporal whole. Sunset Strip emerges as a surface of interchangeable units, of intersections with other disjunct chains. It is impossible to endow it with any horizontal comprehensibility.

Royal Road Test (1967) also works around this nonrelation between parts and whole. The book chronicles the destruction of a typewriter (and the McLuhanesque implications of the work are obviously rich). It is an inventory, an ordered cataloging of components, roles, locations, the methodical description of units and their positions on a field. But it is a table of elements that cannot be reassembled into any wholeness. Some have called his work documentation, but this can only be a negative characterization, for *Royal Road Test*, like *Real Estate Opportunities*, is about what is not shown, what is not documented. The decisive event, the hurling of a typewriter from a speeding car, is exactly what we don't see. Everything in the book is secondary to this pivotal moment of intensity, the colliding of inert surfaces, the "cry" of the machine as it is smashed apart. All that the book represents is absence; images circle around an empty center, enumerating agents, residue, traces. Ruscha's famous final picture, the only one without a caption, shows the shadows of three men looming over the wreckage of the typewriter. Not only does the central violence lie outside the book, but here the subject (the author) becomes only a witness, exterior to the work.

There is an effacement of the author in *Real Estate Opportunities* as well; not, however, in the austere anonymity of its pages but in its status as a mass-produced commodity. The author's name is present, but it stands more as a conventional sign like a brand name than as an indication of an expressive subject, of an authorial entity. Ruscha regretted that he had signed and numbered the initial printing of his first book, *Twenty-Six Gas Stations* (1962), for what he is doing is fundamentally unlike the making of a multiple, an edition of privileged objects. He wanted the polish, the slick finish of a machine-made article, and also the repetitiveness of mass production, which prevents the book from becoming precious or

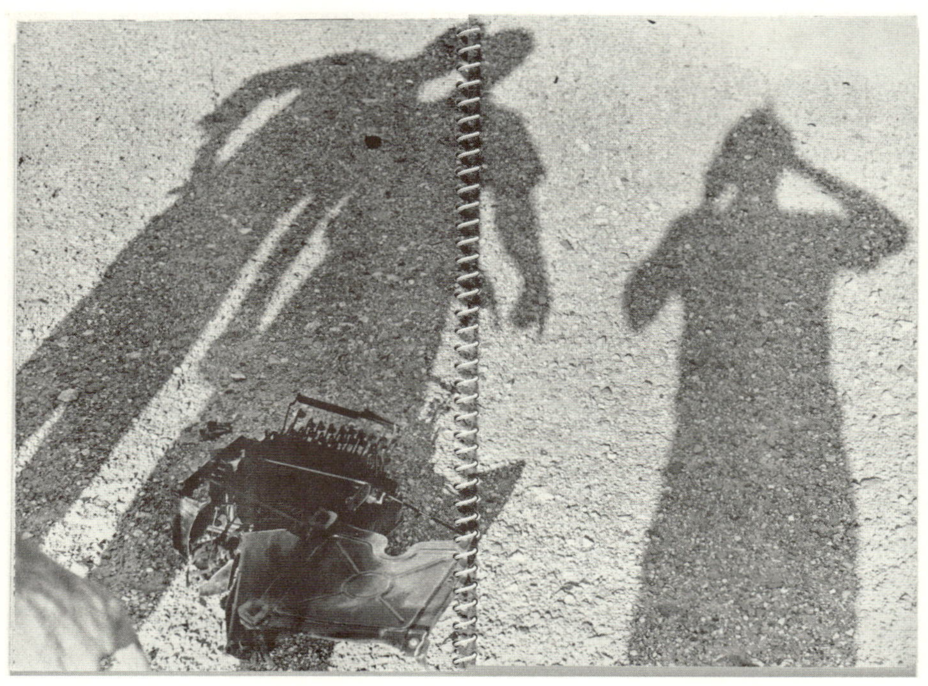

Ed Ruscha, *Royal Road Test*, 1967.

unique. Ruscha's role is, at bottom, different from that of either author or producer. He is more a kind of distributor, one who distributes a given group of signs in a textual space and, more important, one who initiates the distribution of a group of objects over the territory of a social field. He inserts his books into existing networks of circulation, sets them in motion to flow over an unchartable surface where they can interlace with other systems of distribution, inscription, and flows, cross through, and become part of several unrelated structures simultaneously.

The two levels of repetition in *Real Estate Opportunities* might seem to be unconnected: the redundancy of the images within the book and the repetition of the book as a mass-produced object; but book and sign are part of the same machine. The flow of signs and of objects intermingle, become consubstantial and both are consumed the same way, have the same value. Each is the site of some quantity of power and desire and only their patterns of dispersal can be differentiated. Book and sign no longer have a relation of outside and inside, of container and contents. Since neither mediates anything or represents anything, *Real Estate Opportunities* can be made to work however anyone chooses. It becomes an artwork only if we so designate it. By writing about it I inevitably convert it into an object of analysis, but hopefully not to stabilize it or neutralize its own subversive economy.

Originally published in *Arts Magazine*, January 1978.

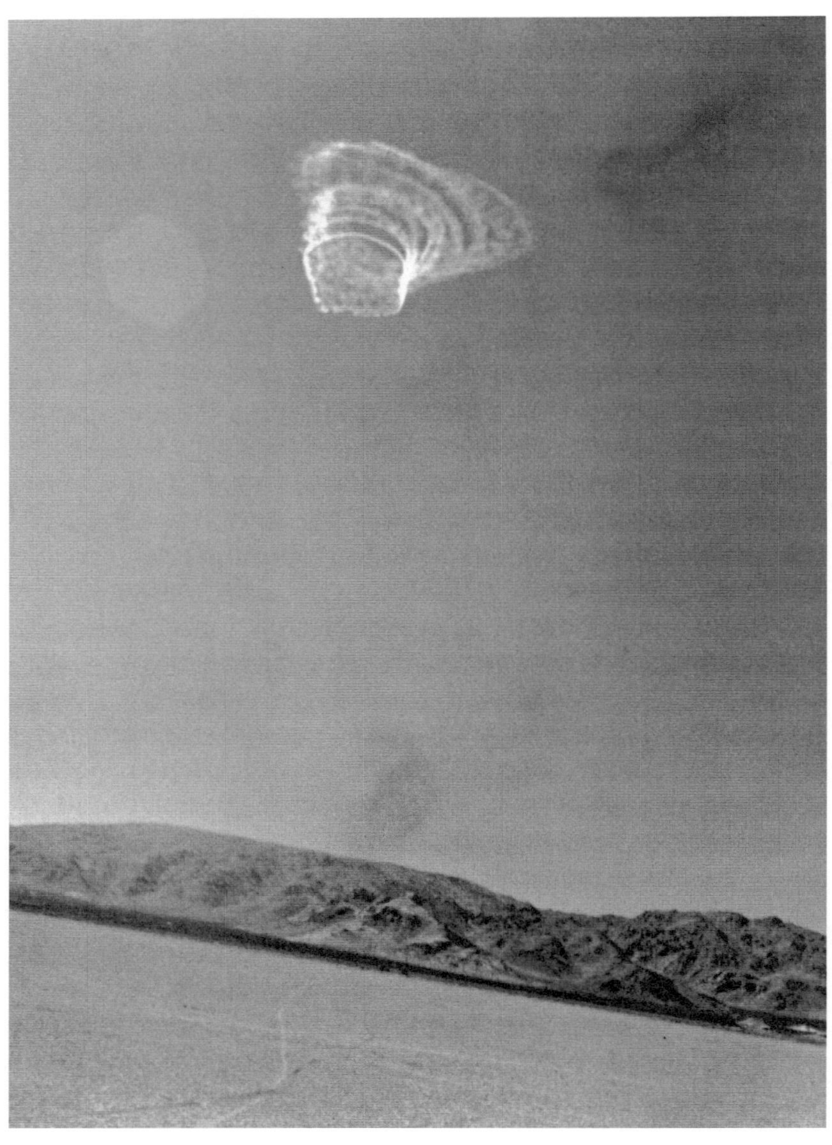

Dennis Oppenheim, *Whirlpool: Eye of the Storm*, 1973. El Mirage dry lake, southern California, ¾- × 4-mile schemata of a vortex (whirlpool), traced in the sky using standard white smoke discharged by an aircraft.

Dennis Oppenheim's Delirious Operations

It is incongruous that Dennis Oppenheim is still often tagged as a "conceptual" artist when his work has always been at odds with such a designation. Not that this label means much anymore, but it's important to stress at the outset that Oppenheim's enterprise seems fundamentally about the dissolution of concepts, about an insistence that abstract systems be treated as physical material to be manipulated. He deals with the corporeality of human experience (including thought), with events that take place on surfaces and in real territories. This is hardly to say that thought is not an issue in his work. But what is central is that thinking is always aligned with physical operations; it is never distinct from an economy of material and forces. This is a question of events rather than ideas. And Oppenheim's venture takes place in the regions that Nietzsche mapped out antagonistically when he wrote, "Philosophers are prejudiced against appearance, change, pain, death, the body, the senses, fate and bondage, the aimless."[1]

Oppenheim's art frustrates attempts to generalize or to structure his activities into coherent periods or types of work. The individual elements of his extremely diverse output spill over into each other, often obsessively repeating specific patterns and practices, only to break off suddenly and begin in a totally new domain. One systematizes his career path only at the cost of losing touch with its essential disjunctions and its disorder. Perhaps one of the best ways of getting a sense of the texture of Oppenheim's career is to study his document called *Catalyst 1967–1974*, a chronological listing of activities, proposed or executed, transcribed from his notebooks. It's a list without consistent punctuation or any clear indication of where the description of one work ends and another begins. The profusion of the activities recorded here merges into one overall chain which, according to Oppenheim, corresponds to "the rhythm underlying my work."[2]

Catalyst is an unruly inventory, a chaotic unfolding of materials, processes, systems, objects, and actions of all kinds. Instead of cataloging distinct "works" or "pieces," it charts a range of experiments or operations that have certain related effects in common. All Oppenheim's projects seem animated by a similar kind of energy, a mobile, disruptive, multiplying desire. Notes for activities indicate some recurring themes: (1) "Interaction of units that do not normally involve each other"; (2) "Seventeen uses for an object"; (3) "Break the law." There are temporary conjunctions of unrelated materials, redirections and overapplications of various inspirations, inscriptions and overlappings of codes and marks on surfaces. Repeatedly we find extensions and expansions of the way objects and systems are dealt with. Persons and objects are defined in terms of use, of relations of force, or points of connection. Whatever he works with, Oppenheim subjects it to a derangement of its established or conventional use or its position in a physical or social field. Materials, language, processes are implicated in reversals, underminings, redistributions, exaggerations, reductions, and collisions. Oppenheim's activity recalls the scope of Richard Serra's *Verb List Compilation* (1967–68), but it also goes beyond that.[3] There is an excessiveness supporting Oppenheim's aspirations, an insistence on the tangibility of everything: a practice that assumes all systems and materials, whether global or microscopic, institutional or anatomical, are open to intervention and modification.

Despite Oppenheim's historical proximity to both minimalism and postminimalism, the kind of operations he performs can be affiliated with some of the innovations of Jasper Johns. The associations and collisions in Oppenheim's work are a radical expansion of the dismantling and overlapping of codes that Johns conducted. By condensing decades of partial experiments (Picasso's *Still Life with Chair Caning*, Duchamp's *Tu m'*, Miró of the mid-1920s, Magritte, etc.), Johns developed a practice in which distinctions between the material and the abstract orders dissolve. Signs and sign systems are detached from a referential function and take on a

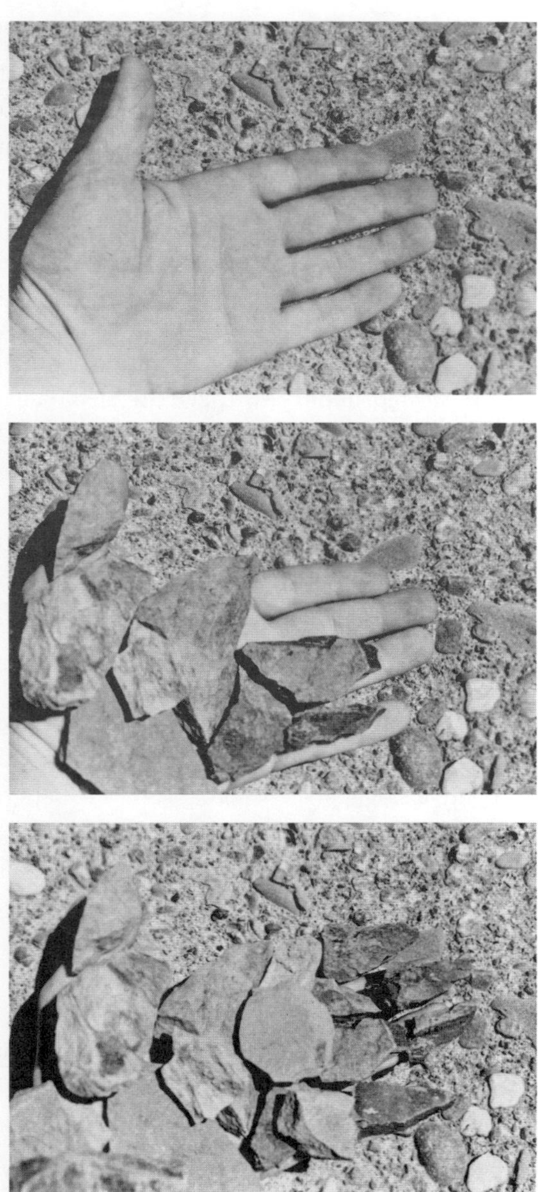

Dennis Oppenheim, *Rocked Hand*, 1970.

floating identity where they can converge with objects and with the activity of the body. What Johns provided for Oppenheim and others was, on the one hand, the indication of a potentially vast array of new vocabularies available for manipulation and recoding; on the other, possible operations that could be carried out on the physical surface of a corporeal, social, or terrestrial field, as well as within the delimited field of painting.

Oppenheim's work, like Johns's, is bound up with a rejection of metaphor and a privileging of surfaces. Obviously, minimalism also discarded metaphor more thoroughly even than Johns, but at the same time it rigorously curtailed the range and diversity of operations and materials that Johns's work had suggested. Johns's so-called literalism seems analogous to certain aspects of Oppenheim's projects, particularly his explicit work with language. For linguistic problems figure, directly or indirectly, in most of Oppenheim's works, whether audio or videotapes, inscriptions of words onto surfaces, or his own written statements accompanying individual pieces. What seems immediately relevant are those activities growing out of a preoccupation with the experience of spoken language, of taking language literally, especially when it is idiomatic. Specific works seem generated by a desire to concretize language: phrases such as "burn up weight," "take my word for it," or "the wrong frame of mind." This makes for two-dimensional dumbness that is akin to Johns, a rechanneling of indirect or figurative speech onto a single plane where it can be experienced without any mediation.

Perhaps it is misleading to discuss Johns in terms of literalism, because what is central in much of his major work is a disquieting snaking *in and out* of representation, of having only a contingent hold on the surface. With Oppenheim and others in the late 1960s we see a sustained, even visceral, effort to get away more completely from representation, and at the same time to leave behind the self-referentiality of minimalism. While Johns's individual signs relinquish an effective referential identity, his work as a whole is still haunted by a preoccupation with language as an apparatus of double articulation, with a hierarchy of signifier/signified. For Oppenheim such a schema is not an issue: problems of signification are supplanted by problems of operation, and what we get in his work is the material or sensuous presence of language, physically intersecting with other systems and networks.[4] His sensibility is wholly different from

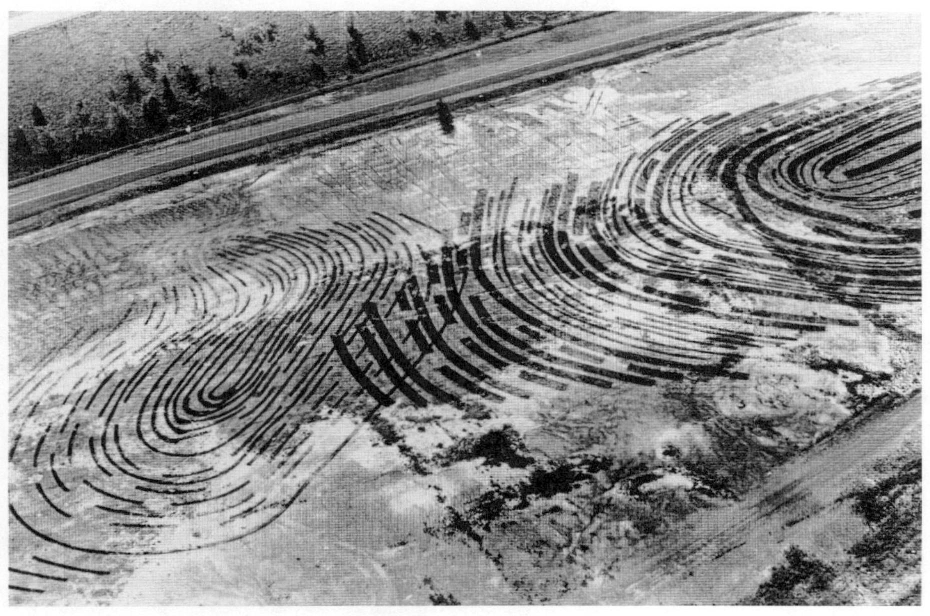

Dennis Oppenheim, *Identity Stretch*, 1970–75. Thumb print of Erik Oppenheim and thumb print of Dennis Oppenheim. Hot sprayed tar, 300 × 1000 feet, Artpark, Lewiston, New York.

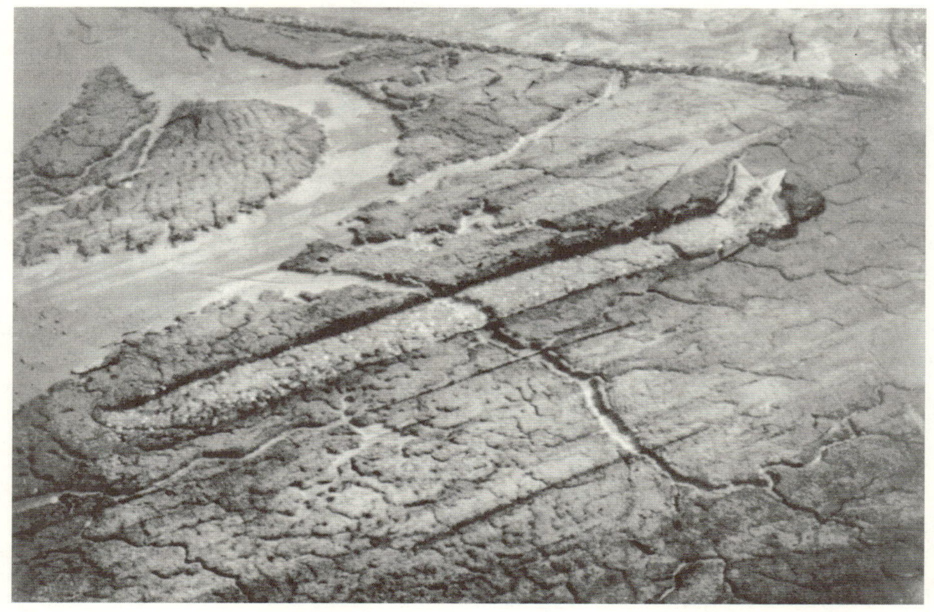

Dennis Oppenheim, *Star Skid*, 1977. Project proposal for western United States, cast concrete and broken glass, 30 feet diameter, 200 feet trench.

Johns's irony. Oppenheim evinces an innocence, as if encountering certain materials and words for the first time and naively inventing new functions and connections for them.

Oppenheim's work in the late 1960s often parallels the work of others, in particular Robert Smithson. Oppenheim and Smithson, working with land during those years, both confronted problems of site and location, using strategies of displacement and doubling. But the apparent closeness of the two artists concealed fundamentally different intellectual positions, as subsequent development made clear. The divergent paths which the two followed are suggested in Smithson's "Sedimentation of the Mind" essay of 1968.[5] This richly ambivalent piece of writing is charged with a vibrant disorder missing from later essays. Shooting out in many directions, Smithson's text sketches an outline of the kind of ideas that would come to characterize Oppenheim's enterprise and, at the same time, elaborates structures in his own thought that would culminate in the dialectical exercises of his 1973 essay on Frederick Law Olmsted. Smithson posited bipolar, categorical frameworks which would become central to his work, such as site vs. nonsite and differentiation vs. dedifferentiation. Yet he also generated a dispersed, noncategorical thought in which language and structures have no stability, caught up in a slow and inexorable disintegration. Smithson wrote: "separate 'things,' 'forms,' 'objects,' 'shapes,' etc. with beginnings and endings are mere convenient fictions: there is only an uncertain disintegrating order that transcends the limits of rational separations." Smithson's dilemma is that the dialectical underpinning of his later work depends precisely on such separations, on the fiction of the opposite and the negative. And the moments when Smithson admits the inadequacy of dialectics are when another order takes over, as in his "Spiral Jetty" essay (1972): an "immense roundness" emerges, out of which the creation of the spiral is possible.

The route Oppenheim traveled is evident: a project of abolishing categorization and separation, of abandoning structural dualities altogether, not one of synthesizing oppositions. When Oppenheim's work involves land, for example, he proceeds without invoking or implying a category or object "nature." He moves independently of a culture/nature polarity. For him earth, nature, people, culture are part of one surface on which all

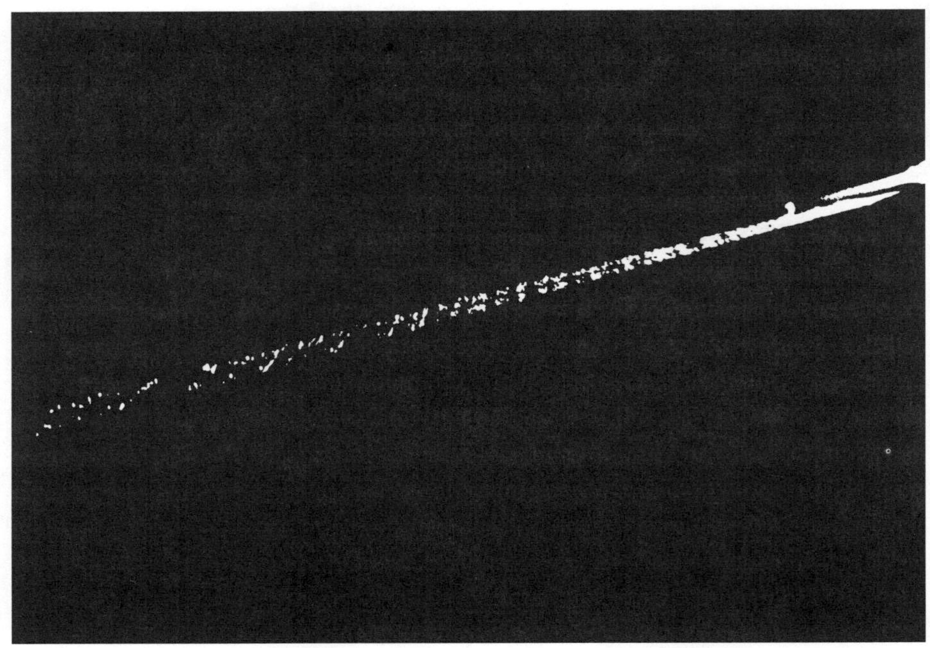

Dennis Oppenheim, *2000′ Shadow Projection*, April 1972. Carbon arc search light and trumpet, performed in Batavia, New York.

boundaries are provisional and fluid. And by staying outside of a man/nature dichotomy Oppenheim frees himself from the implicit humanism that is a tacit but important dimension of Smithson's thinking. Oppenheim challenges the notion of a sovereign or autonomous consciousness behind the work. His activities aim at dissolving divisions between the self and other objects or systems, so that the concept of the human, as an isolable entity becomes unworkable. What minimalism unwittingly supplied Oppenheim and others in the late 1960s and early 1970s was the disclosure of a nomadic subject—a self with an open, shifting relation to the object and free to establish a web of multiple, partial connections with it. Even with Oppenheim's early work, we see a move away from the depositioned status of the self that minimalism heralded, to a self that can interpenetrate or coincide with a diversity of objects, processes, or networks.

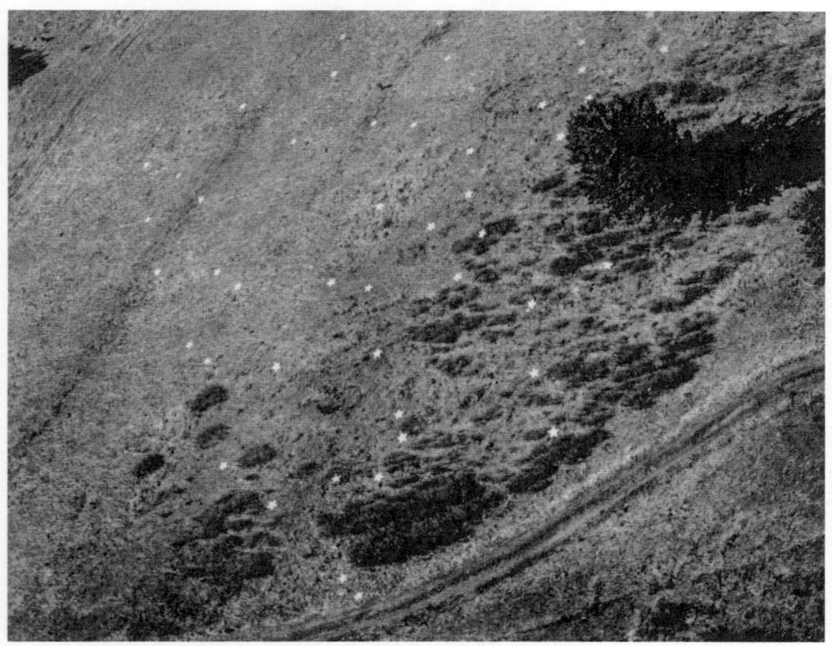

Dennis Oppenheim, *Wishing the Mountains Madness*, 1977. Missoula, Montana, star units 4 × 4 feet, covering four acres.

The titles of his work from around 1970 suggest some of the "material interchanges" he experimented with: *Arm and Wire, Wrist and Hand, Glassed Hand, Leafed Hand*. In *Wishing Well* (1973), Oppenheim's monologue is about the will to merge the body with a concrete wall. *Extended Armor* (1970) is about expanding the body's effectiveness beyond its physical limits. In *2000′ Shadow Projection* (1972), Oppenheim works with light and shadow to destabilize the body's location in space, generating an experience of being in two places at once. He conveys the sense that any substance, body, or sign is always plugged into a constellation of networks and systems as part of a material flux, never discrete. Nothing is articulated as an independent unit but as an element in a field of manifold, encroaching events. The self is defined only by what it is adjacent to, by the objects and forces it connects with.

Around 1973 or 1974 Oppenheim's method of working seemed to change abruptly. He moved into gallery situations, putting together various installations and setups, a number of them involving puppets. Paranoia and despair became part of the experience of his work. But these pieces were not as removed from his previous projects as they may have initially appeared. One objective of this work was to enact the mechanisms of various (especially psychological) traps and enclosures, out of which his earlier work had shown escape routes. The installations present a series of impasses, situations of being locked onto one site or inflexible path. We get the mechanized marionette in *Theme for a Major Hit* (1974), which endlessly performs its redundant song and dance; the toy trains on the circular track in *Predictions* (1973); the conveyor belt in *Wishing Well* (1973); the regimented grid-like set-up in *Lecture* (1976); the figure that ceaselessly smashes its head into a bell in *Attempt to Raise Hell* (1974); the revolving record on a huge turntable in *Early Morning Blues* (1977). In these and other pieces, desire is channeled into deadening and repetitive operations or rigid paranoiac attachments—situations that are the inverse of the multiple and shifting investments of the previous work as well as other work that Oppenheim produced concurrently. One of the principal traps Oppenheim is describing is the experience of being defined as an individual, and of the interiority that individuality implies. Because the puppets that function prominently in many of these works are self-portraits, Jacques Lacan's insistence that the individual is constituted through representation seems relevant: that the individual comes into being only with the manufacture of an image of the body as an enclosed whole, immune to fragmentation. And it is this "armor of an alienating identity" that Oppenheim exhibits as both a physical and a mental prison. At the same time, some of these works hint at the circulation of desire trying to slip out of the walls around it. *Search for Clues* (1976) is built around a monologue recited by Oppenheim's daughter, in which intimations of incest emerge, not as transgression of law, but as a route beyond the twin limits of death and individuality, beyond the confines of an interiorized consciousness.

Much of what Oppenheim does implies an effort of de-defining the self, getting out of the trap of interiority. Instead of the mind reflecting on itself, thought is relocated onto the same surface supporting our bodies—a

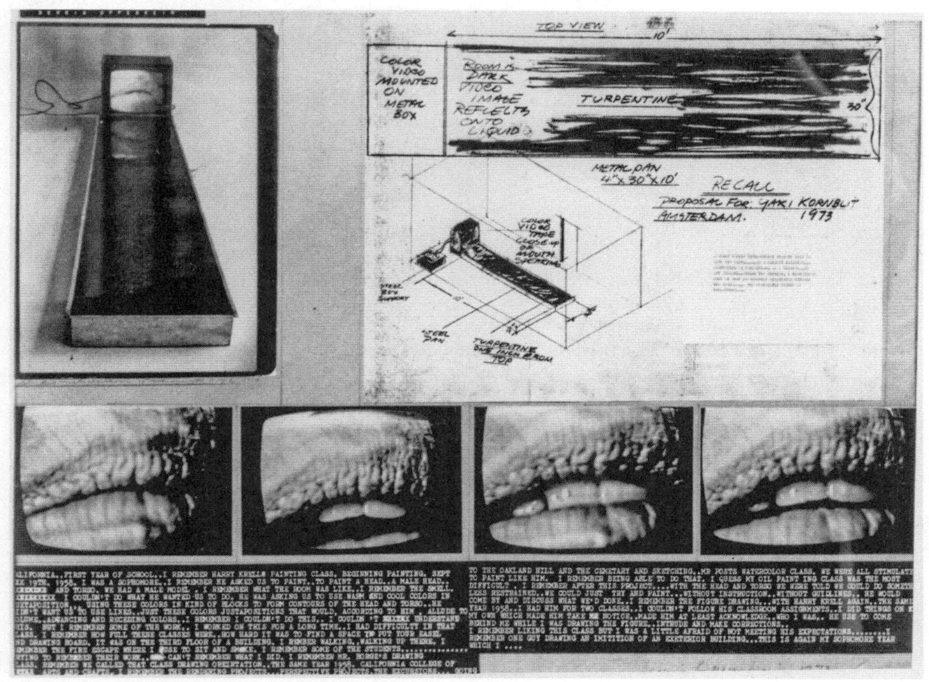

Dennis Oppenheim, *Recall*, 1974. Video monitor, metal pan, turpentine and black tint.

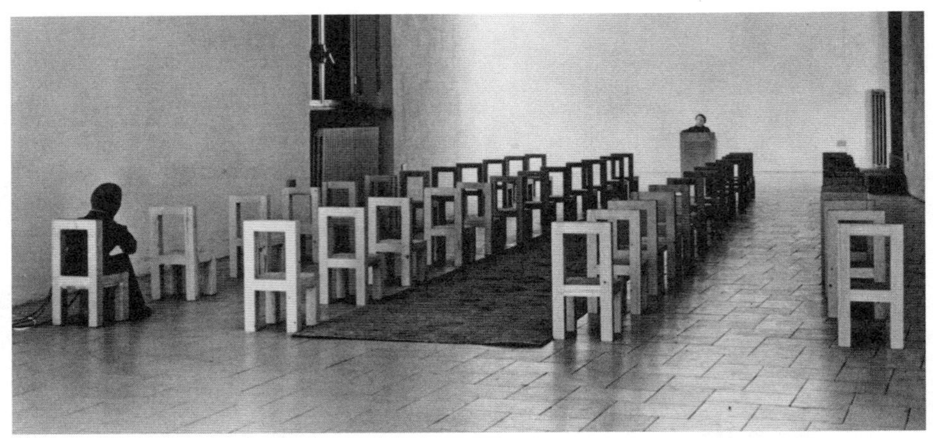

Dennis Oppenheim, *Lecture Piece #1*, 1976. Surrogate figure in the image of the artist supplied with mechanized lip sync voice control, forty 12-inch chairs, lectern, lamp, 20-minute stereo soundtrack.

surface where all kinds of syntheses, breaks, disruptions are possible, where desire is free to make new associations and investments, no longer administered by the ego or by institutions. What he achieves in many of his activities is a situation where we are unable to say whether the self is presented as subject or as object. In this way he evades being turned into a "case," a person with a history who can be studied or analyzed. For if someone is not delimited or individualized, he or she cannot be normalized, made part of a structure, which requires what Michel Foucault calls a knowable, "disciplinary individual." As fewer boundaries are defined, the more forms of control are bypassed or neutralized.

That Oppenheim never works in one area or mode for very long is part of this refusal to be classified; it is a strategy of constantly diversifying the fronts on which he operates. Often his working method is like that of the bricoleur, a handyman or mechanic who works with found materials or spare parts, making new interlockings of unrelated elements. But Oppenheim does not rely on spontaneity or automatic processes.

Like William Burroughs's cut-ups, his work has its own rigorous technology, controlling what is put into it according to definite procedures. Both Oppenheim and Burroughs recognize that the self is cut from reality as long as one is involved in representation. So while Oppenheim may use signs or sign systems, they are no longer representative; and when language figures in his work, it is in terms of operations that are not linguistic. What we get are actions or events that are intensive and nonsignifying. For example, his pieces in which words are spelled out in burning flares over fields and hillsides: they are an experience of language in which questions of meaning or communication are peripheral for Oppenheim engineers an extravagant event in which a fragment of thought, broken off from any rational or discursive practice, is fused onto the earth in a moment of pure expenditure. In another work, *Whirlpool: Eye of the Storm* (1973), a piece that seems both homage and response to Smithson's *Spiral Jetty*, Oppenheim discharged white smoke from an airplane in the shape of a vortex high over a California desert. Here he produces a fleeting inscription that exists only as event, an intensive sign with which the human subject is aligned: both sign and self constitute a single delirious path.

1, Friedrich Nietzsche, *The Will to Power*, trans. Walter Kaufmann (New York: Vintage, 1968), p 220.
2. Dennis Oppenheim, "Catalyst 1967–1974," in *Individuals: Post-Movement Art in America*, ed. Alan Sondheim (New York: Dutton, 1977), pp. 246–66.
3. Richard Serra, "Documents," *Avalanche*, Winter 1971, p. 20.
4. See Félix Guattari, *La révolution moléculaire* (Paris: Éditions Recherches, 1977), pp. 253–56.
5. Robert Smithson, "A Sedimentation of the Mind: Earth Projects," *Artforum*, September 1968, pp. 44–50.

Originally published in *Artforum*, November 1978.

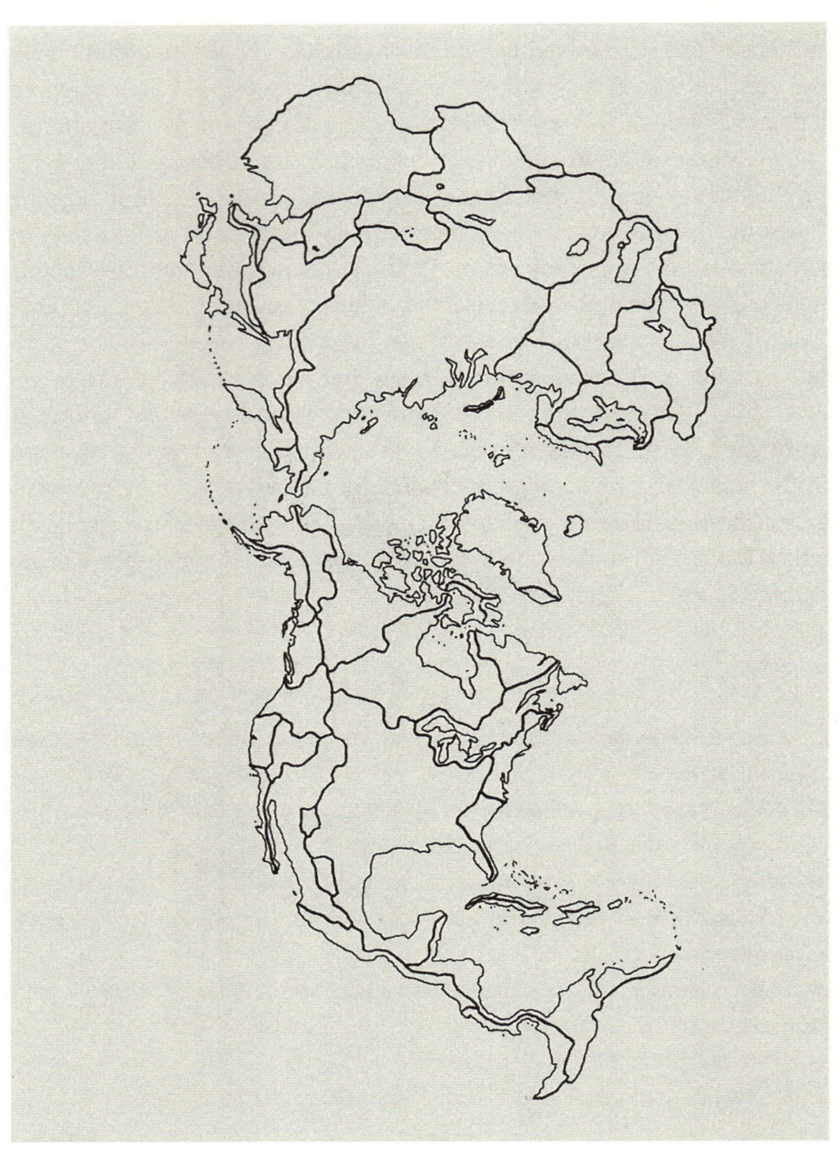

Peter Fend, *Potential Autonomies: Map of Drainage Basin Areas*, 1979.

Peter Fend's Global Architecture

Back in 1963, Buckminster Fuller wrote hopefully that the coming decades might see the emergence of what he called "comprehensive designers," who would be a synthesis of "artist, inventor, mechanic, objective economist, and evolutionary strategist." It may be surprising to find someone meeting Fuller's specifications now active in the labyrinth of artists' spaces in Lower Manhattan. Only thirty years old, Peter Fend is an unusual jack-of-all-trades, even in the plurality of the current New York art scene. He has a formidable background in biology, physics, zoology, history, architecture, urban planning, and economics, and he did regional planning in the midwest, has extensive wilderness living experience, and recently worked nights at the Fulton Fish Market. For the last several years he has participated in a variety of artist-run projects and exhibitions in New York, including the Times Square and Real Estate shows and the New York New Wave Show at P.S. 1.

Taking off from the American landscape tradition of Frederick Law Olmsted and Robert Smithson, Fend's work is based on an understanding of the world as a living earthwork and on the goal of forging a functioning and habitable global environment. In articles, drawings, maps, video, and multimedia proposals, Fend practices architectural thinking on a large scale. For him any kind of urban planning is inseparable from the interconnected physical systems of air, land, and water by which a city lives and breathes, and he integrally links his architecture to working with oceans, farming, and energy sources. Although active in designing urban megastructures, he believes the most immediate task is to make secure and viable the biological underpinning of city life. What distinguishes Fend from other artists involved in large-scale environmental projects are the visionary scope of his work, his insistence that environmental engineering entails major political and economic reorganization, and the seriousness of his efforts to put his plans in practice. While Smithson foregrounded sites and processes of dissipation and collapse, Fend believes in our capacity to initiate regeneration of the environment, and refusing the pessimism of many others, insists that we possess the means to maintain the earth as a life-sustaining system without poisoning or depleting it.

Two of his central concerns are pollution control and renewable energy sources. Fend is highly knowledgeable on waste treatment and conversion methods; in articles and lectures he discusses how urban and chemical wastes can be broken down into hydrocarbons. He emphasizes how this hydrocarbon base not only can be turned into energy but also into food in the form of yeast and fungi. At the same time, Fend sees the oceans offering another, and potentially limitless, supply of both these essentials. He also demonstrates persuasively that meeting food and energy needs through ocean farming of kelp and through waste conversion can be extremely profitable, thus creating financial incentive for keeping the seas unpolluted. The trick, he says, is to convince the public they can eat oil and garbage.

For Fend, such new forms of food production would reduce the need for land-based agriculture. An article he wrote several years ago began, "Agriculture Will Destroy Us," and proceeded to explain how farming depletes soil, reduces diversity of species, removes essentials for higher life from circulation, and releases biocides from fertilizers into rivers, wetlands, and seas. His postagricultural world is a quasi-science-fiction visualization of immense tracts of jungle, marshland, and savanna, all vital components of a living planet. Instead of domesticating farm animals, he proposes vast areas of open range land in which large herds of wild animals would be allowed to repopulate, and he cites recent research proving, much to the dismay of vegetarians, that more meat for human consumption can be produced per acre on wild land than through traditional animal farming. Again, he looks to meet human needs while preserving other species and the land's richness and diversity.

One of the most controversial aspects of Fend's plans is how he links economic and political organization with his proposed ocean-based

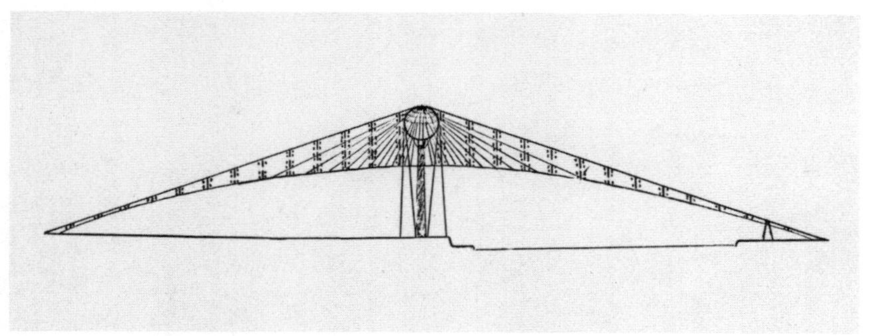

Peter Fend, *Prototype of Windbreak-Canopy for City, Supported by Exhaust Heat Ducted from Buildings*, 1979.

industries. Key to his thinking is the idea of structuring his environmental management schemes on a decentralized and local basis. Much of his recent exhibited work has been about defining viable geographical regions that could support ocean farming programs. After several years of studying world geography and ocean currents, Fend has redrawn the political map of the globe into new configurations defined entirely by topography. Instead of current national boundaries, he sees the world as an aggregate of watershed basin areas, shaped by mountain ranges and the flow of water to the sea. Each of these zones he identifies as a "saltwater polity," economically autonomous territory, self-sufficient in food and energy. Unlike Buckminster Fuller's Dymaxion map, which was a cerebral reconceptualization of the position of the continents, Fend's maps are based on the physical passage of water through land, on the elemental flows generative of all life and culture. His starting point is the sensual and physiological experience of the body's situatedness on the earth, and at the heart of his proposals and designs is a visceral intuition of the world as a living pattern of circulation and biochemical exchanges. Like a twentieth-century physiocrat, Fend believes that an economy is a natural system in which all wealth originates directly from the earth and that economic principles should derive directly from the physiology of the body.

Fend demonstrated that many of his topographically determined "basin states" often closely correspond to regions sought by separatist movements

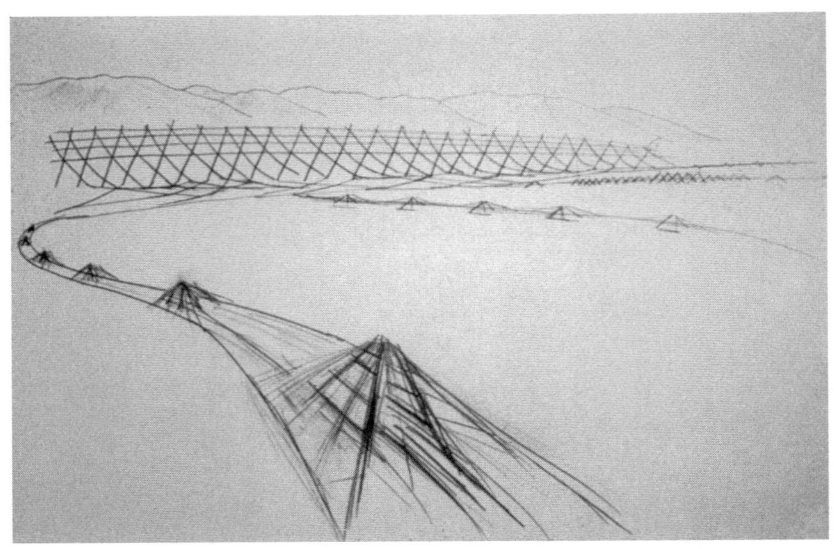

Peter Fend, *Megastructures*, 1979.

or which match the territorial ambitions of various imperial powers throughout history. In a project called *Iran Plan*, he showed how Iran could be split up into five autonomous basin regions that recognize the territory of the Kurds, of oil-rich southwest Iran (the current war zone), and of other identities now subsumed by today's borders. His new regional mappings also suggest solutions for important international problems. Pointing to a mountain-bound area containing most of the Sinai, Fend says confidently, "This will be Palestine," and he elaborates an image of a new Palestinian state with an economy based on fishing industries and ocean production of methane and hydrocarbons. "Underground water sources will be tapped, dry lake areas fertilized, causing increased vegetation. Railways, pipelines, linear megastructural settlements will connect coastal industries with inland cities. The Sinai will be a green land again." Whether such a transformation actually happens is not the issue; what matters to Fend now is to expand notions of the possible in global thinking.

Fend insists that Renaissance ideas of space still govern attitudes to the environment. Just as *quattrocento* painting described a world in which space existed independently of its contents, it also implied a space that would remain constant despite the extraction of material from it, a notion behind present-day exploitation of natural resources. Fend also sees some of these conceptualizations persisting in recent art. For example, he's critical of Alan Sonfist's fenced-off parcel of land, at Houston Street and LaGuardia Place, which purports to recreate the original vegetation of prehistoric Manhattan. Fend sees this circumscribing of space as a falsification in that it denies all the vectors of air, rain, garbage, birds, and insects that weave that space into a much larger environmental mesh. Futurist art was important in giving Fend a sense of space as a field of multiple interpenetrations in which no aesthetic or technical problem can be isolated from the entire active and mobile territory in which it is implicated. Other, more recent art contributed to this view of the world as circulatory, in flux, and intestinal: gravity and flow system pieces by Smithson and Dennis Oppenheim, Joseph Beuys's *Fat Corner*, Carolee Schneemann's *Meat Joy*, and Klaus Rinke's tubing.

Since he became active in the New York art world, Fend has worked almost exclusively in artist-run or artist-controlled undertakings. In 1979 he joined in a collaborative association with five other artists who had all felt the need for a structure to facilitate expanding their activities beyond existing art institutions. Those involved—Jenny Holzer, Coleen Fitzgibbon, Peter Nadin, Richard Prince, Robin Winters, and Fend—formed an organization loosely modeled on a law firm but which offered aesthetic and media guidance rather than legal counsel. Their business card read: "Practical esthetic services adaptable to client situations / Our consultation includes a review of your needs and suggestions for realistic action."

Some of Fend's independent New York projects have been urban planning proposals for specific parts of the city. One of his best-received works was his contribution to the January 1980 Real Estate Show. Titled *Delancey Street Goes to the Sea*, it was a detailed plan about how the Lower East Side actually could secede from Con Ed and restructure its tax payment and rent system to enable it to incorporate separately from the rest of the city (as Beverly Hills is to Los Angeles). At the heart of the plan was a community-owned and operated waste treatment facility that would generate self-sufficient energy as well as marketable food and fuel products. An outgrowth of this project was a stunning proposal, exhibited last fall in

Duisburg, Germany, for a radical reorganization of the steel industry and landscape of the entire Ruhr region. In the much-discussed Times Square Show, Fend displayed an architectural project for midtown Manhattan in which 42nd Street would be leveled and replaced by a green swath of parks, trees, and gardens. Overhead a megastructural skeleton would serve as a constantly changing shopping bazaar and entertainment area. Some Times Square Show participants felt Fend's plan was too respectable for that event and were disappointed that it would have "de-sleazed" the 42nd Street area by wiping out the porno industry.

Recently, Fend initiated what is his potentially most important enterprise to date. He is now coordinating Ocean Earth Construction and Development Corporation, a legally incorporated firm which he hopes will be a credible and effective base from which to deal with business, scientific, and government institutions, as well as a structure to accommodate other artists' projects that reach beyond the gallery. Identified as Ocean Earth Corporation, Fend now can communicate with various companies that have expressed interest in some of his specific designs and can deal with them in a trade secret–protected situation. Some of the ideas he plans to market include an offshore seaweed harvesting rig, waste conversion equipment, and a modular architectural system involving air freight containers. Other plans include tensile canopies for urban climate control, an international video distribution program, and megastructure frameworks. Smithson's work as a consultant for the design of the Dallas–Fort Worth airport is often singled out as an example of the artist breaking out of traditional roles to become a participant in non-art planning. Fend's latest venture seems to realize many of the possibilities implied in Smithson's airport project.

If Fend's corporate undertaking gets nowhere, it can be chalked off as another in a long string of failures by artists to operate effectively outside an art-world context. But even a small measure of success would encourage the hope that artists can have significant influence on economic, scientific, and social planning. Cultural institutions have reduced the artist's role to sideshow performer, one who will never play in the big tent, and most artists, even those who insist they want a joining of art and life, are enamored of their social marginality and have a romantic stake in their own powerlessness. If Marcel Duchamp's fake *Monte Carlo Bonds* of 1924 bespeak the detachment of most artists from major networks of power and exchange, the legal documents and stock certificates inaugurating Fend's corporation signify an alternative conception of the artist's role in which aesthetic and social thinking become indistinguishable.

Originally commissioned by the *Village Voice* in 1980. First published in *Arts Magazine*, June 1981.

Psychopathways: Horror Movies and the Technology of Everyday Life

How is it that *Psycho* remained preeminent for so long? Not that it doesn't continue to hold sway over audiences and filmmakers now, but only recently it has edged back from its position as an unrivaled model for horror movies. For nearly twenty years it loomed as the work that had authoritatively articulated the notion of horror as interior, domestic, familial, lodged within the banal and the familiar. Released in 1960, *Psycho* was immediately a cultural event that exceeded its purely filmic status; it produced effects even on those who did *not* see it. One of its significant repercussions was the launching of the word "psycho" into broad popular usage, where it intersected with other emerging social vectors at that moment. Over two decades later it is difficult to hear afresh the uncertain resonance of this film title, ending in "o" like *Vertigo*. Years of psychological jargon in Hollywood movies had not fully prepared audiences for the sound of this brute, clinical truncation. Did it mean a state of mind, a person, a mental illness; was it an adjective? In the posters and ads for *Psycho*, the juxtaposition of the title with the image of an anxious Janet Leigh in bra and slip set up a volatile confluence of fear, sexuality, and deviance. Even through secondhand verbal description the motel shower murder became emblematic of new experiences of social vulnerability. Appearing in those brief post-1950s but pre-JFK assassination years, Norman Bates came into view before Richard Speck, before Charles Whitman in the Texas tower, before the other quiet loners who would snap became palpable figures at the periphery of our collective awareness. Hitchcock tapped into fears that had not yet

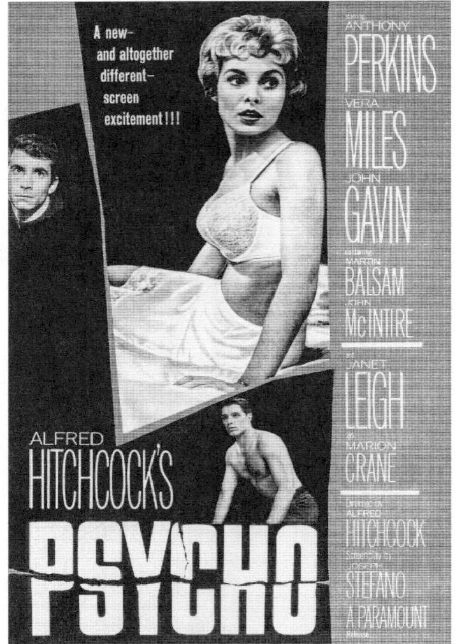

Poster for Alfred Hitchcock's *Psycho*, 1960.

become socially crystallized or fully transformed into objects of mass consumption.

It was also around 1960 that Hitchcock approached the zenith of his popularity and effectiveness. He became a unique cultural entity, both through his own proto-Warholian shrewdness at self-promotion and simultaneous manipulation of film, TV, and print, and because of the unstable, shifting texture of that historical moment. How can we explain that during these few years he made, back to back, the only two horror films out of his more than fifty movies? If Hitchcock, with *The Birds* and *Psycho*, bequeathed to future directors two distinct though often intersecting models (horror as domestic and interior and horror as exterior and alien), he also left them his cynicism about desire and his formal codification of the audience as voyeur/victim. But what Hitchcock kept for his own, and what events would not allow him to bequeath to his heirs was the alibi of entertainment he provided for his audience by virtue of his carefully managed public image. Any screen horror was always linked reassuringly to his pose as clowning showman or to the frivolity of his TV theme music. No one since then has engineered that paradoxical overlapping of pessimism and play.

After the dislocations of the 1960s, new paradigms for horror movies emerged in which the premises of *Psycho* and *The Birds* were intermeshed and expanded. Two films from 1967 and 1968, seemingly incommensurable, opened up a new phase. Jean-Luc Godard's *Weekend* and George Romero's *Night of the Living Dead* posed possibilities for fusing cinematic horror with the contours of contemporary social experience. In visions of an entire self-destructing landscape, fear of death as a source of horror was supplanted by images of a life and culture that were deathlike. Both films helped to install cannibalism as a central motif in subsequent horror movies, with scenes of families or groups eating each other's flesh indicating explicitly the rapacious consumerism of postindustrial capitalism. They each depicted spaces in which onscreen chaos extended indefinitely beyond the frame: Godard's cavalcade of highway carnage and Romero's Pennsylvania farmland populated haphazardly with somnambulant zombies, like an all-over painting.

The surfaces of these films, the intellectual pretensions of *Weekend* and the physical intensity of *Night of the Living Dead*, have influenced other directors for more than a decade with their images of social cataclysm. Even Francis Ford Coppola's *Apocalypse Now* (1979), a kind of "Weekend on the Mekong," mimicked the picaresque itinerary and ambivalent termination of Godard's 1967 film. But as Hitchcock well knew, what constitutes horror must be continually redefined and defamiliarized for its effects to be anything other than the pleasure of repetition. Through reuse, the charged texture of *Night of the Living Dead* was tamed into conventionality. What was a disruptive vitality in 1968 became the deft repackaged assortment of shocks in Romero's *Dawn of the Dead* (1979), severed from the raw, harshly lit panic of his earlier film. *Dawn of the Dead* functions as a formalized mechanism for eliciting a disjointed series of responses from us: the quick, involuntary twinge as we watch some unfortunate's intestines torn out or soporific monsters blown apart by shotguns. A film that posed as an indictment of plastic consumer society (four people besieged in a vast shopping mall by flesh-eating zombies), it never exceeded its own status as a highly consumable collection of special-effects techniques.

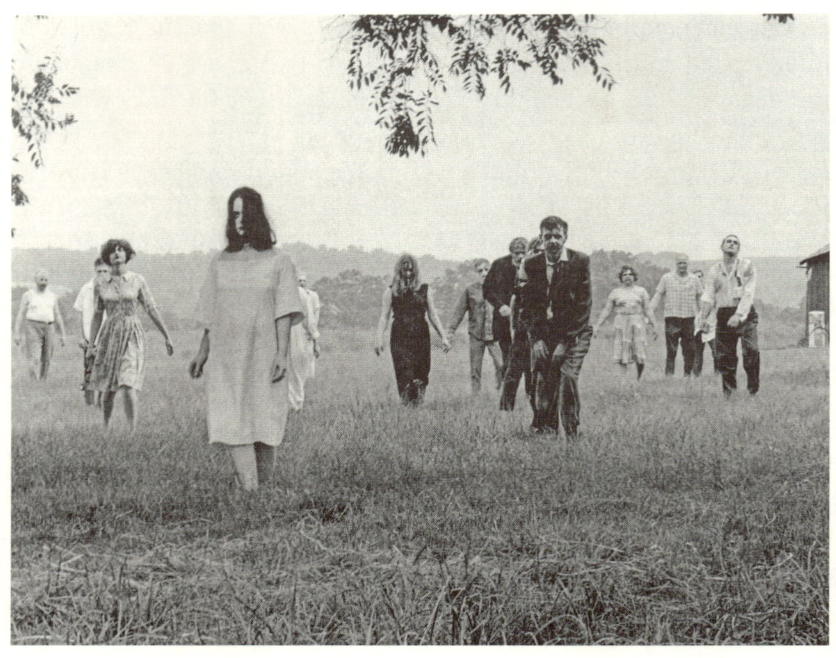

George Romero, *Night of the Living Dead*, 1968.

A recent trend in horror films has been images of bodies and heads exploding (*The Fury*, *Scanners*, *Alien*, *Outland*, *Dawn of the Dead*). Even the Lucas-Spielberg family-oriented *Raiders of the Lost Ark* graphically exhibits people exploding, imploding, and melting. One could possibly argue that the popular fascination with such scenes reflects an affirmative collective appetite: that images of the human form, seen overwhelmingly on TV and in advertising, have become so intertwined with a flat and lifeless object world, so adjacent to commodities, that any violence done to their false unity and inviolable surfaces has a liberating dimension. The gratification of this breakup would be in the dissolution of the repressive insularity of individuality, the smashing of the body as a controllable, marketable structure. But the very currency and pervasiveness of such depictions of corporal fragmentation clearly undermines such speculation. Dismemberment has taken on essentially the same value as car chases, soft-core sex, battling space ships, towering infernos, and the like. Onscreen all these are interchangeable, equivalent quantities. They are simply spectacular substitutes for any real pleasure and evidence of a barely concealed boredom on an immense scale. Narrative is often merely a rack on which to hang units of abstracted slaughter. The concerned debate in the late '60s (*Bonnie and Clyde*, *Straw Dogs*) about the aestheticization of violence seems remote now. The main issue about violence in horror films today is its banalization and neutralization.

Along with timing and texture, the affective core of most horror movies is the nature of the frightening agency or perpetrator. But how often we still hear the same restricted vocabulary to pinpoint the source of horror: the unconscious, the dark side, the return of the repressed, and so on. A striking feature of many recent horror films is the absence or unimportance of intimations of depth, of concealed submersion. Instead, distinctions between the monstrous and the normative have been relocated to simply different locations on the same exposed surface. Our experience now is less one of psychological layers and polarities than it is of positions and pathways in physical territories. Our terror (and pleasure) is of spaces and their margins, of sociopathic zones, of detours off main flows, of deviant patterns of circulation. *Psycho* was transitional; its central architectural amalgam of ancestral home fused onto a motel posed two fundamentally different sites. On one hand, the archaeological, stratified depth of the home; on the other, the motel as an indifferent horizontal extension, a random point on a lateral network of highway and other social circuitry.

John Carpenter's *Halloween*, a film about collisions and intersections on a carefully defined terrain, is prototypical of this new space. Carpenter's killer travels on alternate, disjointed routes of movement against the grain of the planned layout of a suburban neighborhood. Moving at erratic, unpredictable speeds, either slow or very fast, he violates the established lines of sidewalk, street, and hedges so that the transgression of conventional patterns is immediately disruptive and threatening. The psycho-on-the-loose in *Halloween* can be read as a figure who challenged familial structures, resisted institutional confinement, and rejected language, but this antisocial activity and aberrance can only be represented as a grotesque series of violent attacks upon ourselves.

The link between images of deviance and routes through ill-defined territories dominated one of the important horror films of the late 1970s, *The Hills Have Eyes* by Wes Craven, who also made the celebrated post-cathartic *Last House on the Left*. In a tale of a vacationing family whose car and trailer break down in a remote desert area where they are attacked by cannibalistic mutants, the hysteria of *The Hills Have Eyes* is of being in a terrain without roads, where maps are useless, with no demarcations of what area is safe or perilous. Craven overhauls the hackneyed, wagon-train narratives in Hollywood films, and implicit in his revision is an ambiguous sense of space, of the impossibility of establishing any defensive perimeter against what seems to be a menacing otherness. But the otherness here is in fact the dark reflection of the middle-class family under siege. Circling the wagons is a useless strategy when what is outside is already part of what is inside. This nightmare of the sociopathic is generated by the experience of being adrift in an uncentered field without boundaries, without the secure positions, identities, and armature of a recognizable social world. Craven's opening scene, an entropic jumble of gas station, decaying shacks, and rusted auto wrecks, sets up an initial threshold zone where the markers of a "civilized" world begin to erode and collapse, and the distinctions between the two families lose their clarity.

The consequences of making a wrong turn have long been a part of American horror movies, but ever since Janet Leigh said to Tony Perkins that she "must have gotten off the main highway," the status of mobility and circulation take on disturbing resonances. The highway exists as a controlling and channeling apparatus, but at the same time it is also a forking, multiplying network with the built-in possibility of diversion, of convulsive detour. Probably the ultimate wrong turn movie descended from *Psycho* was *Texas Chainsaw Massacre* by Tobe Hooper. Here, in another work whose title was almost as influential as the film itself, the tension between familial home and open road twists in on itself. Both have become sites of chaos; the margins have filled the middle. Beginning and ending on a highway, it unravels an unbroken itinerary of monstrosity throughout. There is less explicit violence than the title suggests: no onscreen dismemberment, no streams of blood. Instead, its terror is built up through its soundtrack of whining chainsaw, the overlapping of a victim's scream, a tormentor's laughter, and one of the most macabre interior sets in any film, all placed within a drought-ridden, contaminated landscape beset by malefic forces of sun and moon.

Hooper's man-machine hybrid of the masked killer coupled with his chainsaw is, in part, a surrogate for a helmeted pilot fused with his F-16 fighter bomber and that ubiquitous and predatory control of space. But this sense of faceless technological terrorism is combined with the enactment of bizarre totemic rituals: self-mutilation, ceremonial burning of photographs, pictograms drawn in blood. At the heart of the film is a distinction between the ascendancy of depersonalized technological violence and a lost past in which violent human instincts had a socially integrated outlet in the slaughter of animals. (We learn that the film's killers lost their jobs at a slaughterhouse after the introduction of new mechanized killing methods.) *Texas Chainsaw Massacre* articulates the dimensions of what René Girard calls "the sacrificial crisis": the chaos and disaster that overtakes any society when sacrificial rites of purifying violence disappear from communal practice. The violence previously channeled into the slaughter of animals spills over to engulf everything, and with a hallucinatory intensity the film unfolds a relentless image of the world as charnel house. One can go to Goya at his most cynical for something comparable.

The wave of movies about psychic powers presents another notion of marginality, revolving around the figure of the gifted individual. For the audience, however, the idea of the "psychic" intermingles with the "psychotic." It becomes another form of deviance, of difference, and the use of these powers is almost always threatening, unleashing chaotic and uncontrollable forces across a wide social field. Recent films about ESP and telekinesis consistently portray the holders of such abilities as helpless and unknowing, often as children who are bewildered, panicked, even destroyed, as in *Carrie*, *The Shining*, *Don't Look Now*, *The Fury*, *The Medusa Touch*, *The Shout*, *Eyes of Laura Mars*, *The Heretic*, *The Last Wave*. It is a curious inversion of the characters descended from Caligari and Mabuse, whose hypnotic authority and mental strength shaped events and were instruments of control and mastery. Why big commercial films continually show psychic powers as fraught with terror is an intriguing question. Brian De Palma's *Carrie* is paradigmatic: it superficially satisfies fantasies of power while insisting on the underlying impotence and failure of the person so gifted. On the surface there is a superficial valorization of the psychic individual, but more significantly there is a stronger fear of difference and of heightened individual agency.

Stanley Kubrick's *The Shining* and Nicolas Roeg's *Don't Look Now* are perhaps the most notable recent ESP movies. But while Roeg is fundamentally interested in the phenomena of psychic experience, Kubrick uses the story of a telepathic child as the basis for another of his baroque and equivocal meditations on the winding down of Western civilization. The late-1960s symphonic expansiveness of *2001* is inverted in *The Shining*, in the confinement of its claustrophobic interiority. As a horror film it opens up a more intricate and problematic field in its delineation of a complex, shifting system of entrapment, controlling and paralyzing those within it. It is a trap constituted by architectural space, by the family, by social hierarchies of domination, by history, and above all by a cultural milieu overloaded with multiple levels of images and representation.

The Overlook Hotel is in a lineage of great but doomed houses from Poe's House of Usher to Orson Welles's Xanadu. Here it's also an emblem of the violent imposition of Western culture on land already inhabited. The gilt opulence of the hotel, decorated with trophies of conquered races and species, Navajo rugs, and buffalo heads, is not as remote from the monster house in *Texas Chainsaw Massacre* as its well-groomed surfaces might seem. It reveals itself as a citadel of white patriarchal power with an explicitness unusual for Kubrick. Not since *Lolita* has he so elaborated

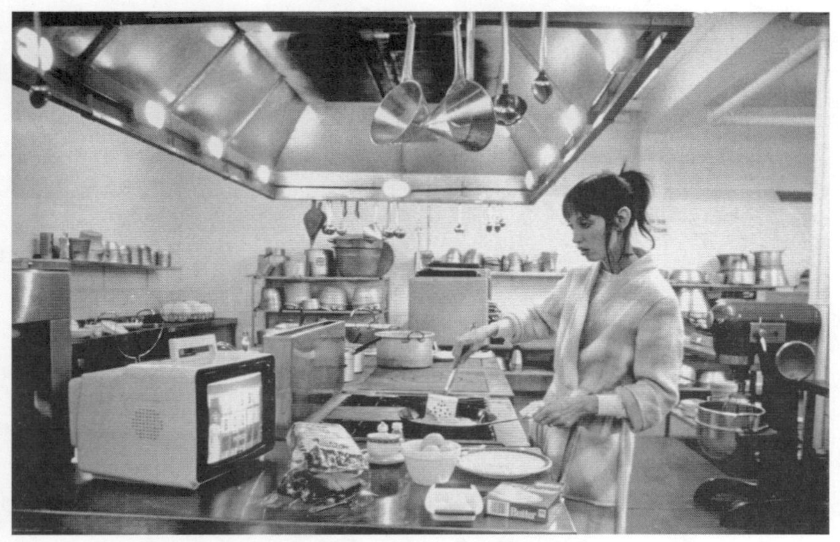

Stanley Kubrick, *The Shining*, 1980.

the texture of American life, carefully choosing every detail of language, clothing, and objects. The hotel's immense overstocked kitchen and pantry situates us in a postscarcity, commodity-saturated space, with emotional hunger in the midst of abundance. A reference to the Donner Party is more than just a throwaway; an image of the original American pioneering impulse ending in a snowbound debacle of cannibalism, it comes as the Torrance family also journeys into the mountains. A lunchbox decorated as a covered wagon seen in Danny's bedroom before this car ride emphasizes the link between hunger, consumption, and an American past. But the allusions to a brutal national history also are an anticipation of a future cataclysm of terrifying scale. Kubrick's baffling image of a deluge of blood surging from the hotel's elevator shafts like some biblical retribution is a dream of annihilation and oceanic terror, apparently experienced by all four major characters.

The crisis of the nuclear family is prominent in *The Shining*, and it is tempting to oedipalize the film, to plot out its lines of movement according to the dynamics of a familial triangle. But Kubrick insists on setting the family and its wreckage within a larger network of relationships of subservience and authority, in the key figures of Black chef, bartender, waiter, hotel boss, and pediatrician. We first see the family literally arrayed into a pyramid, cramped in the privatizing confines of a small car, but the visual structure of the rest of the film involves a destabilizing, centrifugal energy, generating lines of flight out of the family unit: we see the three of them moving on divergent paths and in disconnected spaces and levels of the hotel, intersecting with fragments of other forces and other times. *The Shining* shares much with Nicholas Ray's *Bigger Than Life*: both are broad-daylight horror films in which murderous and megalomaniacal fathers are the products not just of familial constraints but also of the oppressive demands of their larger social environment.

As narrative, *The Shining* is an odd transposition of Stephen King's overinflated novel into a pared down Borgesian puzzle. A kind of "Last Year in the Rockies," it recalls other horror movies about architecture and cyclical repetition, such as Roman Polanski's *The Tenant* and Richard Longcraine's *Full Circle*. Its often-seamless interweaving of different levels of reality and its elliptical structure are fundamentally counter to the naturalism on which most horror films are predicated. Kubrick's enigmatic

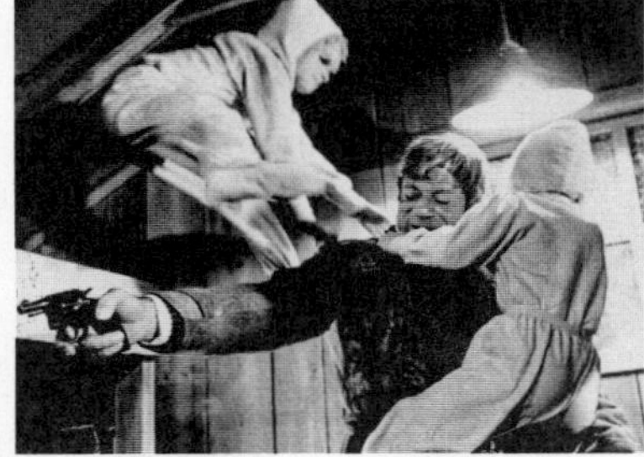

David Cronenberg, *The Brood,* 1979.

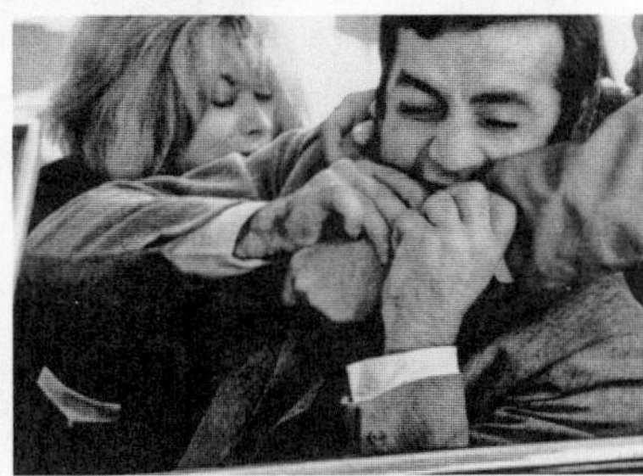

Jean-Luc Goddard, *Weekend*, 1967.

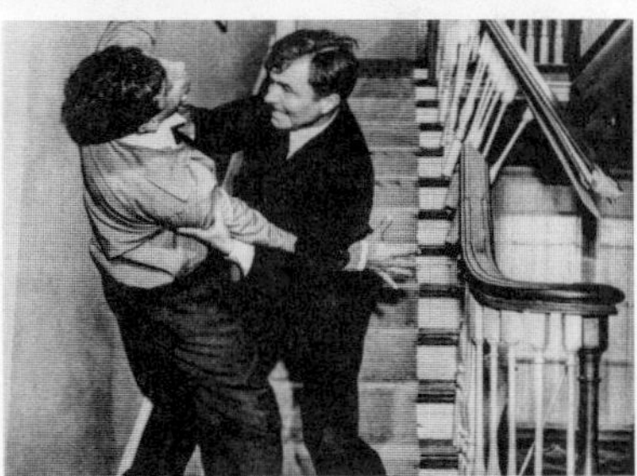

Nicholas Ray, *Bigger Than Life*, 1956.

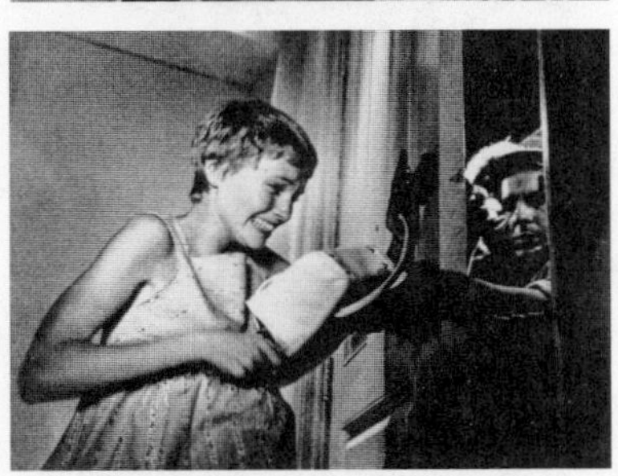

Roman Polansky, *Rosemary's Baby*, 1968.

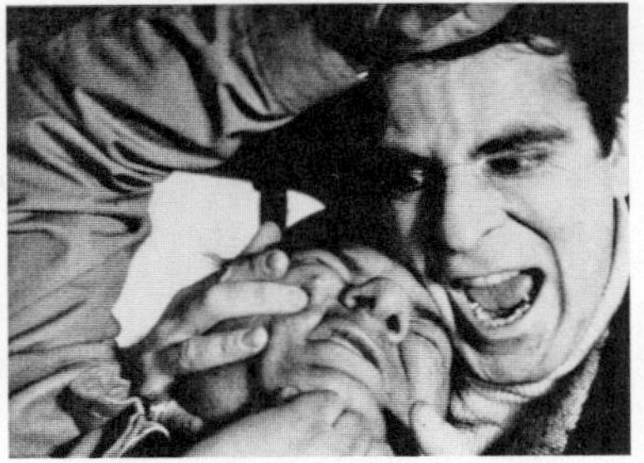

David Cronenberg, *Rabid*, 1977.

amalgam of past, present, future, of memory, dream, clairvoyance, and hallucination makes efforts at decipherment unproductive, if not impossible. Polanski's *Rosemary's Baby*, a film Kubrick has praised highly, worked with this kind of semantic texture in which Rosemary's "real" experiences and her paranoiac projections become virtually indistinguishable. Kubrick's movie is more complicated; the overlapping delirium of several people often occupies the screen simultaneously so that we cannot follow any character as a unified separate consciousness.

The Shining is essentially a movie about images, about an environment constituted by representation, whether in photographs, films, television, or an unconscious made up of images. Much of its horror derives from an encircling web of disconnected representations which tyrannizes the characters in the film, determining the shape of their desires and lives. The "shining" of the title is not, as some suggest, simply a byword for cinema but rather a suggestion of the nature of an image in general: the image as that luminous, seductive, and fictitious point of reproduction from which power emanates and onto which desire fastens itself. Kubrick crystallizes some of the discussion by film critic Raymond Bellour about the fundamental interconnection between photography, hypnosis, psychoanalysis, and cinema in the late nineteenth century. The position of television in *The Shining* is especially significant. Kubrick uses the glowing TV tube frequently as a crucial counterpoint to other categories of images suggested in the film. At two points a television picture completely coincides with the film frame, and with these intersections Kubrick emphasizes television's centrality and the authority of its effects.

In the first of these scenes, the camera pulls slowly back from a television image revealing Wendy and Danny near the set, gradually showing us more of an immense room flooded with daylight. The centrally situated television set here is what Paul Virilio calls the "third window." Noting the American habit of having a TV set turned on perpetually, he describes television as an essentially architectural element and that it signals a new historical phase in the conception of an architectural aperture. (First window: a cut in a fortress wall; second window: an opening to admit sunlight.) So it is as a kind of portable window that the TV set functions in this scene. Kubrick's exposure for interior light renders the room windows into shimmering but opaque panels, elevating the television into the sole visual access to an outside. The tectonic structure of this take (which recalls features of Michael Snow's *Wavelength*) establishes the visual pyramid of Renaissance perspectival space, but within it everything converges, not on a potentially infinite point seen through a window but on the pivotal TV tube, an object incompatible with the possibility of such illusory deep space. A key premise of *The Shining* as a whole is this closing off and disappearance of open and extensive space and the autonomy it implied. Movement can take place only in circular, convoluted, or labyrinthine routes.

The image on the television is actually a movie, transformed into a continuum of charged phosphors, demonstrating TV's assimilating and homogenizing power. But this scene also underlines television's role in the formation of consciousness and the process through which its representations become internalized. The movie Wendy and Danny are watching is *Summer of '42*, and the scene shown involves the sexual tension between an adolescent boy and an older woman. Here television is not only a window but also a mirror, allowing its viewers to see themselves in its images. Film or television, what is at stake are the mechanisms which "personify" and structure desires and then prohibit them after having incited them originally. Danny and Wendy's relationship, like any familial bond, is inseparable from this external imposition of needs and roles.

Later in the film Kubrick cuts to another TV picture, also filling his entire frame. This time it is a split screen, with images flipping in and out of its three divisions: palm trees, sailboats, tall buildings, a golf course. We soon realize it is the formulaic visual intro to a local news show on a TV set in Halloran's Miami apartment. As the camera drifts back, with Halloran on his bed, trancelike and inert like Mantegna's *Dead Christ*, a newscaster comes on with the top story: severe snowstorms in the Rockies. Apparently, this triggers something in Halloran, for he starts to "shine" and is gripped with fear as Jack, back in Colorado, enters the sinister Room 237. There is an obvious similarity between Halloran's telepathic experience and the images he is watching. The conventionality of visual information and forms such as split screens presupposes a viewer who can follow unquestioningly the utter discontinuity of television, who can make the vast jump as a "live" picture shifts from Florida to Denver. Television's radical reformulation of temporal and spatial consciousness, its fragmentation and recombination of previously unrelated signs, codes, images, and spaces parallels the notion of an uncontrollable mental capacity to similarly override categories of space and time.

Halloran on his bed is a captive of more than his television. Organized like a ceremonial altar, a table in his room supports his TV in the center with two large ornate lamps at each side, while two oil paintings of nude, young Black women hang over it. The paintings amplify the notion of desire locked onto an image, on a symbol completely cut from its referent. What he desires is attainable only through these mediating signs. Halloran then is as much a prisoner as the family in the snowbound hotel. In his darkened, sealed-off apartment, with phone and TV his only links to the outside, he is caught in the same system of representations as Jack, organized around images of women. This is the moment at which Halloran psychically witnesses Jack's experience in Room 237. Shot with an ominous languor in a lush greens and purples, Jack invokes an image of woman as seductress, as Venus rising from the sea, as a long-thighed vampire, or as a fertile muse to rouse him from his creative torpor. But for Jack and Halloran the horror of this dream is the instability of the image, of this reified point of desire. Helplessly, Jack watches her dissolve into a laughing, decaying corpse in his arms. It is a terror of change, of lived time, of the corporeality behind the image. Death suddenly reveals itself to Jack not as Ophelia floating among flowers, but as an aging body rotting in a half-filled bathtub. In a society that has desocialized and repressed the fact of death, he is completely unequipped to cope with the disparity between a static, culturally imposed image and the reality of physical decay.

One of our few glimpses of the world at large in *The Shining* is at a gas station owned by a friend of Halloran's. While the friend is on the phone, a man in the background stands motionless as if in a stupor, holding up a page of a nude pin-up calendar, frozen into an inescapable circuit with the picture. Linked with Jack, with Halloran and his paintings, with Danny and Wendy at their TV sets, with Halloran's fellow plane passengers plugged into headphones or leafing through fashion magazines, this anonymous, entranced figure focalizes part of the crisis Kubrick describes in the film as a whole. A narcotic consumption of images and paralysis of desire perpetuates a death-in-life more unsettling, more threatening than the zombies or pod people of other horror movies.

Clearly, *The Shining* also expands themes examined before by Kubrick in *2001* and *Clockwork Orange*: the ambivalent status of biological man in modern society where instinctual life is circumscribed and rechanneled. Other recent films explore this same conflict between man's animal origins and the demands of culture, such as *Altered States* and *Mon oncle d'Amerique*. It is also the familiar subject of a whole class of horror movies (*Wolfen, The Howling, American Werewolf*) about man-animal aggregates. Kubrick's direction amplifies a sense of this tension and Nicholson becomes a volatile bundle of symptoms and impulses, with each facial expression and bodily contortion more pronounced as the film progresses. It is a kind of hyperbole recalling Eisenstein's direction of Nikolai Cherkasov in *Ivan the Terrible*.

Jack's character, as an agent of all that the hotel represents, embodies a death instinct, and Kubrick plays freely with Freud's link between repetition and a death drive. Jack's paranoiac delirium is one of repetition, repeating the actions of the previous caretaker and his own earlier violence to Danny, his desire to stay at the hotel "for ever and ever," his language of clichés and jingles and his typing of a single sentence over and over. This inertia, his wish not to change, leads to an entropic winding down in the climactic chase through a maze. This chase is Jack's "circuitous path to death," a return to an inanimate state. He freezes to death, and, in a twist on the notion of "freeze frame," he is preserved forever in a photograph. This terminal image, light caught in particles of silver, becomes a final kind of death, of "shining." That Danny, the schizo to Jack's paranoid, survives and extricates himself from the labyrinth is a lone hopeful note, as if his nomadic mobility and fluid subjectivity were a route out.

The social claustrophobia of *The Shining* comes through in David Cronenberg's films in a wholly different visual language: unconstrained, visceral, chaotic, and frequently comic. Another director preoccupied with civilization and its discontents, he deals directly with the incompatibility between human biology and the civilizing structures that control and delimit instinctual life. For Cronenberg, the body is the site of both an individual and a cultural crisis. His thinking turns on the body's production of signs and symptoms, on its fragility and potential for disorder. Cronenberg's work descends in part from William Burroughs in the kind of

Nova landscape his films portray, a world dominated by bizarre corporate and scientific institutions which subject the body to extravagant medical and psychiatric interventions. Prey to contagion and strange pharmaceuticals, the body is an objectified territory onto which new organs and technologies are appended. In *They Came from Within* biologists develop a new parasite that is half-aphrodisiac, half-venereal disease and spreads like a virus; the ominous Somafree Institute for Psychoplasmics in *The Brood* employs a therapeutic technique for materializing neurosis as physical growth on the body's surface; in *Rabid* the aftereffect of experimental surgery cause a patient's body to grow a syringe-like organ that emerges from an aperture in her armpit, turning her into a blood-drinking sexual predator. He works with an imagery of corporal anarchy: we see bodies splitting open, fissuring under internal pressure, generating growths and lesions. But Cronenberg would be relatively uninteresting if his work was simply a series of shocks calculated to elicit disgust or revulsion. At the core of his films is a sense of the body as a positive productive force and of its radical disorganization as an affirmative rebellion against social domestication and its prohibitions.

Biological insurrection is in fact the theme of Cronenberg's *They Came from Within*, a film made for less than $200,000. Here the revolt is directed against the confinement and enervating sterility of life in a luxury apartment complex. Located on an island, the setting is like the shopping mall in *Dawn of the Dead* or the self-sufficient hotel in *The Shining*. It is a microcosmic world of stores, golf course, restaurants, but also of tranquilizers, monotony, and anxiety. The crux of the plot is a scientific experiment gone awry which disrupts the routine life of its residents. In another part of the city, biologists are attempting to produce a "useful" parasite as an alternative to organ transplants, so that the functions of an impaired organ could be taken over by the parasite. "It's crazy but who cares," says one of the scientists about this plan. What emerges from their work, however, is an "instinctual parasite" that renders its host sex-crazed and threatens "to turn the world into one huge orgy." Needless to say, someone in the island condominium becomes infected.

Slimy, six-inch-long, wormlike creatures with mobile snouts, Cronenberg's parasites synthesize a profusion of sexual and excremental fears. Like his other work, *They Came from Within* is about an assault on the political organization of the body in which instinctual systems are under the rule of rationalizing imperatives. Early on, an insurance executive infected by the parasites stands over his desk, unable to respond to his secretary as blood trickles from his mouth, his head is no longer in command of his body. Later the same man is totally in the grip of the virus, and his stomach bulges and balloons out as the parasites migrate through his insides. Paralleling this subversion of the body's circulatory and intestinal workings is the parasite invasion of the apartment building itself. They enter into its hidden functional systems, traveling through plumbing, air shafts, garbage dumps, and mail slots, and eventually emerge to inch along immaculate walls and corridors, leaving a trail of blood and slime.

As the parasites spread, the number of those eroticized grows. But rather than suggesting a Reichian fantasy of sexual utopia, Cronenberg introduces a new form of horror: the saturation of society with compulsive eroticism. The parasite attack is initially disruptive to the fabric of everyday life and challenges the normative hierarchies of the body. But at the end of the film, the corporal derangement is routinized and a new means of control asserts itself. Eroticism becomes another bland form of consumption and conformity. The film concludes with the residents of the apartment complex driving out at night in a caravan of cars to infect the rest of the city with a virus of sex addiction. A trade-in of one boredom for another.

Cronenberg's *The Brood* has less of the wild, comic book pace of *They Came from Within*, and it expands the scope of his imagery and social critique. He sketches out a desolate world of loneliness, alcoholism, cancer, madness, and paranoia. His characters: a near-autistic child in the harmful clutches of a psychiatric establishment, a husband who says of his wife, "She married me for my sanity, hoping some of it would rub off," an infantile mental patient "addicted" to his shrink, an unbalanced cancer patient obsessed with his body's circulatory systems, and a pop psychologist, hailed as a genius, who performs one-on-one therapy in a packed auditorium. Like *The Shining*, *The Brood* traces the submerged channeling of anger within a familial setup. Focusing on three generations of the Carveths, it reveals the family as an instrument in the social perpetuation of repression, as a mechanism that keeps rage unexpressed. Like Jack Torrance in *The Shining*, employed as a hotel caretaker, Frank Carveth, the husband in *The Brood*, has a related kind of job as an architectural restorer, mirroring his futile efforts to prop up the collapsing edifice of his family.

Again, Cronenberg comes up with a startling set of images for concretizing interior drives. His narrative revolves around Psychoplasmics, a therapy so efficient in concentrating emotional pain that it manifests itself on the body's surface as growths or skin eruptions. The film's opening scene establishes its effectiveness when a patient breaks out in proliferating scabrous rashes as his suppressed pain surfaces. But Psychoplasmics is too successful in the case of one patient whose anger generates a series of external wombs on her abdomen. These wombs in turn engender a brood of creatures who become the violent emissaries of her own murderous feelings. The creatures are small, sexless hooded dwarfs who enact Nola Carveth's deadly desires, uttering hissing reptilian sounds. Cronenberg cast a group of ten-year-old gymnasts for these roles, utilizing acrobatic jumping as an image of the explosive emotions they embody. When Nola reveals the astonishing transformation of her body to her husband, the aversion he initially feels mixes with awe at her new creative powers.

Cronenberg's most recent film, *Scanners*, carried the vocabulary of his earlier work to new limits. Its narrative concerns a global corporate battle for control of telepathic individuals, as in De Palma's *The Fury* or Philip K. Dick's novel *Ubik*. A mythic fable, it discloses hopeful flickers of light in the harsh savagery of a futuristic urban night world. The plight of the telepath, Cameron Vale, is in one sense that of an interiorized consciousness cut off from any integral connection to his body or the world. But Cronenberg is making more than simply a Cartesian nightmare. The telepath's difference is essentially one of heightened receptivity, of sensitivity, an inability to tune out a flood of stimuli, the immense overload of language and information invading the mind. "It's these voices . . . how do you stop them?" Vale's struggle is not only against corporate power and its telecommunication systems but also, like Danny in *The Shining*, against familial and patriarchal forces. In the climactic mental combat between the rival telepaths, flesh and veins crack open and the body dissolves into blood and flame, as Vale shatters the walls of an oppressive subjectivity.

A shot of milk and orange juice mixing together on the floor of a ransacked kitchen in *The Brood* sets the dissonant tone for much of Cronenberg's work. As Kubrick did in *The Shining*, Cronenberg describes structures that control individuals and shape consciousness. In *The Shining* power was exerted through the manipulation of desire with images; for Cronenberg, individuals are regulated through a social administration and constraint of their bodies. Horror in these movies is not in what is repressed but in the networks of images and institutions that function to "normalize" individuals. *Psycho*'s formal insularity and Hitchcock's essential conservatism individuated the experience of horror, interiorized and circumscribed the field of its effects. For directors like Kubrick and Cronenberg, horror is no longer a dehistoricized experience of the human psyche but rather the manifold product of a specific technological and social landscape.

Originally published in *Wedge 2*, Winter 1982.

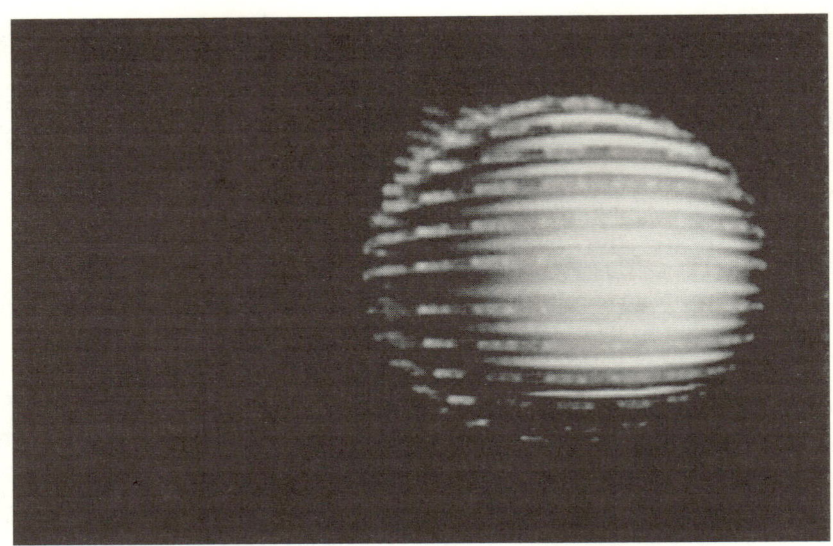

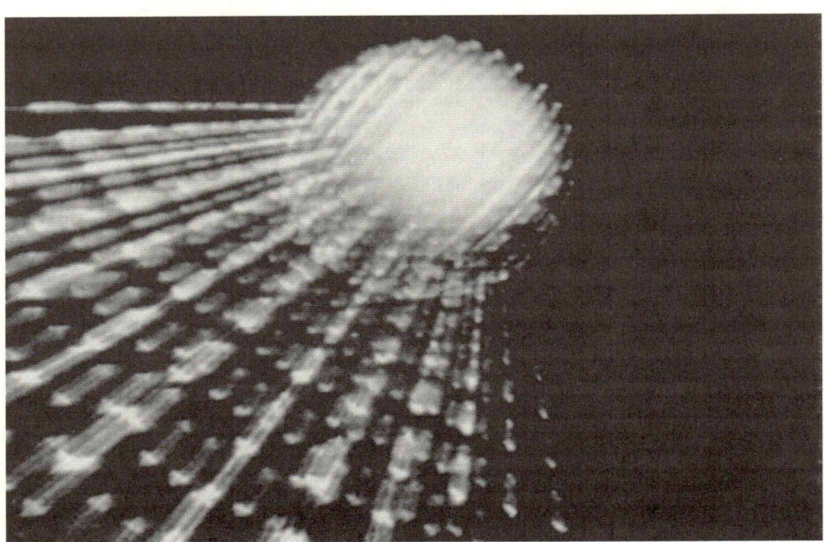

Gretchen Bender, *AT&T in Slow Motion* (from *Dumping Core*), 1984.

Eclipse of the Spectacle

The pervasive imagery now enveloping us of a rationalized world of digitized life and languages mediated by video display screens, is prefigured in Nikola Tesla's 1901 plan for a World System of totally interconnecting planetary communications.[1] Although bound up with other futurist dreams of simultaneity, Tesla's ideas had more of an affinity with the needs of state and corporate power than other projects of modernization. He believed he could engineer a globe unified by the universal registration of time and traversed by flows of language, images, and money—all reduced to undifferentiated streams of electrical energy. Backed by J.P. Morgan, Tesla's first transmission station rose on the North Shore of Long Island: two hundred feet high, the Wardenclyffe Tower stood only from 1902 to 1917, never to be capped by the immense copper dome Tesla planned for it. No piece of sculpture better embodied the synchronous, history-rending aspirations of Western modernity in the early twentieth century than this tower. It could well be posed alongside Tatlin's *Monument to the Third International* and Brancusi's *Endless Column* to represent three variants of modernist absolutism: corporate, utopian, and aestheticist.

Although Tesla's vision was to prove the most durable of these three, its full realization was postponed for nearly a century. A major oil discovery at Spindletop, Texas, also in 1902, helped assure the continued dominance of the extensive, vehicular space traversed by the railroad and then the automobile well into the twentieth century. Nonetheless, Tesla's achievement was to transform Thomas Edison's relatively pedestrian notion of electricity as a commodity to be sold in units to consumers into

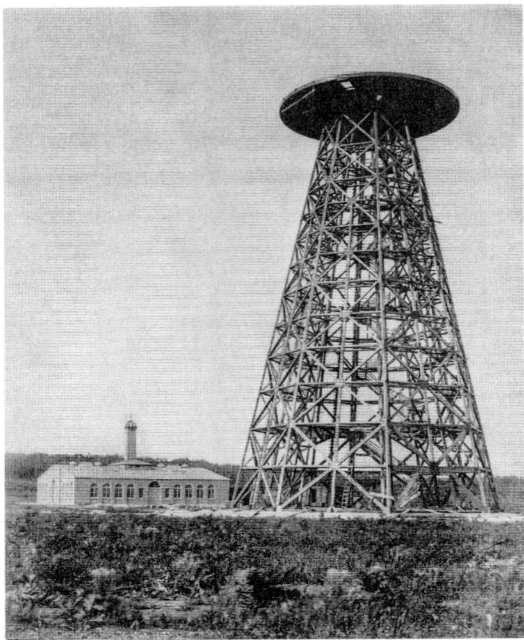

Tesla's Wardenclyffe transmission tower, Shoreham, Long Island, extant 1902–17.

an apprehension of electricity as an immanent substance into which anything was transcodable and which could instantaneously intervene anywhere, even to literally occupy the full body of the earth and atmosphere.[2] Tesla's was a primal understanding of the totalizing logic of capital, and television would emerge as a key component of the "world system" whose outlines he foresaw so presciently.

Today all of us are implicated in the practice of giving a conceptual solidity and unity to the evasive and seemingly ubiquitous entity that is television. We maintain an illusory coherence around what is a shifting coalescence of powers, objects, effects, and relations. Even though all that is subsumed by television has historical specificity, technological underpinnings, and lines into multiple economies, we have mystified it and situated it beyond the grasp of critical analysis, while at the same time endowing it with a despotic identity insulated from the vicissitudes of social processes. Television has always been an aggregate of bodies, institutions, and transmissions in continual transformation. We could more clearly apprehend

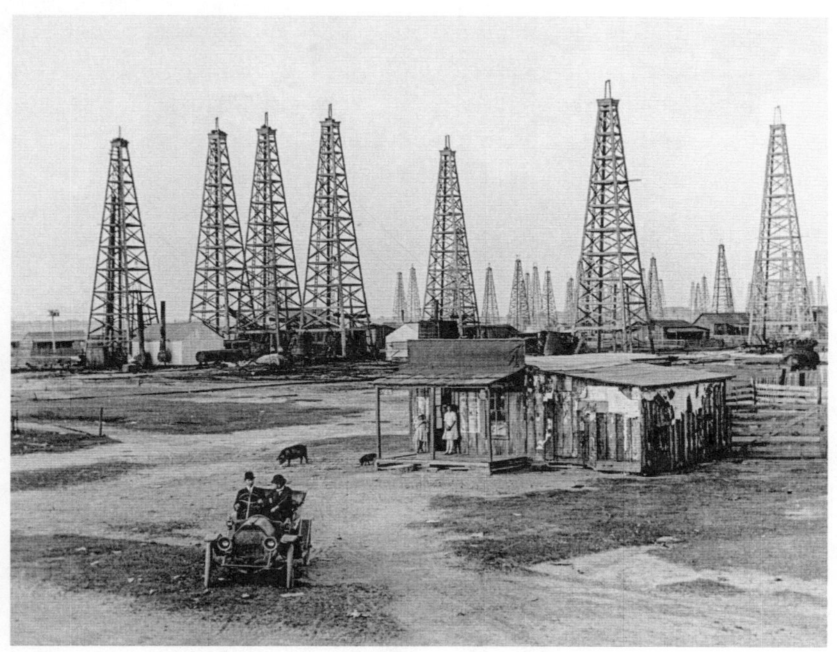

Oil field, Spindletop Texas, 1903.

television if instead of seeking an elusive formal structure, we identify the conjunctions it forges, the circulations it controls, and more importantly, the accelerating mutations it is currently undergoing.

Because of the increasing adjacency of television to telecommunications and computers, any investigation of its prospects can easily become entwined with an ideology of technological determinism and with a discourse of prefabricated futures that ultimately serve present powers. This essay seeks to relocate the problem of television and its metamorphosis, not merely within the study of technological change but also in relation to the larger remapping of other zones: cultural, economic, geopolitical. Addressed here is the extent to which television as a system which functioned from the 1950s into the 1970s is now disappearing and being reconstituted at the heart of another network in which what is at stake is no longer representation, but distribution and regulation.

Modernist habits led many critics to seek out properties deemed intrinsic to television, to articulate it as a medium like painting or sculpture, and to isolate a new entity called "video art." Television was conceptually stabilized as a semiotic system one could "read" or as a superstructural element through which power was exercised.[3] Yet developments in recent years have controverted accounts that once seemed durable. Marshall McLuhan's famous formulations of the 1960s, for example, show how one discourse about television was founded on features that proved to be transient peculiarities of a technology still in its infancy. Television was "cool" because of the low definition of its image and its small size; its image quality effectively blurred intellectual and perceptual distinctions on the part of the viewer.[4] However, as is well known now, the ongoing refinement of high-resolution TV and of large home screens promises soon to diminish significant experiential differences between film and television.

For other critics, television is so thoroughly constitutive of the social that its operations are indistinguishable from those of an entire hegemonic order. But no matter how pervasive and inwrought are the mechanisms of television, one danger is to totalize it. Of course, television is a global tracery of linkages that produces truth and that increasingly dominates the arena of the lived; but, at the same time, as with any deployment of power, the surface that television mobilizes also encompasses barely visible alcoves, striations, and folds. Thus, on one hand, we can consider the moment in July 1982, when 2.5 billion people watched the World Cup soccer final, welded together in real time before the same image, and participating for two hours in a perfectly regulated mega-circuitry. But, on the other hand, there also exist very different kinds of circuits that may be defective or contingent: when television is conjoined with multiple events exterior to it, when television becomes an object like a piece of furniture, when it functions as no more than an architectural aperture, or when it is simply a metronome of the quotidian.[5] These, then, are the overlapping spaces to be comprehended: a circuit of power that can be uniform and seamless as a macro-phenomenon, but that is broken, diversified, and never fully controllable in its local usage.

The totalizing response to television grew in part out of Frankfurt School texts on the "culture industry." Adorno and Horkheimer, as exiles in Los Angeles, disclosed the "ruthless unity" of a "system that is uniform and whole in every part," an inescapable and voracious web that absorbs and commodities everything according to a logic that, for them, was perilously close to fascism.[6] This model, retuned and disseminated by Herbert Marcuse, merged in the United States with indigenous left-holistic ideas to produce books like Jerry Mander's *Four Arguments for the Elimination of Television* (1977). But the most influential stepchild of the Frankfurt School is Jean Baudrillard, who has relentlessly revitalized a vision of the irredeemability of contemporary (consumer) culture.[7]

Like science fiction about new ice ages or the crystallization of organic life, Baudrillard's recent texts narrate a related triumph of the inanimate. As in an updated evocation of Caspar David Friedrich's *The Wreck of the Hope*, Baudrillard paints the specter of implosion. A kind of negative eschatology, Baudrillard's implosion announces the nullity of all opposition, the dissolution of history, the neutralization of difference, and the erasure of any possible figuration of alternate actuality. And, at the cold, super dense core of this anti-finale is not absolute knowledge, but rather the absolute dominion of digitized memory-storage banks, not even dimly fathomable through the aqueous screens of video display terminals. Philip K. Dick, in his novel *A Scanner Darkly* (1977), touched on what is also crucial in Baudrillard's work: "Biological life goes on, everything else is dead. A reflex machine. Like some insect. Repeating doomed patterns over and over. A single pattern."[8]

For Baudrillard, television is a paradigm of implosive effects. It collapses any distinction between receiver or sender or between the medium and the real. Like Mallarmé's Herodiade caught in a sterile closed circuit with her mirror, Baudrillard's subject is locked into an "uninterrupted interface" with the video screen in a universe of "fascination." Television, for Baudrillard, exists as an abstract and invariant function from which any principle of disorder is excluded. The materiality of both viewer and television apparatus dissolves, along with any multiple or contradictory layers of institutional texture. His perfect circuit of viewer–TV subsists on a single, formalized plane solely as an index of the nonworking of power and of the illusory essence of all signification.

Implosion announces the collapse of capital's ability to expand; it is an unprecedented social contraction and paralysis, the last unmasking of a long sequence of representational illusions in operation since the Renaissance. But perhaps it is not even a question of "the end of capitalism" or of "late capitalism." Deleuze and Guattari, for example, propose that capitalism is by its very nature always "neo-capitalism."[9] While Baudrillard sees technological miniaturization as a symptom of implosion, Deleuze and Guattari read it as part of the reorganization of a global system of domination and circulation.[10] Following from their model, geographical frontiers no longer exist and in their place are being manufactured vast microelectronic territories for expansion. Telecommunications is the new arterial network, analogous in part to what railroads were capitalist accumulation in the nineteenth century. And it is this electronic substitute for geography that corporate and national entities are now carving up. Information, structured by automated data processing, becomes a new kind of raw material—one that is not depleted by use.[11] Patterns of accumulation and consumption now shift onto new surfaces. Against this scenario, implosion, in all its sublimity, seems like the death wish of a failed humanism, in which capitalism and mass culture are guilty, above all else, of the "liquidation of tragedy."[12]

However, Baudrillard is not wrong to suggest the waning of what Guy Debord called "the society of the spectacle." Clearly, a certain period in the initial deployment of television is over, a phase roughly coinciding with post–World War II US hegemony. It is in the mid-1970s that the transformation of television and its insertion into a wholly different set of structures logins, alongside the reorganization of world markets on a nonbipolar model.[13] The convergence of home computer, television, and telephone lines as the nexus of a new social machinery testifies to an undoing of the spectacular consumption of the commodity. And paradoxically, television, which had elevated the commodity to the height of spectacular space, is now implicated in the collapse of that space and the consequent evaporation of aura around the body of the commodity.

For Debord writing in 1967, at the last high tide of the "Pax Americana," the auratic presence of the commodity was bound up with the illusion of its utter tangibility.[14] But since that time, we have witnessed the gradual displacement of aura from images of possessable objects to digitized flows of data, to the glow of the video display terminal and its lure of unbounded access. This is a reversal of the process indicated by Debord in which the seeming self-sufficiency of the commodity was a "congealment" of forces that were essentially mobile and dynamic. Now, however, with pure flux itself a commodity, a spectacular and "contemplative" relation to objects is undermined and supplanted by new kinds of investments. There is no more opposition between the abstraction of money and the apparent materiality of commodities: money and what it can buy are now fundamentally of the same substance. And it is the potential dissolution of any language of the market or of desire into binarized pulses of light or electricity that unhinges the fictive unity of spectacular representation. Figurative images lose their transparence and are consumed as simply one more code.

Consider *General Hospital*, allegedly the most widely watched afternoon soap opera. It is consumed essentially as strings of representations that never surpass their functioning as an abstract code. In its construction and effects, *General Hospital* announces the disappearance of the visual and narrative space that might seem to have authorized it and points toward a programmable calculus of continually switching syntheses of figural and narrative units. The consistent repetition of "formulas" is no longer even a possibility. In *General Hospital* any character, relationship, identity, or situation is reversible, exchangeable, convertible into its opposite. With the eradication of any simulation of interiority, one invests not into images of actors but onto the formal management of those images. Discontinuities, substitutions, and duplications shatter the illusion which once would have been called bourgeois verisimilitude. More and more the so-called "content" of television shifts in this direction; it is not at all a question of the replication of life, but of its reduction to abstract and manipulable elements ready to be harmonized with a plethora of other electronic flows. Television was not destined finally for analogic tasks, but when it first appeared, how could the networks in which it is now positioned have been foreseen? It seemed then, according to what McLuhan calls "rear view mirrorism," like one more refinement in five centuries of space-simulating techniques. Yet as reproductive technology attains new parameters of mimetic "fidelity" (holography, high-resolution TV) there is an inverse move of the image toward pure surface, so that whatever drifts across the screen of either television or home computer is part of the same homogeneity.[15]

Up through the 1960s television collaborated with the automobile in sustaining the dominant machinery of capitalist representation: in the virtual annexation of all spaces and the liquidation of any unified signs that had occupied them. The TV screen and car windshield reconciled visual experience with the velocities and discontinuities of the marketplace.[16] As windows they seemed to open onto a visual pyramid of extensive space in which autonomous movement might be possible. Instead, both were apertures that framed the subject's transit through streams of disjunct objects and affects, across disintegrating and hyperabundant surfaces. These latter are the vehicular trajectories that run through Straub and Huillet's *History Lessons* and many of Godard's films. Although both car and TV were primary disciplinary instruments for the production of normalized subjects, the subject they produced also had to be competent to consume and coexist with a tremendous field of free-floating signs that has previously been grounded. Privatization and control on one hand and deterritorialization on the other were engineered by the same machines. But the channeling horizontality of the highway (e.g., the conclusion of Godard's *Made in U.S.A.*) and the sequentially of TV images masked the actual disorganization and nonlinearity of these networks. The vortex of overlapping cloverleaf interchanges and the delirious circularity of the channel dial are more authentic concretions of the impacted itineraries perpetually available on both roadway and TV, an infinity of routes and the equivalence of all destinations.

This was the proliferating field of post–World War II capitalism in the United States, the car defined a dominant socioeconomic mapping. It shaped forms of labor and temporality; codified a primary experience of space, its margins, and of access to the social; was the site of multiple intensities; and spawned a mass culture of its own. But beginning in the 1970s, this vehicular space began to lose its predominance. Television, which had seemed an ally of the automobile in the maintenance of the commodity-filled terrain of the spectacle, began to be grafted onto other networks. And now the screens of home computer and word processor have succeeded the automobile as "core products" in an ongoing relocation and hierarchization of production processes.[17] Videogames may initially have dominated consumer software sales, but in the early 1900s the automobile was also originally inserted as a recreational form until the

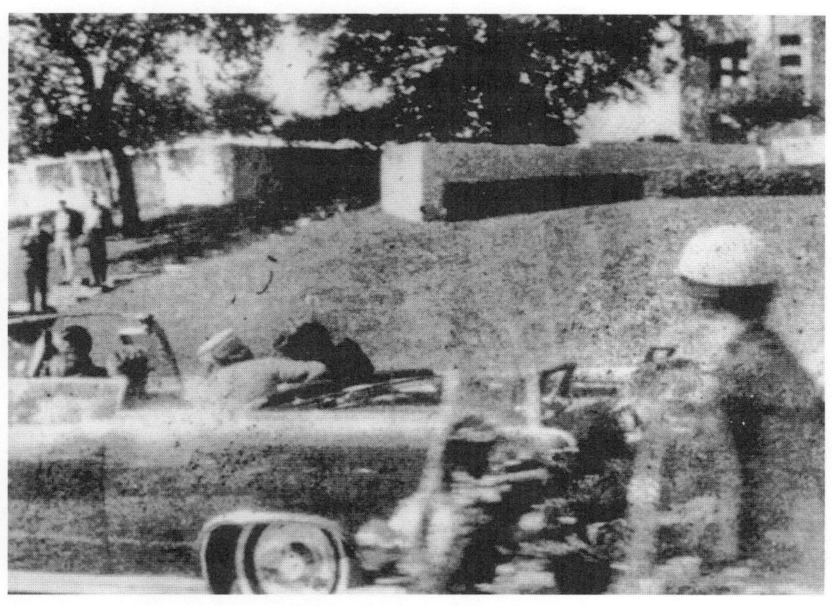

Photograph of the assassination of President John F. Kennedy, taken by Mary Ann Moorman, November 22, 1963.

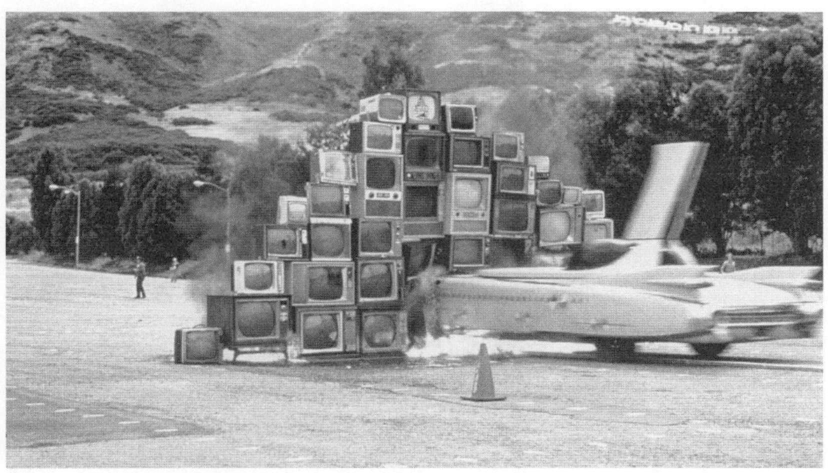

Ant Farm, *Media Burn*, 1975, videotape, single-channel video, color, with sound, 37 min.

infrastructure of gas stations, parking lots, and the massive reshaping of urban spaces made car ownership synonymous with social participation. Similarly, the establishment of data services and information "utilities" has only just begun. But videogames have been crucial in the reeducation and formation of a new subject ready to assume "interactive" links with VDTs, links altogether different from the prosthesis of body and automobile.

The charade of technological "revolution" is founded on the myth of the rationality and inevitability of a computer-centered world. From all sides, a postindustrial society is depicted that renders invisible the very unworkability and disorder of present "industrial" systems of distribution and circulation. Telecommunications and Paul Virilio's world of absolute speed will not supplant highway/railroad space, but instead these two domains will coexist side by side in all their radical incompatibility. It's within the dislocation of this unthinkable interfacing that the present must be conceived: a planetary data-communications network physically implanted into the decaying, digressive terrain of the automobile-based city. One of the key roles of the expanding electronic "grid" (how this image of modernity endures) is exclusionary—to articulate a new social and geopolitical stratification based on the privileges of access to transmitted data.[18] And it is precisely the interstices of this grid, the diversity of rifts within its net, that its totalizing pretensions would disown and efface.

But it is the very persistence and immediacy of the crumbling edifices of a previous theater of modernization that Baudrillard eliminates from his panorama of a flawlessly self-regulating world. His virtuoso delineation of the monolithic surfaces of contemporaneity becomes complicit, at a certain point, in the maintenance of the myths of the same cybernetic omnipotence he intends to deplore. What his texts exclude is any sense of breakdown, of faulty circuits, of systemic malfunction; or of a body that cannot be completely colonized or pacified, of disease, and of the colossal dilapidation of everything that claims infallibility or sleekness. This is the particular importance of Dick's novels and the films of David Cronenberg; they describe a world no less congested with the technology of everyday life than Baudrillard's, but they insist on a threshold at which the social domestication of the body produces unmanageable disruption, as in psychosis or contagion. For both, television and the sovereignty of the hyperreal are so effective in building a delusional world that the mechanisms of social rationalization rapidly corrode, including even Baudrillard's "circularity of media effects."

Another work signaling a limit to the hyperreality of spectacular space is J.G. Ballard's *The Atrocity Exhibition* (1969).[19] This exemplary psychotic text details the collapse of a landscape through which lines of deterritorialization have proceeded to absolute thresholds. Ballard explores fractured zones in which sheer contiguity replaces syntax and which extend only in terms of the ceaseless conjugation of bodies, architecture, and images that briefly abut, then detach to make new connections. *The Atrocity Exhibition* coincides with a dissolution of legibility generated by the very efficacy and supremacy of the spectacle. Ballard's landscape—the city interpenetrated by image-events of car crashes, assassinations, celebrities, astronauts, and war crimes—demands an unremitting effort of decipherment, an effort rendered impossible, however, by the equivalence of everything glutting the field. A saturated spectacular space neutralizes the interpretive delirium of paranoia at the very moment of inciting it. Key events of the 1960s, those which authenticated the spectacle and guaranteed its efficacy (Kennedy assassination, moon landing, Vietnam War, Zapruder frames, etc.) become part of an opaque text that cannot be read and no longer claims significance.

For Ballard, the crisis of the spectacle in the late 1960s follows from the disengagement of desire, its desultory floating-free from anchoring structures, thus exploding the possibility of cathecting with anything because every surface is available for investment. "Sex is now a conceptual act," says the omnipresent Dr. Nathan. "The perversions are completely neutral—in fact, most of the ones I've tried are out of date. We need to invent a series of imaginary perversions just to keep the activity alive." And it was the schizo interregnum of those years that necessitated the fashioning of new apparatuses and networks with which to manage potentially dangerous flows and to rechannel them productively. The late 1960s, whether in China or the West, witnessed a situation requiring more efficient management and the imposition of new regulatory grids: in China it necessitated recontainment of the forces unleashed by the Cultural Revolution; in the West it demanded a rationalization of the spectacle.

The lists running through *The Atrocity Exhibition* are like Foucault's description of Borges's Chinese Encyclopedia: they indicate the absence of any "homogeneous and neutral space in which things could be placed so as to display at the same time the continuous order of their identities or differences as well as the semantic field of their denomination."[20] The violence of Ballard's text occurs in this kind of absence. Founded on the heterotopia of television, it maps a space in which relations of proximity and of resemblance are hopelessly convoluted onto a single plane. For Ballard, empirical and quantitative practices become the flip side of psychosis and its loss of identities. The simulation of coherence for him results only from the blank accumulations of clinical data, laboratory recording techniques, and the "objective" observations of scientific research. And as we now know, the computer was to be central to the remaking of the spectacle by offering the semblance of a "homogenous and neutral" table on which one could know and manipulate the contents of the world without reference to the visible.

When Ballard writes, "The obsession with the specific activity of quantified functions is what science shares with pornography," he anticipates features of *Gravity's Rainbow* (1973). Thomas Pynchon's work is important here for its exhaustive disclosure of the processes and lines of force which remade the world after World War II, producing the conditions for landscape of *The Atrocity Exhibition*. When Pynchon particularizes the chemical and armaments industries and the German film industry, they stand for a much wider range of technologies and institutions which sought to render any subject or substance controllable and exchangeable, whether it was languages, raw materials, or neural reflexes. "How alphabetic is the nature of molecules.... These are our letters, our words: they too can be modulated, broken, recoupled, redefined, co-polymerized one to the other in worldwide chains that will surface now and then over long molecular silences like the seen part of a tapestry."[21] For Deleuze and Guattari, this is a shift from a linguistics of the signifier to a linguistics of flow. It's a transition coinciding with the processes of rationalization that Pynchon describes, the abstract coding of anything that would claim singularity, and also with television's annihilation of the "semantic field" in Ballard. What *Gravity's Rainbow* tells us better than any other text is how World War II was an operation of modernization, how it was the necessary crucible for the obliteration of outdated territories, languages, filiations, of any boundaries or forms that impeded the installation of cybernetics as the model for the remaking of the world as pure instrumentality. And it cannot be overemphasized how the development of cybernetics ("a theory of messages and their control") is intertwined with the commodification of all information and with the hegemony of what Pynchon calls the "meta-cartel."[22]

The masquerade television performed is over: we can no longer privilege as an independent agency what has now become primarily a switching device, one which derives meaning solely from the connections it makes, breaks, or modifies. The operation of television suggests similarities with the semiconductor, that quintessential object of 1980s capitalism. A product of "postindustrial" industry, the semiconductor chip is a conductive solid with infinitely alterable logical properties that amplifies and codifies flows of power. Unique specifications are produced, as Pynchon's German chemists would have understood, by actually rearranging the atoms of the substances used to make them, like silicon. And recently it has become clear how some semiconductor materials (e.g., gallium arsenide) are optically as well as electronically active: circuits of light and circuits of electricity are interchangeable, subject to the same digitation, dollar quantification, and maximizations of speed. According to the same axioms, television and the semiconductor operate by decomposing and remaking a field to achieve optimum patterns of circulation. Both intensify distribution and flows while at the same time imposing intricate circuitries of control.

The liquefaction of signs and commodities has advanced to a point where liquidity no longer spawns the nomadic or the fugitive. The repositioning of television within the web of telecommunications both facilitates the reduction of commodities to pure flux and simultaneously reroutes these flows, previously managed haphazardly and partially, into more easily controllable channels. The passive consumption of images that characterized the 1960s spectator is over. If television then still allowed aleatory experiences of drift and anomie, the video display terminal imposes a highly articulated, coercive apparatus, a prescriptive mode of activity and corporal regimentation. Yet this more developed form of sedentarization, of cellular space mapped out on a global scale, is less the consequence of new technologies and inventions, than the banal legacy of the nineteenth century, and the dream fabricated then of the complete bureaucratization of society.[23]

The compulsory, even carceral underpinning of cellular space is obscured by the overwhelming mass-marketing of the computer and its sham of "interactive" technology, of the "extensions of man," and the fraudulent homology between the computer "revolution" and the advent of printing.[24] But in rejoinder to critics like Hans Magnus Enzensberger, who prematurely celebrated the egalitarian and emancipatory potential of "interactive" media, stands Roland Barthes's contention that whatever compels speech is intrinsically fascist.[25] Most often advocacy of "alternative" uses of telecommunications and computers goes hand in hand with a naive belief in the neutrality of digital languages and a blindness to the immanence of binary notation within a specific system of technocratic power. The imperatives of that system were disclosed by nuclear war strategist Herman Kahn in identifying the key vocation of the future: "the extraction of the maximum information from whatever data is on hand."[26]

Perhaps the most fragile component of this future, however, lies in the immediate vicinity of the terminal screen. We must recognize the fundamental incapacity of capitalism ever to rationalize the circuit between body and computer keyboard, and realize that this circuit is the site of a latent but potentially volatile disequilibrium. The disciplinary apparatus of digital culture poses as a self-sufficient, self-enclosed structure without avenues of escape, with no outside. Its myths of necessity, ubiquity, efficiency, of instantaneity require dismantling: in part, by evading the separation of cellularity, by refusing productivist imperatives, by inducing slow speeds and inhabiting silences.

1. For the text of Tesla's Wardenclyffe Plan, see John J. O'Neill, *Prodigal Genius: The Life of Nikola Tesla* (New York: McKay, 1944), pp. 210–12.
2. Compare Tesla's plan for converting earth and atmosphere as natural conductors with a Nazi scheme for a war-winning weapon through transforming the atmosphere into a high-voltage conductor, recounted in Albert Speer, *Infiltration*, trans. Joachim Neugroschel (New York: Macmillan, 1981), pp. 146–47.
3. See, for example, John Fiske and John Hartley, *Reading Television* (London: Methuen, 1978), and Colin McArthur, *Television and History* (London: British Film Institute, 1978).

4. Marshall McLuhan, *Understanding Media: The Extensions of Man* (New York: McGraw-Hill, 1965), pp. 22–27 and 317–19.
5. Paul Virilio proposes an architectural model for television in "La troisième fenêtre: Entretien avec Paul Virilio," *Cahiers du Cinéma* 322 (April 1981): 35–40. In the late 1960s Jean Baudrillard insisted on television's status as physical object in "Sign Function and Class Logic." See his *For a Critique of the Political Economy of the Sign*, trans. Charles Levin (St. Louis, MO: Telos, 1981).
6. Max Horkheimer and Theodor Adorno, *Dialectic of Enlightenment*, trans. John Cumming (New York: Seabury, 1972), pp. 120–24.
7. See, in particular, Jean Baudrillard, "The Ecstasy of Communication," in *The Anti-Aesthetic: Essays on Postmodern Culture*, ed. Hal Foster (Port Townsend, WA: Bay Press, 1983); *Simulations* (New York: Semiotext(e), 1983); *In the Shadow of the Silent Majorities* (New York: Semiotext(e), 1983); and *Les stratégies fatales* (Paris: Grasset, 1983).
8. Philip K. Dick, *A Scanner Darkly* (New York: Doubleday, 1977), p. 83.
9. Gilles Deleuze and Félix Guattari, *Mille plateaux: Capitalisme et schizophrénie 2* (Paris: Éditions de Minuit, 1980), p. 30.
10. Ibid. pp. 572–75. Deleuze and Guattari outline an unfolding cybernetic phase of capitalism in which telecommunications and computers are part of a world apparatus of "generalized enslavement." They cite Lewis Mumford, *The Myth of the Machine*, 2 vols. (New York: Harcourt Brace Jovanovich, 1967–1970), for his account of the "megamachine."
11. Ernest Mandel's distinction between commodity production and a services sector is no longer tenable. He saw distribution of gas, electricity, and water as part of the former and the distribution of "communications" part of the latter. In *Late Capitalism*, trans. Joris De Bres (London: New Left Books, 1978), pp. 401–403. The emergence, for example, of information "utilities" and their circulation of what Fredric Jameson calls "nonphysical and nonmeasurable 'commodities'" demand analysis outside of Mandel's categories. See, for example, Jacques Attali, *Les trois mondes* (Paris: Fayard, 1981), pp. 342–64.
12. Horkheimer and Adorno, *Dialectic of Enlightenment*, p. 154.
13. See Immanuel Wallerstein, "Crisis as Transition," and Giovanni Arrighi, "A Crisis of Hegemony," in *Dynamics of Global Crisis*, eds. Samir Amin et al. (New York: Monthly Review, 1982). See also the overview in Jean-François Lyotard, *The Postmodern Condition: A Report on Knowledge* (Minneapolis: University of Minnesota Press, 1984), pp. 3–6.

14. Guy Debord, *Society of the Spectacle* (Detroit: Black and Red, 1977). Original French publication in 1967.
15. Video art, paradoxically, depends for its intelligibility on its isolation from television. It can exist only in the cloister of gallery-museum space or wherever the video monitor claims autonomy and independence from major networks of distribution. A case in point was the fate of Nam June Paik's *Good Morning Mr. Orwell*, broadcast January 1, 1984, on network TV. Its insertion into that system rendered it invisible, indistinguishable from the adjacent texture of flow. Yet, as if to preserve its separate identity and visibility, a "live" viewing was organized at the art gallery space of The Kitchen in New York.
16. Virilio alludes to the affinity of windshield and TV screen in "La troisième fenêtre." See also his discussion of the automobile as an instrument of mass mobilization in *Vitesse et politique* (Paris: Galilée, 1977), pp. 33–37.
17. See Andre Gunder Frank, *Reflections on the World Economic Crisis* (New York: Monthly Review Press, 1981), pp. 111–42.
18. See Juan F. Rada, "A Third World Perspective," in *Microelectronics and Society: A Report to the Club of Rome*, ed. Günter Friedrichs and Adam Schaff (Elmsford, NY: Pergamon, 1982), pp. 213–42.
19. J.G Ballard, *The Atrocity Exhibition* (London: Jonathan Cape, 1970). Many parts of the book were published separately between 1966 and 1969. Ballard has called it "a collection of partially linked condensed novels." The first American edition was *Love and Napalm: Export U.S.A.* (New York: Grove Press, 1972), with a foreword by William Burroughs.
20. Michel Foucault, *The Order of Things: An Archaeology of the Human Sciences* (New York: Random House, 1970), pp. xv–xiv. Also relevant here is Roman Jakobson's "Two Aspects of Language and Two Types of Aphasic Disturbances," in Roman Jakobson and Morris Halle, *Fundamentals of Language* (The Hague: Mouton, 1971).
21. Thomas Pynchon, *Gravity's Rainbow* (New York: Viking, 1973).
22. Ibid., pp. 239 and 566.
23. Foucault writes: "Never, I think, in the history of human societies—even in the old Chinese society—has there been such a tricky combination in the same political structures of individualization techniques, and of totalization procedures." See "The Subject and Power," *Critical Inquiry* 8, no. 4 (Summer 1982): 777–95.
24. See, for example, Douglas Hofstadter, *Gödel, Escher, Bach: An Eternal Golden Braid* (New York: Basic Books, 1979). This Pulitzer Prize–winning work is typical of hundreds of current books in its thorough mystification of the words "language,"

"systems," and "knowledge" and its rhapsodic assertion of the "natural" compatibility of mind and machine. Hofstadter's own account of human intelligence is founded on the terms "hardware" and "software."

25. See "Constituents of a Theory—of the Media," in Hans Magnus Enzensberger, *Critical Essays*, trans. Stuart Hood (New York: Continuum, 1982). For Barthes, see "Lecture," *October* 8 (Spring 1979), pp. 5–16.
26. Herman Kahn, *The Coming Boom: Economic, Political, and Social* (New York: Simon & Schuster, 1982), p. 73.

Originally published in *Art After Modernism: Rethinking Representation*, ed. Brian Wallis (New York: David R. Godine/New Museum, 1984).

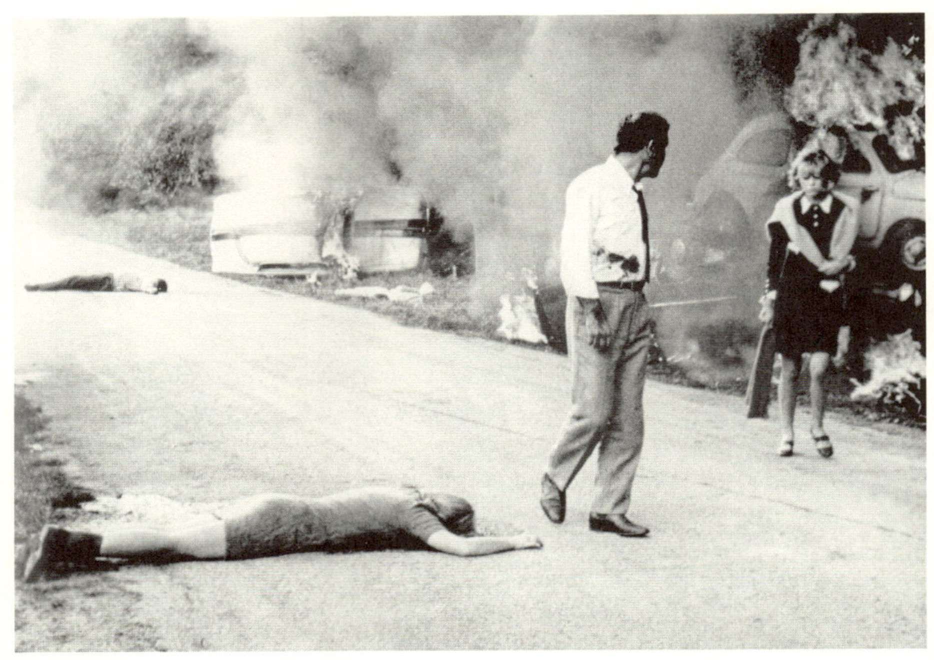

Jean-Luc Godard, *Weekend*, 1967.

J.G. Ballard and the Promiscuity of Forms

In the late 1960s the legibility of the city appeared near a threshold of oblivion. Discourses on urbanism multiplied seemingly in inverse proportion to the dissolution of the city's coherence. It was a moment in which the Western city, beset by one "crisis" after another, increasingly became a function of networks and forces surpassing it; the city retained an objective shape only if obsolete maps were used. Lodged amidst these transformations is the work of J.G. Ballard; nowhere is the disappearance of the axial city and its replacement by a new fragmented yet homogenous consistency more evident than in his novels *Atrocity Exhibition* (1969), *Crash* (1973), *Concrete Island* (1974) and *High Rise* (1975). Ballard renounced the possibility of understanding the city as an extensive configuration of fixed positions and instead chose to describe new regularities and distributions of events across a discontinuous and decentered field, of which no objective view was possible.

His texts are intertwined with the fate of urbanism in the 1960s. He decomposes the ground on which urbanist discourses attempted to salvage or to beget a form for the city, to delineate a cohesive object whose structure was intrinsically adequate to perceived social or human needs. But urbanism collided with that moment in capitalism when the rationalization of built space became secondary to problems of speed and the maximization of circulation. Urbanism continued to operate in an increasingly bereft domain; it sought to impose spatial intelligibility onto a locale that was being transformed by the antiterritoriality of capital. Urbanists found their own thought accommodating itself, in the guise of new forms,

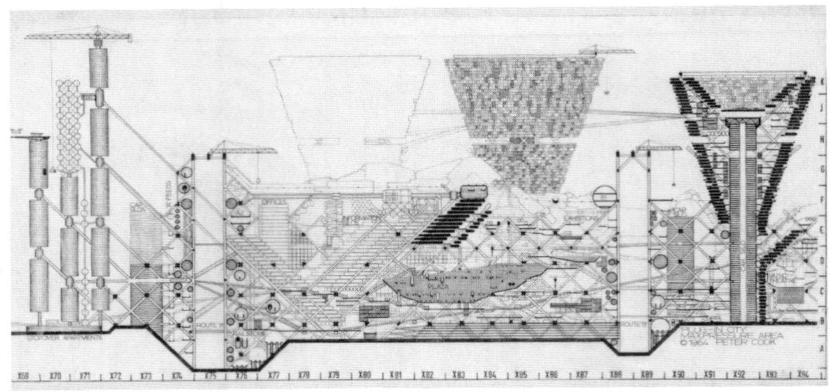

Peter Cook/Archigram, *Plug-in City, Section, Maximum Pressure Area*, 1964.

to developments it was powerless to affect. At one extreme, for example, are the technocratic fantasies of Buckminster Fuller (e.g., his Tetrahedonal City), the World City or global Ecumenopolis of Constantin Doxiadis, his vision of total planetary urbanization, and Paolo Soleri's immense vertical Arcologies. Such models presumed to incarnate a still sovereign human reason and the preeminence of the designer, but their plans actually entailed the full subordination of the city's inhabitants to the immensity of their systems.

If Fuller, Doxiadis, and Soleri attempted in vain to rationalize or contain the phenomenon of urban sprawl, at another extreme the British group Archigram sought to emulate and participate in the "irrationality" of the capitalist city. Borrowing from earlier machine aesthetics, Archigram envisioned the city as "a kit of parts," in which standardized industrial elements could be playfully deployed according to the dictates of individual desires. Along with others (e.g., the Austrian group Coop Himmelblau) they propagated the fantasy of a "responsive" environment, of "feedback," and were bound up in '60s fantasies that the city could be rendered adaptable to the needs of its population. Specifically, Archigram sought to reconcile individual desire with the physical texture and dynamics of a throwaway consumer society, but the reconciliation they attempted began to put in question the very externality of body and city to one another.

Along with related work by Japanese Metabolist architects, Archigram projects seriously undermined notions of the city as a functional integration of parts; instead they posed models of adjacent semi-autonomous systems, operating at different rates of speed so that ideas of an underlying structural or organic unity to the city became unworkable.

Both Ballard's *Crash* and Archigram projects share common roots in the general mechano-morphic eroticism of British Pop, and one must remember Ballard's association in the late 1950s and 1960s with British art circles that included Richard Hamilton, Eduardo Paolozzi, and Reyner Banham. Thus it's not difficult to see *Crash* as a convulsive consummation of Archigram's Plug-In City—as Ballard's paroxysm of functionalism in which city and body form one visceral aggregate of technical systems and organs. But the sheer density of the field it describes distinguishes *Crash* from the kinetic mobility of Archigram work. Rather than an open-ended set of possibilities to be determined by an independent subject, Ballard's terrain presupposes the evaporation of any distance between bodies and their environment. Once the city had been reduced to "a kit of parts" only a humanist mirage could prevent its inhabitants from becoming one more relay in this new network.

Jean Baudrillard has rightly characterized *Crash* as "a purely immanent mix of the body and technology," but the nature of the "mix" needs to be made clear. Most critics situate it as a terminal image of consumer society, and obviously on one level it is. However, it must be insisted that the automobile or the automobile-as-commodity is incidental to Ballard's text. The "product" that finally concerns him is the human subject in whom are fulfilled some of Marx's speculations in the *Grundrisse*: "the discovery, creation and satisfaction of new needs arising from society itself; the cultivation of all the qualities of the social human being, production of the same in a form as rich as possible in needs...production of this being as the most total and universal possible social product, for in order to take gratification in a many-sided way, he must be capable of many pleasures."

The existence of a being able to make a statement like "I love my Buick" is hardly the recent result of media manipulation; rather, it is the triumphant production over a century and a half of a logic internal to capitalism itself. Ballard provides a delirious description of this literally

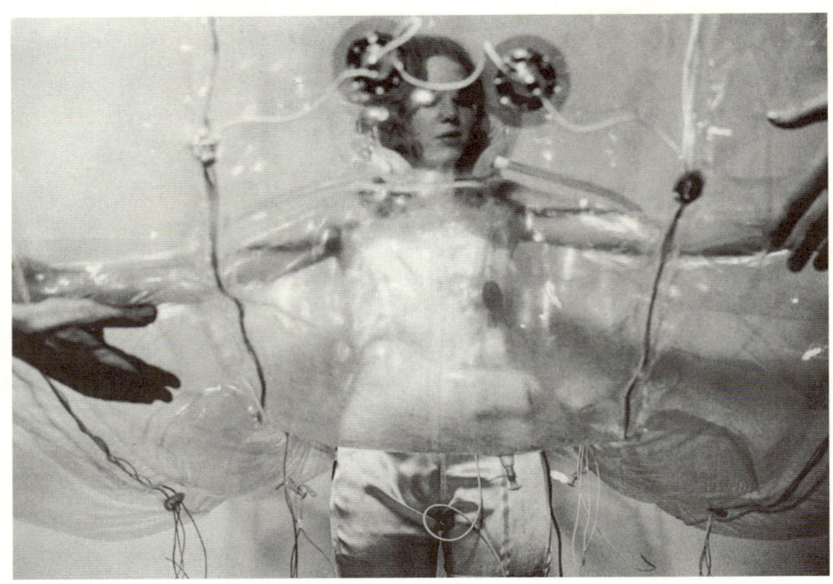

Coop Himmelblau, *Astroballoon*, 1969.

"many-sided" capacity of a subject to conjoin with any object or surface. Thus the perforation of the body's physical integrity in *Crash*, through wounds and orifices, discloses a condition of permanent openness and receptivity. Ballard presents the body as the last domain of an external nature to be made over into what Marx called "purely a matter of utility."

Ballard takes to a limit effects that Jean-Luc Godard examined in *Weekend* (1968) and *Two or Three Things I Know About Her* (1967). The title of the latter film referred to, among other things, Paris, prostitution, and "neo-capitalism"; it emphasized the inseparability of the body and representations of it from the multiple economies of the city. In fact, Godard explicitly avoided using the word "city" in the film, specifying instead "la region parisienne." He presents Paris less as a built environment than as a modulating, heterogenous texture, experienced only as periphery, interwoven with flows of images, money, and desire. But at the same time, the antiurbanism of *Two or Three Things,* with its recurrent images of an older Paris under demolition, of bulldozers and new construction sites, showed

Godard coping with a familiar modernist dilemma (that goes back to Baudelaire's response to Haussmann's demolitions). In the words of Manfredo Tafuri, this recurring problem was "how to come to terms with the anguish of urban dynamism."

But for Ballard the city's physical metamorphoses are not an issue. In spite of its title's connotation of speed, *Crash* and Ballard's related novels disclose (*High-Rise*, *Concrete Island*) a fundamental dereliction and inertia of what once constituted the city. Everything in *Crash* occurs within a field that is defined spatially by proximity to the airport. Nothing even hints at the existence of an urban center. Ballard never takes us into the airport itself but travels ceaselessly around its fringes: a boundary-less world of access roads, shopping malls, hotels, parking garages, prostitutes. It is a permanent in-between, an in-transit, adjoining both the speed of air travel and the dissipation of the axial city. The artist Robert Smithson was also drawn to the airport as a nonsite implanted on an urban periphery, located ostensibly in the suburbs yet radically distinct from them. Like the Orly observation deck in Chris Marker's film *La Jetée* (1964), the layout of the airport was an entrance onto another network of vectors, viewpoints, languages, and temporalities. Ballard and Smithson understood how the airport, in spite of its geographical sprawl, was a machinery of displacement, that it rested not on extensive terrain but "on a firmament of statistics."

One perplexing feature of *Crash* is the apparent convergence of two radically dissimilar realms, two different models of circulation. On one hand, Ballard delineates a wholly vehicular city, dominated by the extensive (and seemingly anachronistic) space of the automobile, its labyrinth of routes and support structures. On the other, he outlines what might be called the "televisual" city, a setup constituted by simulation and reproductive technologies, and as insubstantial as the purely projected *Instant City* (1969) of Archigram. But Ballard assigns no priority to either of these, insisting on the interpenetration of these "incompatible" spaces. As much as the text is littered with the carnage of the car crash, so it is also with cameras, viewfinders, stacks of photographs, video screens, slow-motion replays. Everyone in the novel is equally entangled with the lure of the automobile and the business of television or film, especially the presiding figure of Vaughan, "one of the first of the new style of TV-scientists," whose dubious vocation is "the application of computerized techniques to the control of all international traffic systems." But in his obsession with assassinations and the deaths of celebrities in car crashes, that is, with the corporeality of the image, Vaughan's real project is to explore the congruence of these overlapping zones.

One of Ballard's crucial images is the automobile coupled with recording apparatus: a movie or TV camera bolted to a car dashboard, with the human body at the same time merged with both vehicle and viewfinder. But Ballard is not describing a subjection of the body to either car (commodity) or image (spectacle). Rather, he diagrams how events, trajectories, and their reproduction all circulate indifferently on the same isotropic surface; and Ballard is ultimately less interested in outlining the homogeneity of space and of surfaces than he is the interchangeability of operations, connections, and syntheses. The potential singularity and intensity of the car crash (which André Breton had suggested in a footnote at the end of his novel *Nadja*) are neutralized by being merely one of innumerable modes of conjunction.

One is sometimes tempted to position Ballard as a late twentieth-century Lautréamont, and certainly his ambivalent, even nostalgic relationship to surrealism is a conspicuous part of his work, including *Crash*. But if his writing is haunted by surrealism, it is also marked by a recognition of the inability of surrealist operations to achieve the same effects that were once sought. For Breton the city offered "certain juxtapositions, certain combinations that greatly surpass our understanding." In Breton's *Nadja* or Louis Aragon's *Le paysan de Paris* the city allowed the exercise of a *gout d'errer*: a wandering through its (magnetic) field always held the possibility of a transfiguring encounter with a given site or person, of paths or itineraries punctuated by combinations of talismanic objects. But the kind of deterritorialization that Ballard outlines is taken to such limits that anything can conjoin with anything, thus exploding an aesthetic of juxtaposition (or of perversion). In *The Atrocity Exhibition,* "Talbert has accepted in absolute terms the logic of the sexual union. For him all junctions, whether of our own soft biologies or the hard geometries of these walls and ceilings, are equivalent to one another. What Talbert is searching for is the primary act of intercourse, the first apposition." There is a fundamental regularity to the field in spite of the heterogeneity of its contents, and it is the very uniformity of exchange values that derails what once might have been surrealism.

A paradox of *Crash* is the remoteness of its violence from a modernist experience of shock, which presupposed a subject autonomous enough to maintain a distance from the ceaselessly evolving collage-city, founded on the chaos of anarchical industrial production. Ballard's derelict and amorphous city is concurrent with the global dispersal of the body of the multinational corporation into shifting mobile arrangements, and the relation of the subject to this new city is not one of opposition. Rather, he outlines the subject's decomposition, scattering and remapping onto its new surfaces, paralleling related processes in Thomas Pynchon's *Gravity's Rainbow*, published the same year as *Crash*. There are then no independent agents, defining their own trajectories and meeting in random collisions. Instead, Ballard details a permanent condition of interface, of sheer contiguity, an invasion of the subject so thorough that his frequent use of the word "dream" no longer describes anything interior. The city coincides with this promiscuity of forms, an infinity of intersections, in which the accidental is no longer possible. It is not so much a text to be read and interpreted as a delirium of conjugations to be named and enumerated. Even the bare recitation of these new syntactical formations generates a constellation of epiphanies. And Ballard the writer has the superb tact never to impose on his reader the beauty or horror of this syntax.

Originally published in *Zone 1/2: The Contemporary City* (New York: Zone Books, 1986).

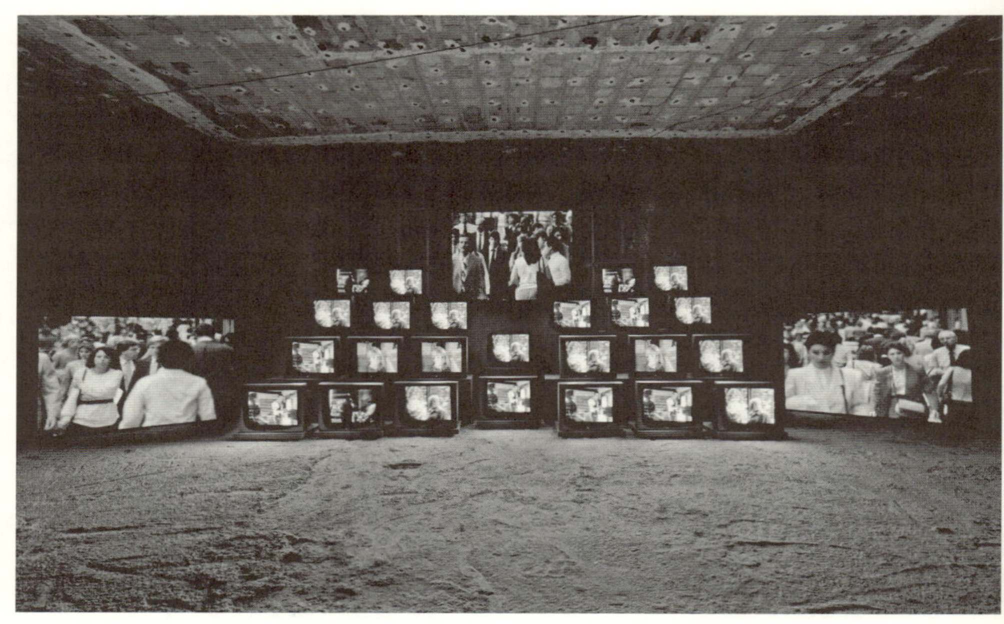

Gretchen Bender, *Total Recall*, 1987.

Gretchen Bender's *Total Recall*

In retrospect, it is easy to say that Gretchen Bender's *Total Recall* is about the social and perceptual experience of watching television. But whether this would occur to any of us in the midst of viewing it is another question. The delirium, the sensory overload, and the structural extravagance of *Total Recall* deranges our customary habits of television viewing and explodes it into fragmented and multiplied configurations. She seems to say to us, "You think you know about TV? Well, let me show you a few things." By upending our familiar, domestic relationship to the TV screen she intensifies our physiocognitive involvement to a threshold at which it becomes acute. In doing so, she does not make a critical or objective statement about television, but enters into its laws of operations and effects, pushing them to extremes, exploring their limits and boundaries.

Although many video artists have worked with multiple monitors, Bender's use of them does not share a concern for the formal problems of video art. In fact, part of her stance as an artist is a refusal to acknowledge any significant distinctions between video and television; she sees both as inextricably bound up in a homogeneous and ubiquitous media culture. Nonetheless, her deployment of so many television screens is clearly an extension of a modernist strategy of "defamiliarization." That is, she disrupts certain features of our experience of television to attain a new perspective from which to comprehend its possibilities and effects. Multiplying the number of screens before us and maximizing the audio volume might lead us to assume that Bender is only heightening our subjugation and control by television; but the opposite may, in fact, be the case. Researchers have shown that television is probably most powerful when the eye is immobile for long periods of time. This is the normal situation of television viewing and it produces what some neurologists call an Alpha state, characterized by slow brain-wave activity, passivity, and even trancelike fixation. *Total Recall* precludes this possibility. Bender's setup forces us to become active, responsive viewers whose eyes continually move from one screen to another, never resting, never lulled into an arrested state. She allows us a glimpse of the awesome fascination of television, almost submerges us in it, but simultaneously preserves for us the autonomy of stimulated, alert, and analytical observers. Our visceral and intellectual experience becomes not unlike that of the narrator in Edgar Allan Poe's "Descent into the Maelstrom," who discovered that envelopment in the chaos of a sublime disaster had the effect of sharpening his perceptions, rather than disorienting and overwhelming him.

All television watching has the structure of performance, but Bender puts us in an explicitly theatrical situation. We are an audience in front of a stage, and the assembled video monitors are the performers in a mega-spectacle of sound and image, volume and void. At the same time, *Total Recall* is a sculptural or architectonic installation. The cubic, geometric layout of the video monitors recalls some of the crystalline structures by the artist Robert Smithson from 1967 to 1968. The connection with Smithson is actually more than formal similarity. Like Smithson, Bender is interested in how the physical or spatial setup of a site is displaced or negated by the very material objects that constitute it. Smithson's work with mirrors, with the repetition of inert minimal forms that bespoke their own emptiness, eventually leads to his idea of a nonsite. Bender also plays with a paradoxical structure in which the plurality of televisions generates a sense of negation and absence. A single image can sustain an illusion of presence, but the profusion of luminous, dematerialized images that coexist in time effaces the screen as object and the space it occupies. It is a vision of television as a black hole that absorbs energy and collapses in on itself.

The content of *Total Recall* has not yet been described, not because it is unimportant, but because it is inseparable from the conditions under which it is presented. For Bender, integral parts of an image are the phenomena of its proliferation, repetition, and distribution. Although there are many recognizable images in *Total Recall* (for example, a General

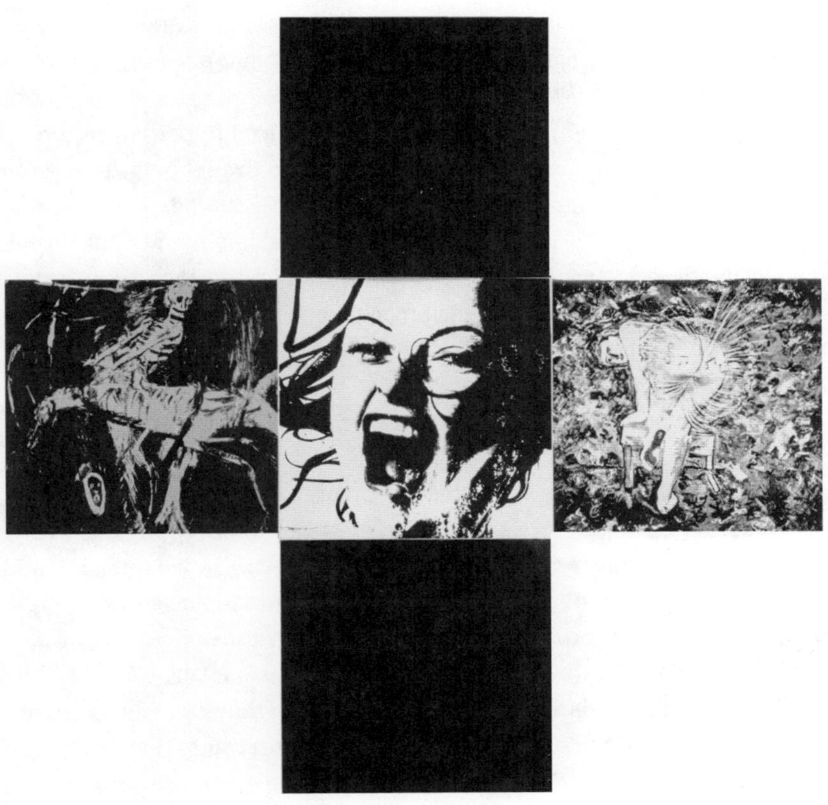

Gretchen Bender, *Untitled "The Pleasure is Back" Series*, 1982, enamel ink silkscreened on sign tin, 72 × 72 in.

Electric commercial; scenes from Oliver Stone's film *Salvador*), Bender stresses our remoteness from traditional problems of representation. Her images are so processed, treated, and manipulated, through an astonishing array of techniques, that they assume a reality of their own. A corporate logo or network emblem asserts a haunting corporeality yet exists fully outside of what might have once been thought of as perspectival space. We see a new vocabulary and grammar of forms, with an increased velocity to perceptually complex optical transformations. We gradually sense the inertia of our own physical responses, the slowness of our bodies versus the speed of images and their mutations. She works in the area of overlap between everyday perception and communication-information technology. *Total Recall* evokes some of the pathos and tragedy of this gap, the imposition of an electronically induced hyperperception on human beings. In the words of filmmaker David Cronenberg, television has become "the retina of the mind's eye." And Bender, expanding upon the critical thought of writers such as Walter Benjamin and Paul Virilio, makes us visually aware that the present is a historical moment, a time when technology is forcing wrenching change in human perception from which there is no going back.

Bender also works within the logic of television's visual flow, where anything can be connected to anything else, which produces what William Burroughs has called "image haze." Indirectly, her piece is a reflection on the once radical aesthetic strategies of montage. Bender's work shows how the techniques of juxtaposition and fragmentation have long been fully assimilated by mainstream mass media. Developed to a new intensity and sophistication, they now constitute the dominant language of corporate culture. She hardly proposes a return to earlier forms of realism or narrative; rather, she outlines survival tactics for artists to maintain a mobile position at the boundaries of mass culture, where they can engage in, but remain uncoerced by, its technological transfigurations. Her work is an acknowledgment that there is no zone of pure aesthetic activity outside a highly impure arena exemplified and dominated by television. Bender does not approach television as a medium that distorts or falsifies a view of the true or real world. She explores how television produces, rather than represents, a world of experience that, increasingly, becomes more real than so-called everyday life.

Originally published in a brochure for the exhibition *Gretchen Bender: Total Recall* at the Contemporary Arts Museum and the Museum of Fine Arts in Houston, Texas, February 1988.

Spectacle, Attention, Counter-Memory

Whether or not the term "spectacle" was originally taken from Henri Lefebvre's *Critique de la vie quotidienne*, its currency emerged from the activities in the late 1950s and early 1960s of the various configurations now designated as presituationist or situationist. The product of a radical critique of modernist art practice, a politics of everyday life, and an analysis of contemporary capitalism, its influence was obviously intensified with the publication of Guy Debord's *Society of the Spectacle* in 1967. And twenty-two years later, the word "spectacle" not only persists but has become a stock phrase in a wide range of critical and not-so-critical discourses. But assuming it has not become completely devalued or exhausted as an explanation of the contemporary operation of power, does it still mean today what it did in the early 1960s? What constellation of forces and institutions does it designate? And if these have mutated, what kind of practices are required now to resist their effects?

One can still well ask if the notion of spectacle is the imposition of an illusory unity onto a more heterogenous field. Is it a totalizing and monolithic concept that inadequately represents a plurality of incommensurable institutions and events? For some, a troubling aspect about the term "spectacle" is the almost ubiquitous presence of the definite article in front of it, suggesting a single and seamless global system of relations. For others, it is a mystification of the functioning of power, a new opiate-of-the-masses type of explanation, a vague cultural-institutional formation with an ill-defined structural autonomy. Or is the concept of spectacle a necessary model for mapping a systemic shift in the way power functions noncoercively within twentieth-century modernity? Is it an indispensable means of revealing as related what would otherwise appear as disparate and unconnected phenomena? Does it not show that a patchwork or mosaic of techniques can still constitute a homogenous effect of power?

Debord's book did not include any kind of historical genealogy of the spectacle, and that absence may have contributed to the sense of the spectacle as having appeared full-blown out of the blue. The question that concerns me is, then: assuming the spectacle does in fact designate a certain set of objective conditions, what are its origins? When might we say it was first effective or operative? And I don't ask this simply as an academic exercise. For the term to have any critical or practical efficacy depends, in part, on how one periodizes it, that is, the spectacle will assume quite different meanings depending on how it is situated historically. Is it more than just a synonym for late capitalism? For the rise of mass media and communication technology? More than an updated account of the culture or consciousness industry and thus chronologically distinct from these?

The early work of Jean Baudrillard provides some general parameters for what we might call the prehistory of the spectacle (which Baudrillard sees as having disappeared by the late 1970s). For Baudrillard, writing in the late 1960s, one of the crucial consequences of the bourgeois political revolutions was the ideological force that animated the myths of the Rights of Man: the right to equality and the right to happiness. In the nineteenth century, for the first time, observable proof became necessary to demonstrate that happiness had in fact been obtained. Happiness, he says "had to be measurable in terms of signs and objects," signs that would be evident to the eye in terms of "visible criteria."[1] Several decades earlier, Walter Benjamin had also written about "the phantasmagoria of equality" in the nineteenth century in terms of the transformation of the citizen into consumer. Baudrillard's account of modernity is one of an increasing destabilization and mobility of signs beginning in the Renaissance, signs which previously had been firmly rooted to relatively secure positions within fixed social hierarchies.[2] Thus, for Baudrillard, modernity is bound up in the struggle of newly empowered classes to overcome this "exclusiveness of signs" and to initiate a "proliferation of signs on demand." Imitations, copies, and counterfeits are all challenges to that exclusivity. The problem of mimesis, then, is not one of aesthetics but one of social power, and the emergence of the Italian theater and perspective painting are at the start of this ever-increasing capacity to produce equivalences. But obviously, for Baudrillard and many others, it is in the nineteenth century, alongside new industrial techniques and forms of circulation, that a new kind of sign emerges: "potentially identical objects produced in indefinite series." For Baudrillard "the relation of objects in such a series is equivalence and indifference...and it is on the level of reproduction, of fashion, media, advertising, information and communication (what Marx called the unessential sectors of capitalism)...that the global process of capital is held together." The spectacle then would coincide with the moment when sign-value takes precedence over use-value. But the question of the location of this moment in the history of the commodity remains unanswered.

From a very different theoretical vantage point, T.J. Clark has made one of the most influential contributions to a historical understanding of spectacle. In his book *The Painting of Modern Life*, he uses the images of Edouard Manet to identify the conditions of possibility for its emergence. Writing about the 1860s and '70s, Clark explores the inseparability of Manet's art from a newly emerging social and economic configuration. This society of the spectacle, he writes, is bound up in "a massive internal extension of the capitalist market—the invasion and restructuring of whole areas of free time, private life, leisure and personal expression.... It indicates a new phase of commodity production—the marketing, the making-into-commodities of whole areas of social practice which had once been referred to casually as everyday life."[3] In Clark's chronology, then, the spectacle also coincides with the rise of late nineteenth-century Western imperialism, that is, with two parallel expansions of a global marketplace, one internal, one external. Although he rightly calls "neat temporality" impossible, he does sees elements of the spectacle taking shape in the late 1860s and '70s, citing the emergence of commercialized aspects of life and leisure that are themselves due to a shift from one kind of capitalist production to another. This shift, he says, was "not a matter of mere cultural and ideological refurbishing but of all-embracing economic change."[4]

Guy Debord recently offered a surprisingly specific indication of when he sees the comprehensive operation of society of the spectacle as fully underway. In his *Commentaires sur la société du spectacle* (1988), Debord reflects that in 1967, when the original book appeared, the spectacle "had barely forty years behind it."[5] Not a more approximate kind of number like fifty, but forty. Thus, 1927, or roughly the late 1920s. He doesn't provide any details about the importance of this moment, and it would be misguided to overread an isolated remark. Nonetheless it might still be valuable to consider provisionally what it could mean to designate the late 1920s as a historical threshold. This essay offers some brief and fragmentary speculations on historical developments that could possibly have been implicit in Debord's remark.

1.

The first is both symbolic and substantive. The year 1927 saw the technological consolidation of television. Vladimir Zworykin, the Russian-born, American-trained engineer and physicist, patented his iconoscope—the first electronic system of a tube containing an electron gun and a screen made out of a mosaic of photoemissive cells, each of which produced a charge proportional to the varying light intensity of the image focused on the screen.[6] Also, in 1927, the American inventor Philo Farnsworth successfully conducted the first transmission of television signals with his own scanning tube. Right at the moment when an awareness arose of the age of mechanical reproduction, a new model of circulation and transmission appeared that was to exceed that age, one that had no need of silver salts or permanent physical support. The spectacle was to become inseparable from this new kind of image and its immateriality, ubiquity, and simultaneity.

But equally important was that by the late 1920s, when the first experimental broadcasts occurred, the vast interlocking control of corporate, military, and state control of radio and television was effectively in place. Never before had the institutional regulation of a new technique been planned and divided up so far in advance. So, in a sense, much of the territory of spectacle, the intangible domain of the spectrum, had already been diagrammed and standardized before 1930. Ownership of the means of communication, in Debord's words, "gave them the tools to lie about everything, and to confirm their lies by falsifying the actual content of all production."[7]

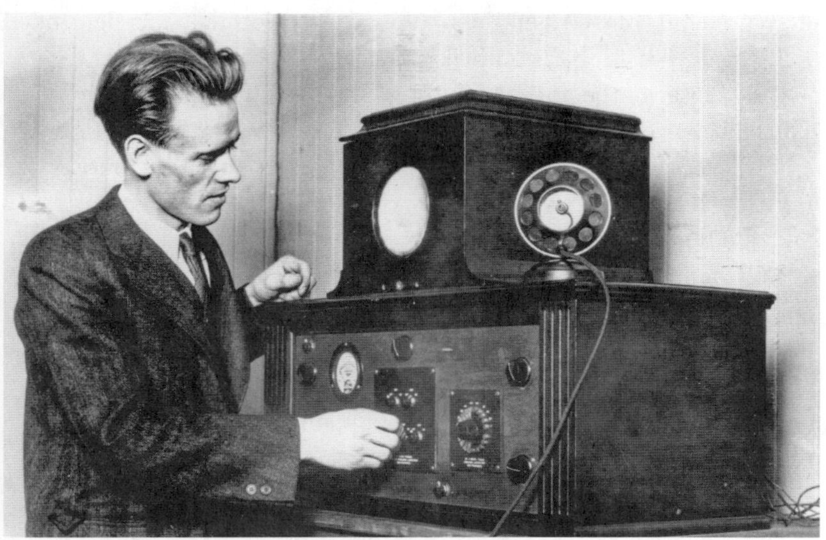

Philo Farnsworth with his television receiver, 1927.

2.

Equally significant, the movie *The Jazz Singer* premiered in 1927, signaling the arrival of the sound film, and specifically of synchronized sound. This was not only a transformation in the nature of subjective perceptual experience. It was also an event that accelerated the complete vertical integration of production, distribution, and exhibition within the film industry and its amalgamation with the corporate conglomerates that owned the sound patents and provided the capital for the costly move to the new technology.[8] These were often the same companies that already controlled radio networks. Again, as with television, the nascent institutional and economic infrastructure of the spectacle was set in place. This also confirms Clark's emphasis on the transformation of small entrepreneurial capitalism into increasingly monopolistic forms.

Specifying sound here obviously suggests that spectacular power cannot be reduced to an optical model but is inseparable from a larger organization of perceptual consumption. Sound had of course been part of cinema in various additive forms from the beginning, but the introduction of sync sound transformed the nature of attention that was demanded of a viewer. Possibly it is a break that makes previous forms of cinema actually closer to the optical devices of the late nineteenth century. The full coincidence of sound with image, of voice with the human face, not only was a crucial new way of organizing space, time, and narrative, but it instituted a captivation of the observer through the imposition of a new kind of attention.

And from the 1890s well into the 1930s one of the central problems in mainstream psychology had been the nature of attention: the relation between stimulus and attention, problems of concentration, focalization, and distraction. How many sources of stimulation could one attend to simultaneously? How could novelty, familiarity, and repetition in attention be assessed? It was a problem whose position in the forefront of psychological discourse was directly related to the emergence of social and industrial spaces increasingly saturated with sensory input. Initially much of this research was bound up in the need for information on attention in the context of rationalizing assembly-line production, but as early as 1910 hundreds of experimental laboratory studies had been done specifically on the range of attention in advertising (including titles such as "The Attention Value of Periodical Advertisements," "Attention and the Effects of Size in Street Car Advertisements," "Advertising and the Laws of Mental Attention," "Measuring the Attention Value of Color in Advertising").

The year 1927 was also when Benjamin began his *Arcades Project*, a work in which he would eventually point to "a crisis in perception itself," a crisis that is the result of a sweeping remaking of the observer by a calculated technology of the individual, derived from new knowledge of the body. In the course of writing the *Arcades Project*, Benjamin himself became preoccupied with the question of attention and the related issues of distraction and shock, and he turned to Henri Bergson's *Matter and Memory* for a way out of what he saw as the "standardized and denatured" perception of the masses. Bergson had fought to recover perception from its status as sheer physiological event; for him attention was a question of an engagement of the body, an inhibition of movement, a state of consciousness arrested in the present. But attention could become transformed into something productive only when it was linked to the deeper activity of memory:

> Memory thus creates anew present perception...strengthening and enriching [it].... If after having gazed on any object, we turn our eyes abruptly away, we obtain an "after-image" [image consecutive] of it. It is true we are dealing here with images photographed on the object itself, and with memories following immediately upon the perception of which they are but the echo. But behind these images which are identical with the object, there are others, stored in memory which only resemble it.[9]

Bergson sought to describe the vitality of the moment when a conscious rift occurred between memory and perception, a moment in which memory had the capacity to remake the object of perception. Deleuze and Guattari have described similar effects of the entry of memory into perception, for example in the perception of a face: one can see a face in terms of a vast set of micromemories and a rich proliferation of semiotic systems, or, what is far more common, in terms of bleak redundancies of representations, which, they say, is where connections can always be effected with the hierarchies of power formations.[10] That kind of redundancy of representation, with its accompanying inhibition and impoverishment of memory, was what Benjamin saw as the standardization of perception, or what we might call an effect of spectacle.

Although Benjamin called *Matter and Memory* a "towering and monumental work," he reproached Bergson for circumscribing memory within the isolated frame of an individual consciousness; the kind of afterimages that interested Benjamin were those of collective historical memory, haunting images of the out-of-date which had the capacity for a social reawakening.[11] And thus Benjamin's apprehension of a present-day crisis in perception is filtered through a richly elaborated afterimage of the mid-nineteenth century.

3.

Given the content of Debord's work, we can also assume another crucial development in the late 1920s: the rise of fascism and, soon after, Stalinism, and the way in which they incarnated models of the spectacle. Important, for example, was Joseph Goebbels's innovative and synergetic use of every available medium, especially the development of sound/image propaganda, and his devaluation of the written word, because reading implied time for reflection and thought. In one election campaign in 1930, Goebbels mailed fifty thousand phonograph records of one of his own speeches to specially targeted voters. Goebbels also introduced the airplane into politics, making Hitler the first political candidate to fly to several different cities on the same day. Air travel thus functioned as a conveyor of the image of the leader, providing a new sense of ubiquity.

As part of this mixed technology of attention, television was to have played a crucial role. And as recent scholarship has shown, the development of television in Germany was in advance of that of any other country.[12] German TV broadcasting on a regular basis began in 1935, four years ahead of the United States. Clearly, as an instrument of social control, its effectiveness was never realized by the Nazis, but its early history in Germany is instructive for the competing models of spectacular organization that were proposed in the 1930s. A major split emerged early on between the monopolistic corporate forces and the Nazi Party with regard to the development of television in Germany. The Party sought to have television centralized and accessible in public screening halls, unlike the decentralized use of radio in private homes. Goebbels and Hitler had a notion of group reception, believing that this was the most effective form of reception. Public television halls, seating from forty to four hundred, were designated, not unlike the subsequent early development of television in the USSR, where a mass viewing environment was also favored. According to the Nazi director of broadcasting, writing in 1935, the "sacred mission" of television was "to plant indelibly the image of the Führer in the hearts of the German people."[13] Corporate power, on the other hand, sought home viewing, for maximization of profit. One model sought to position television as technique within the demands of fascism in general as a means of mobilizing and inciting the masses, whereas the agents of capitalism sought to privatize, to divide, and to impose a model of separation.

It is easy to forget that in *Society of the Spectacle* Debord outlined two different models of the spectacle; one he called "concentrated" and the other "diffused," preventing the word spectacle from simply being synonymous with consumer or late capitalism. Concentrated spectacle was what characterized Nazi Germany, Stalinist Russia, and Maoist China while the preeminent model of diffused spectacle was the United States. "Wherever

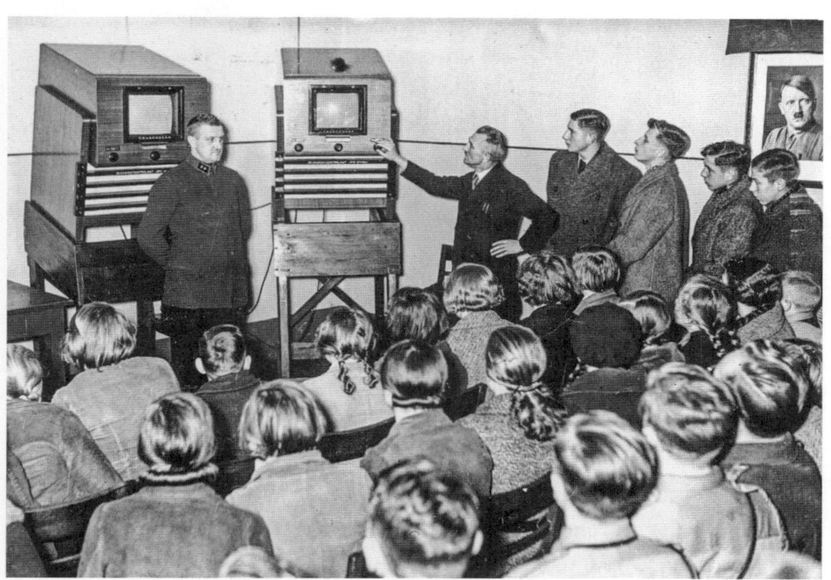

Television viewing center for Berlin Hitler Youth, 1936.

the concentrated spectacle rules so does the police...it is accompanied by permanent violence. The imposed image of the good envelops in its spectacle the totality of what officially exists and is usually concentrated in one man who is the guarantee of totalitarian cohesion. Everyone must magically identify with this absolute celebrity-or disappear."[14] The diffuse spectacle, on the other hand, accompanies the abundance of commodities. And certainly, it is this category to which Debord gives most of his attention in his 1967 book.

I'll note in passing Michel Foucault's famous dismissal of the spectacle in *Discipline and Punish*: "Our society is not one of spectacle, but of surveillance; under the surface of images one invests bodies in depth."[15] But the spectacle is also a set of techniques for the management of bodies, the management of attention (I am paraphrasing Foucault) "for assuring the ordering of human multiplicities," "its object is to fix, it is an anti-nomadic technique," "it uses procedures of partitioning and cellularity...in which the individual is reduced as a political force."[16] It would not be difficult to make a case that television is a further perfecting of panoptic technology. In it, surveillance and spectacle are not opposed terms, as he insists, but collapsed onto one another in a more effective disciplinary apparatus. Recent developments have confirmed literally this composite model: television sets that contain advanced image recognition technology in order to monitor and quantify the behavior, attentiveness, and eye movement of a spectator.[17]

But in 1988 Debord sees his two original models of diffused and concentrated spectacle becoming indistinct, converging into what he calls "the integrated society of the spectacle."[18] In this deeply pessimistic book, he describes a more sophisticated deployment of elements from those earlier models, a flexible arrangement of global power adaptable to local needs and circumstances. In 1967 there were still marginalities and peripheries that escaped its reign. Today, he insists, the spectacle has irradiated into everything and has absolute control over production, over perception, and especially over the shape of the future and the past.

As much as any single feature, Debord sees the core of the spectacle as the annihilation of historical knowledge—in particular the destruction of the recent past. In its place, there is the reign of a perpetual present. History, he writes, had always been the measure by which novelty was assessed, but whoever is in the business of selling novelty has an interest in destroying the means by which it could be judged. Thus, there is a ceaseless appearance of the important, and almost immediately its annihilation and replacement: "That which the spectacle ceases to speak of for three days no longer exists."[19]

In conclusion, I want to briefly note two different responses to the new texture of modernity taking shape in the 1920s. The painter Fernand Léger writes, in a 1924 essay titled "The Spectacle," published soon after the making of his film *Ballet mécanique*:

> The rhythm of modern life is so dynamic that a slice of life seen from a cafe terrace is a spectacle. The most diverse elements collide and jostle one another there. The interplay of contrasts is so violent that there is always exaggeration in the effect that one glimpses. On the boulevard two men are carrying some immense gilded letters in a hand cart: the effect is so unexpected that everyone stops and looks. There is the origin of the modern spectacle…in the shock of the surprise effect.[20]

But then Léger goes on to detail how advertising and commercial forces have taken the lead in the making of modern spectacle, and he cites the department store, the world of fashion, and the rhythms of industrial production as forms that have conquered the attention of the public. Léger's goal is the same: wanting to win over that public. Of course, he is writing at a point of uncertainty about the direction of his own art, facing the dilemma of what a public art might mean, but the confused program he comes up with in this text is an early instance of the ploys of all those—from Warhol to today's so-called simulationists—who believe, or at least claim, they are outwitting the spectacle at its own game. Léger summarizes this kind of ambition: "Let's push the system to the extreme," he states, and offers vague suggestions for polychroming the exterior of factories and apartment buildings, for using new materials and setting them in motion. But this ineffectual inclination to outdo the allure of the spectacle becomes complicit with its annihilation of the past and fetishization of the new.

The same year, 1924, the first *Surrealist Manifesto* suggests a very different aesthetic strategy for confronting the spectacular organization of the modern city. I'm referring to what Benjamin called the "anthropological" dimension of surrealism.[21] It was a strategy of turning the spectacle of the city inside out through counter-memory and counter-itineraries. These would reveal the potency of outmoded objects excluded from its slick surfaces, and of derelict spaces off its main routes of circulation. The strategy incarnated a refusal of the imposed present, and in reclaiming fragments of a demolished past it was implicitly figuring an alternative future. And despite the equivocal nature of many of these surrealist gestures, it is no accident that they were to reappear in new forms in the tactics of situationism in the 1960s, in the notion of the derive or drift, of detournement, of psychogeography, the exemplary act, and the constructed situation. Whether these practices have any vitality or even relevance today depends in large measure on what an archaeology of the present tells us. Are we still in the midst of a society that is organized as appearance? Or have we entered a non-spectacular global system arranged primarily around the control and flow of information, a system whose management and regulation of attention would demand wholly new forms of resistance and memory?[22]

1. Jean Baudrillard, *La société de consommation: Ses mythes, ses structures* (Paris: Gallimard, 1970), p. 60. Emphasis in original.
2. A well-known passage from Baudrillard amplifies this: "There is no such thing as fashion in a society of caste and rank since one is assigned a place irrevocably. Thus class-mobility is non-existent. A prohibition protects the signs and assures them a total clarity; each sign refers unequivocally to a status.... In caste societies, feudal or archaic, the signs are limited in number and are not widely diffused.... Each is a reciprocal obligation between castes, clans, or persons." *Simulations*, trans. Paul Foss (New York, Semiotext(e), 1983), p. 84.
3. T.J. Clark, *The Painting of Modern Life: Paris in the Art of Manet and His Followers* (Princeton, NJ: Princeton University Press, 1984), p. 9.
4. Ibid., p. 10.
5. Guy Debord, *Commentaires sur la société du spectacle* (Paris: Éditions Gerard Lebovici, 1988), p. 13.
6. Philosopher of science François Dagognet cites the revolutionary nature of this particular development in his *Philosophie de l'image* (Paris: J. Vrin, 1986), pp. 57–58.
7. Guy Debord, *Oeuvres cinématographiques complètes, 1952–1978* (Paris: Éditions Champ Libre, 1978).
8. See Steven Neale, *Cinema and Technology: Image, Sound, Colour* (Bloomington: Indiana University Press, 1985), pp. 62–102; and Douglas Gomery, "Toward an Economic History of the Cinema: The Coming of Sound to Hollywood," in *The Cinematic Apparatus*, ed. Teresa de Lauretis and Stephen Heath (London, Macmillan, 1980), pp. 38–46.
9. Henri Bergson, *Matter and Memory*, trans. N. M. Paul and W. S. Palmer (New York: Zone Books, 1988), pp. 101–103.
10. See, for example, Félix Guattari, "Les machines concrètes," in *La révolution moléculaire* (Paris: Encres, 1977), pp. 364–76.
11. "On the contrary he [Bergson] rejects any historical determination of memory. He thus manages above all to stay clear of that experience from which his own philosophy evolved or, rather, in reaction to which it arose. It was the inhospitable, blinding age of big-scale industrialism." Walter Benjamin, *Illuminations: Essays and Reflections*, trans. Harry Zohn (New York: Schocken Books, 1969), pp. 156–57.
12. I have relied on the valuable research in William Uricchio, "Rituals of Reception, Patterns of Neglect: Nazi Television and its Postwar Representation," *Wide Angle* 10, no. 4 (1989), pp. 48–66. See also Robert Edwin Herzstein, *The War That Hitler Won: Goebbels and the Nazi Media Campaign* (New York: Paragon, 1978).

13. Cited in Uricchio, "Rituals of Reception," p. 51.
14. Guy Debord, *Society of the Spectacle*, trans. Donald Nicholson-Smith (New York: Zone Books, 1994), p. 42.
15. Michel Foucault, *Discipline and Punish: The Birth of the Prison*, trans. Alan Sheridan (New York: Pantheon Books, 1976), p. 217.
16. Ibid., pp. 218–19.
17. See, for example, Bill Carter, "TV Viewers, Beware: Nielsen May Be Looking," *The New York Times*, June 1, 1989.
18. Debord, *Commentaires*, pp. 17–19.
19. Ibid., p. 29.
20. Fernand Léger, *Functions of Painting*, trans. Alexandra Anderson, (New York, Viking, 1973), p. 35.
21. Walter Benjamin, *One Way Street and Other Writings*, trans. Edmund Jephcott and Kingsley Shorter (London: New Left Books, 1979), p. 239. The late 1920s would also likely be crucial for Debord as the moment when surrealism became coopted, that is, when its original revolutionary potential was nullified in an early instance of spectacular recuperation and absorption.
22. See my "Eclipse of the Spectacle," in *Art After Modernism: Rethinking Representation*, ed. Brian Wallis (Boston: David R. Godine, 1984), pp. 283–94. Reprinted in this volume.

This text was originally presented at the Sixth International Colloquium on Twentieth-Century French Studies, "Revolutions 1889–1989," at Columbia University, March 30 – April 1, 1989. It was first published in *October* 50 (Autumn 1989).

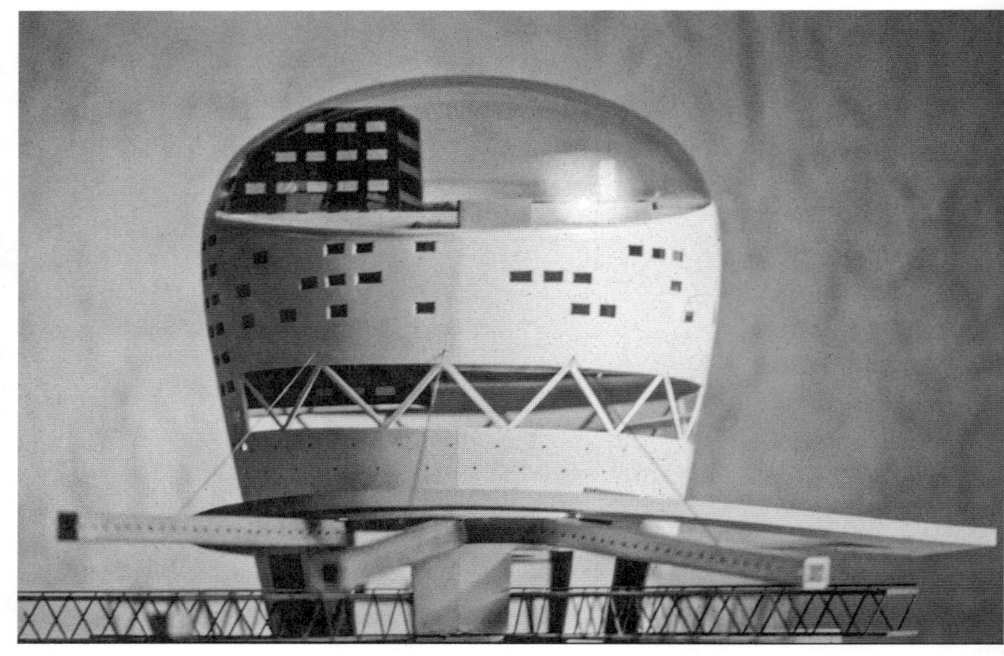

Rem Koolhaas, *Zeebrugge Sea Terminal*, 1989, project proposal.

Notes on Rem Koolhaas and Modernization

By now it is customary to engage the work of Rem Koolhaas in terms of its creative alignment with processes of cultural transformation, its planned instabilities and flexible components—an architecture designed as a dynamic ingredient of perpetual social flux and reorganization. *Delirious New York* is frequently read as a manifesto outlining how architecture (and by implication other forms of cultural invention) could become immanent to a mutating field of modernization rather than function as static or enduring monuments exterior to it. And certainly Koolhaas, as an antireformist urbanist, proposes collaborating with, if not emulating, uncontrolled forces of development rather than formulating anything self-consciously remedial that would attempt to rationalize or "solve" social disorder.

But given this recognizable profile of Koolhaas's work, it is also important to track the less conspicuous ways in which he is simultaneously working "against the grain" of modernization. For his apparent immersion in strategies of pushing or riding the logic of development (and playing the role of "developer") coincides with a rich understanding of the paradoxes and traps of modernization. In particular, his clear recognition of the obsolescence of the modern (as a style, strategy, affect, hope) is inseparable from his understanding of the overwhelming persistence and continuity of modernization, of neo-capitalism. In other words, for him the vicissitudes of the city, of architecture, of experience in the past few decades are the sign not of a new era in which modernity has somehow been exceeded, but rather a phase characterized by a shifting and reorganization of ongoing currents of rationalization. These are processes that jettison and destroy whatever obstructs flux and circulation, that transform the singular into the exchangeable, that incessantly create expand existing patterns of commodification and consumption, that, in Koolhaas's words, transform identity into the generic. A few obvious contemporary examples would be the continuing implantation of global communications and information networks and the steady dissolution of national boundaries—NAFTA, GATT, and EEC are merely acronyms for the reconfiguring effects of modernization. But Koolhaas seems to understand that the drifts, uprootings, and migrations caused by the opening up of streams of "free" trade or of images and data are not only indications of the emergence of an increasingly smooth planetary field of exchange but also of new distributions, demarcations, exclusions, and hierarchies, and, important for Koolhaas, cultural vacancies and derelict spaces.

Since the nineteenth century, a crucial dimension of the experience of modernization has been the precarious psychic and social accommodation to the relentless processes of destruction and creation through which the city mutates according to the shifting requirements of capitalism. But while some might want to position Koolhaas and *Delirious New York* in the context of the "melting" or evaporating vision of modernity (first sketched out by Marx) , he is in fact staking out a very different relation to modernization and history. Baudelaire gave paradigmatic expression to two reciprocal poles of response to modernization that have had a curiously enduring half-life: on one hand, the exhilarating experience of unfamiliar velocities and itineraries, the apparent freedoms of their sensations and perceptual frontiers (exemplified by today's cyberspace cheerleaders); on the other, lament at the immense richness of what modernization had eradicated forever (e.g., rain forests, tradition-based communities, epic poetry). Koolhaas's career is bound up in a deployment of historical memory that is neither paralyzed by the weight of nostalgia and loss nor dissipated in a celebratory abandonment to the kaleidoscopic momentum of technological innovation. Baudelaire's swan, doomed by the spirit of gravity, flapping its wings wretchedly in the dust of urban work sites and demolitions, has as its flip side the false lightness of the man of the crowd, surrendering to the latest rhythms and force lines of capitalist reorganization. Working outside of this polarity, one of Koolhaas's achievements is allowing architecture to become involved in the practical elaboration of the composite lifeworlds of urban collectivities, letting his work operate as a medium between the volatile possibilities of modernization and a more enduring set of routines, patterns, and desires. If Koolhaas's work incarnates a certain cool-headed social optimism, it is also anti-utopian and relentlessly demystifying about notions of progress. An unflinching engagement with the history of the twentieth century, its layers of savagery, stupidity, and intellectual failure, pervades his writing. It is possible to speak of Koolhaas's thinking as "untimely," recalling that for Nietzsche untimeliness was not about forgetting but rather about creating a new kind of historical vision, the invention of different eyes and senses with which to survey the past, the difficult acquisition of new viewpoints on how to transform human experience and activity in "the perspective of life." Clearly Koolhaas has no hesitation in exploiting the latest technological contrivances. Some of his projects, such as the Center for Art and Media Technology at Karlsruhe, would be unthinkable without them. But his work, for all its impressive utilization of cutting-edge technique, is not driven by the breathless "futurism" exhibited by some of his contemporaries who believe, *a priori*, that telecommunications and data manipulation will be the primary components of emerging social environments. In his encounter with technological modernity he seems strongly opposed to arrangements based on the physically isolated individual and cellular model of the social that digital networking entails. For Koolhaas, though, it is not a question of choosing the material over the dematerialized or the tectonic over the electronic. His pragmatic strategies allow him to move fluidly between these options, based on local conditions and requirements, even if his priorities are, finally, to facilitate the mutually supportive activity of human collectivities within urban assemblages.

One of the many achievements of his Très Grande Bibliothèque de France competition entry is how it sustains a resonant coexistence of two incommensurable realms—the atopic (and sublime) domain of data storage and, nested in unmappable proximity, spaces that affirm the potency of human aggregates and flows. The inclusions of features such as communal screening rooms could seem to some an anti-modernizing archaism, but it is a willful repudiation of the contention that, given a global film archive, the standard method of film viewing will be isolated individuals ordering them over the internet for home consumption. Even simply the

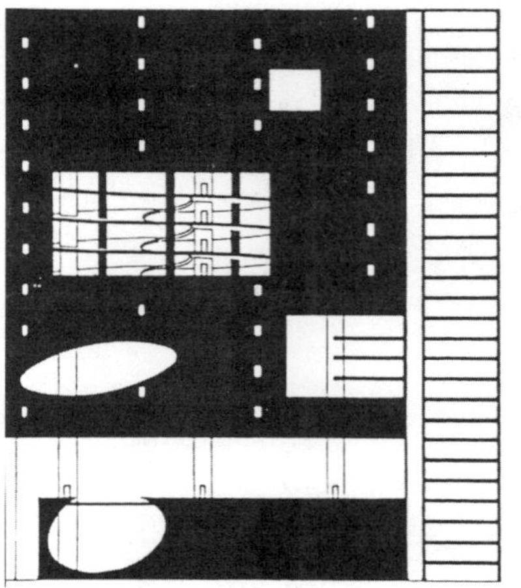
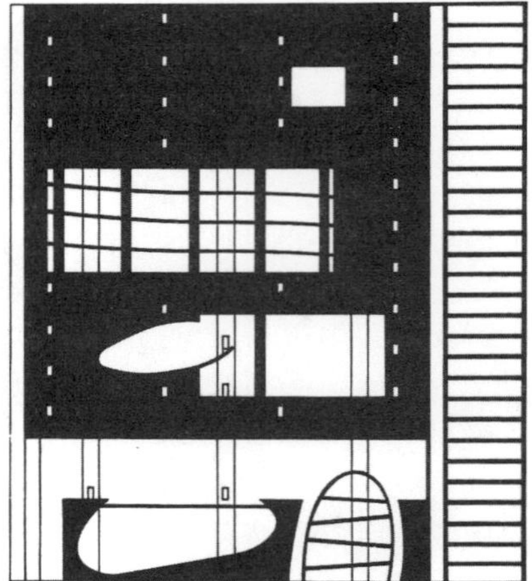

Rem Koolhaas, *Très Grande Bibliothèque*, 1989, project proposal.

notion of a library with a great hall to accommodate thousands of people is an indication of how the "rationalizing" logic of miniaturization and dematerialization is interrupted by diagramming the library-archive as a powerful social and communal apparatus.

The library, like his other public proposals, allows a polyphony of unforeseen zones and temporalities to emerge within the unstable mechanosphere we still call the city. They produce changing configurations and meetings. Collisions, not in the sense of shock or defamiliarization but of a montage of openings of the imagination onto other possible social ecologies. To say that Koolhaas works against the sedentarization now being imposed by modernization (i.e., the remodeling of the body into an electronic consumer) implies that he is committed to a certain general model of the human nervous system—the body as an integrating spatiotemporal system, whose perceptual and cognitive structures are decisively linked to motor patterns. In other words, an individual both shapes and is shaped by an environment in terms of an evolving relation between memory and sensorimotor activity. (Forms of cyberspace pose a very different model of the nervous system in which there is an indiscriminate mix of sensory and the locomotor on a flattened-out surface of digital information.)

Some of Koolhaas's most provocative and stunning plans, like Yokohama, Lille, and Zeebrugge, amplify the importance of a locomotor experience of movements, trajectories, and intersections of many kinds. In spite of all we have heard about the annihilation of distance and absolute speed, these projects (involving harbors, train stations, highways, ferry boats) affirm the persistence of "outmoded" vectors and vehicles, of other relations of motion and stasis, acceleration and slowness, that coexist with hyperspeeds and instantaneity. The nineteenth-century model of travel, as Paul Virilio has shown, is irrecoverable, but for Koolhaas the routines of everyday life are still composed of unrepresentable transitive moments, of the enigmatic passages that once linked arrivals and departures, which so fascinated artists and thinkers like de Chirico, Einstein, and Duchamp. But even if some works, like Zeebrugge, are "terminals," they are effectively intermediary elements of larger social machines, defined by the adjacencies and intermixings that occur through them, by their effective permeability (and this was part of Koolhaas's admiration of the Pan Am building). *Delirious New York* appeared in 1978 just when the Western city, as a theater of modernization, began to cede its primacy to another more pervasive and placeless arena of transformation and rationalization: the digital circuitry of telematics and informatics. Obviously the city, whether in the West or the Global South, has not and will not cease to be a space of instability and mutation. But as the physical map of the city is being overlaid by another radically different set of cognitive and sensory coordinates, the cultural effects of the city's dynamism have atrophied and deteriorated in comparison with the fermentation of the first seventy years of the twentieth century, as the models of theme park, shopping mall, and movie set increasingly redefine the texture of urban space.

Koolhaas's work inhabits this hybrid field in which diverse and historically distinct forces of modernization both interact and operate autonomously, and his notion of the "culture of congestion" comes into play here in crucial ways. For modernization continues to generate many different and even incompatible notions of congestion—some of which hold forth the possibility of livable and workable human environments even as others are producing experiences of social segmentation and separation, such as those Toni Negri has described in terms of the consequences of Reaganism and Thatcherism. At the same time, Koolhaas is not privileging the congestion of an image- and data-saturated environment, which is also founded on the cellurization and productive separation of human beings. One of the valuable features of Émile Durkheim's analysis of anomie was the insistence that social cohesiveness depended on the richness and flexibility of the contacts between individuals in a given society, rather than the sheer number of contacts. The computer terminal seems to open onto a profusion of potential points of contact and linkage, but it is a site on which communication and sensation are reduced to a single plane of affect and energy, to impoverished modalities of exchange and interface, and to anomic forms of redundancy. Koolhaas seeks to produce congestion in which a palpable heterogeneity of social/environmental contact, psychical and sensory feedback, and kinesthetic stimulation launch the individual out of the isolation that is the lot of the modernized "interactive" and amnesiac inhabitant of the Generic City.

Originally published in *Any: Architecture New York* 9 (1994).

Dr. Mabuse and Mr. Edison

In a 1988 interview with Serge Daney, Jean-Luc Godard surveys the life span of cinema. For him it is essentially "a nineteenth-century concern resolved in the twentieth."[1] He locates its last flowerings in Italian neorealism, the Nouvelle Vague, and, finally, in the work of Fassbinder. With the ubiquity of television, it was no longer a question of how one looked at the world, for television "quickly replaced the world and didn't look at it anymore."[2] Godard is only one of many, in the last decade, who have insisted that, even though films obviously continue to be made, their effects, their significance, the way they are consumed and produced now occurs amid such qualitatively different conditions that they bear only a depleted formal similarity to film in the first half of the twentieth century. Whether or not one agrees with Godard's historicization here, or with related arguments by others, one of the assumptions of his polemic is the instability and transience of cinema as a cultural form within modernity.

In spite of such reminders we nonetheless have a tendency, even a need, to define certain visual practices in terms of enduring formal structures or innate characteristics. Many analyses of film, television, and photography make them into essentialized objects of analysis. There is also a persistent, and most often unexamined, Kantian prejudice that perceptual and cognitive capacities are ahistorical; that is, they are unchanging and permanent, and most significantly are independent of an external social/technological milieu that is in constant flux. Thus there are difficult historical problems in attempts to posit anything more than a temporary subjective identity for a cinematic spectator, a television spectator and so on.

One has only to think of the influential meditations written in the 1970s on the philosophical and semiotic status of the photograph, which seemed so persuasive then, and of how they have been rendered quaintly obsolete by the spread of various digital techniques for image production. The mimetic dimension of photography (actually challenged from the 1840s on) will perhaps one day seem like a peculiar digression within a larger trajectory of image making in the West. Television, partly because of the immediate physical presence of the TV set, seemed for several decades like a stable object when in fact the institutional relations of which it was a part were changing continuously during that time. But during the past ten years even the possibility of giving television a coherent identity has evaporated as monitors and screens of many kinds proliferate and intersect with a broad range of expanding flows and electronic networks. Of course, critical analyses of practices such as film, video, or photography may at times need to work with synchronic assumptions or to pose provisional stable models for explanatory purposes, but a falsification occurs if these practices are treated as autonomous formal structures or independent visual media. They must also be thought of in terms of their inseparability from the intrinsic instability of larger processes of modernization.

More specifically, since the late nineteenth century, and increasingly during the last two decades, one crucial dimension of capitalist modernity has been a constant remaking of the conditions of sensory experience, in what could be called a revolutionizing of the means of perception. For the last hundred years perceptual modalities have been, and continue to be, in a state of perpetual transformation or, some might claim, of crisis. If visual experience can be said to have any enduring characteristic within twentieth-century modernity, it is that it has no enduring features; rather, it is embedded in a rhythm of adaptability to new technological relations, social configurations, and economic imperatives. What we familiarly refer to as film, photography, and television are transient and malleable elements within an accelerating sequence of displacements, amalgamations, and obsolescences within the destabilizing processes of modernization. Modernization here is distinct from a notion of progress and which is instead a self-perpetuating, directionless creation of new needs and desires, new production, new consumption.

To step back for a moment to the late nineteenth century, it is worth noting that it is just when the dynamic logic of capital begins to systematically undermine any normative model of perceptual performance that dominant institutions simultaneously attempt to impose a disciplinary regime of attentiveness. The late nineteenth century is also when the human sciences, particularly the emerging field of scientific psychology, prioritize the question of attention. Attention was a problem whose importance related directly to the emergence of a social, urban, psychic, industrial field increasingly saturated with sensory input. Inattention, especially within the context of new forms of industrialized production and consumerism, begins to be seen as a threat and as a serious problem. It's possible to see one crucial aspect of modernity as a continual crisis of attentiveness, a crisis in which the changing configurations of capitalism push distraction to new limits and thresholds, with unending introduction of new organizations of sensory experience, new sources of stimulation and streams of information, and then respond with new methods of regulating but also productively harnessing perception.

By the late nineteenth century, capitalism in the West begins to spawn arrangements that require attentiveness of a subject in terms of a wide range of new tasks, but, at the same time, its internal movement was continually to dissolve the binding cognitive synthesis that was the basis of a disciplinary attentiveness. New environments and technologies of many kinds demand that we accept as natural switching our attention rapidly from one thing to another. Capital as high speed exchange and circulation is inseparable from this kind of human perceptual adaptability, and it imposes a regime of reciprocal attentiveness and distraction. The last decade has been a mere hint of the rapidity with which new forms of visual consumption will continue to supplant one another. Whether there are inherent social or psychic or even physiological limits to this acceleration remains to be seen.

One of the places where this particularly "modern" system of perceptual mutation can first be located is in the work of Thomas Edison. Edison stands not simply as a participant in the making of cinema but for a specific swerve that separates earlier nineteenth-century techniques of exhibition and attention from what would follow in the twentieth. What needs to be identified is not some sequence of optical devices running from the magic lantern, diorama, phenakistoscope, cinemascope, or 3-D movies to contemporary, head-mounted displays, but the emergence, beginning in the 1870s, of a new system of quantification and distribution. For Edison, cinema had no significance in itself; it was simply one of a potentially endless stream of ways in which a space of consumption and circulation could be dynamized and exploited. Edison saw the marketplace in terms of how images, sounds, energy, or information could be reshaped into measurable and distributable commodities, and how a social field of individual subjects could be arranged into increasingly separate and specialized units of consumption. Now, the assumptions that defined the Kinetoscope and the phonograph—an arrangement of perceptual experience in terms of solitary rather than collective (movie theater audience) reception—is now replayed in the increasing centrality of a small screen as the primary vehicle for the distribution and consumption of electronic entertainment commodities.

At the same time, Edison was one of the first to intuit the economic interrelation between hardware and software (i.e., the machines to make movies, the machines with which to view movies, and the movies themselves), establishing as he did enduring patterns of vertical integration of these spheres of production within a single corporation. Edison's first technological product, a hybrid teletype machine-stock ticker of the early 1870s, is paradigmatic for what it foreshadows in subsequent technological setups—the indistinction between information and visual images, and quantifiable flow as the object of consumption. Edison's understanding of some of the key systemic features of capitalism underscores the abstract nature of the products he "invented"; his work was about the continual manufacture of new needs and the consequent restructuring of the network of relations in which such products would be consumed. Steve Jobs, Bill Gates, and so on are simply later participants in this same project of perpetual rationalization and modernization. In the late twentieth century, as in the late nineteenth century, the management of attention depends on the adaptive capacity of an observer in the face of continual repatternings of the ways in which a sensory world can be consumed.

Critics such as Siegfried Kracauer and Walter Benjamin brought the notion of "distraction" to the forefront of debates about the effects of cinema in twentieth-century mass culture. In a general way, their work, and much that followed, poses distraction as a term opposed to the idea of a

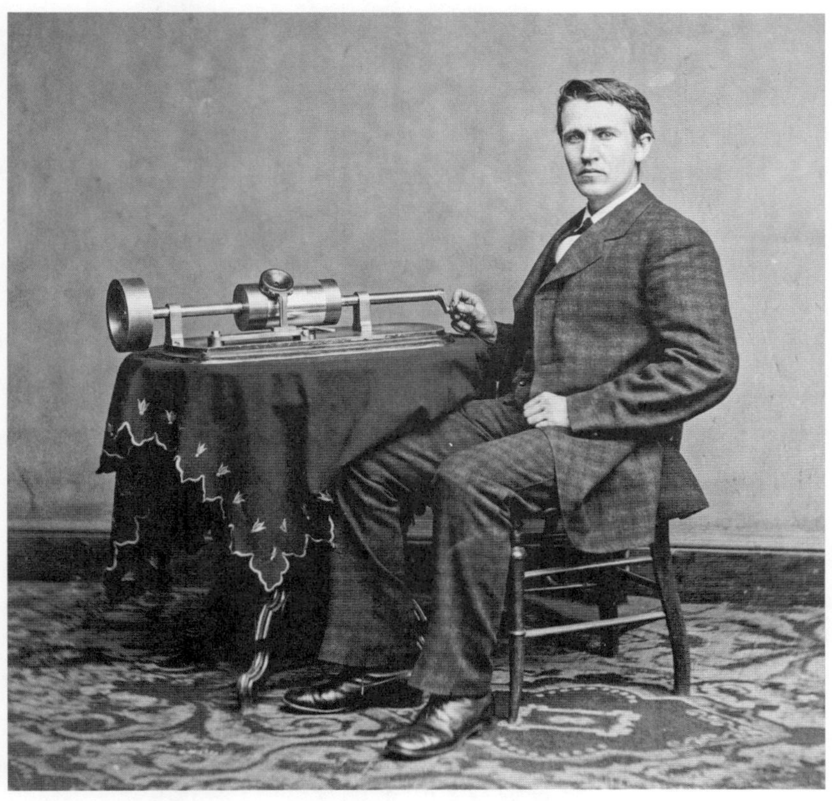

Thomas Edison with early model of his phonograph, ca. 1878.

contemplative perception, a self-conscious apperception. Movies, as products of an incipient culture industry, seemed to signal the transformation of perception into a debased form of mere external stimulation, very different from an older, more sustained, self-aware modality of looking. In the context of music, a related distinction was made by others between "higher" (deeply attentive) and "lower" (distracted) forms of listening. In both cases, works of high modernism were cited as examples in which some kind of purified, even ethically superior, perceptual engagement was possible.

But some of those in the nineteenth century who most deplored the distracted qualities of an emerging mass culture sought to push their own art in the direction of a kind of attentiveness remarkably close to what popular cinema would claim in the twentieth century, especially after 1930. For example, Richard Wagner's frustrations with the experiential reality of opera in the mid-nineteenth century were in part about the general problem of inattentiveness of spectators who were given multiple points of attraction, of theaters constructed so that audiences delighted in looking at each other, at the orchestra, at the diverse texture of attractions in addition to those on the stage (which was the case with the variety show and music hall contexts of early cinema as well).[3]

One aspect of Wagner's "reforms," incarnated in the design of Bayreuth, involved the transformation of the nineteenth-century theater into a proto-cinematic space. Bayreuth diagrammed a new kind of viewing machine which more rigorously controlled the spectator's perceptual experience. It not only integrated the sightlines of the audience with the orthogonals of scenic space (eliminating the lateral views of older theater design), but also helped initiate the idea of relative darkness as a way of heightening the intensity of lighting effects on stage. Wagner's insistence on lowering the orchestra out of sight is another part of the thoroughly "phantasmagoric" character of his work discussed by Theodor Adorno and others. As many have noted, there was a sizable gap between Wagner's ambitions and the technical resources that were available to him in his lifetime. He never was reconciled with having to work with the clunkiness of mundane stagecraft, with greasepaint on the singer's faces and with how these interfered with the absorption of an audience into the performance. Wagner's project, despite its archaizing surfaces, stands for a new will to mastery over all aspects of spectacle that would incite states of regression, fascination, dream, the very kind of attentiveness that would belong to cinema half a century later. Nonetheless, his control over emotional response was potent enough to provoke Nietzsche's insistence that Wagner furnished "the first example, only too insidious, only too successful, of hypnotism by means of music…persuasion by the nerves."[4]

The institutional and technological shifts in the late nineteenth and early twentieth centuries, briefly suggested here, were bound up in new knowledge about perception, cognition, and the subjective experience of vision. For several hundred years up into the nineteenth century, a wide range of ideas about vision had tended to emphasize those features of

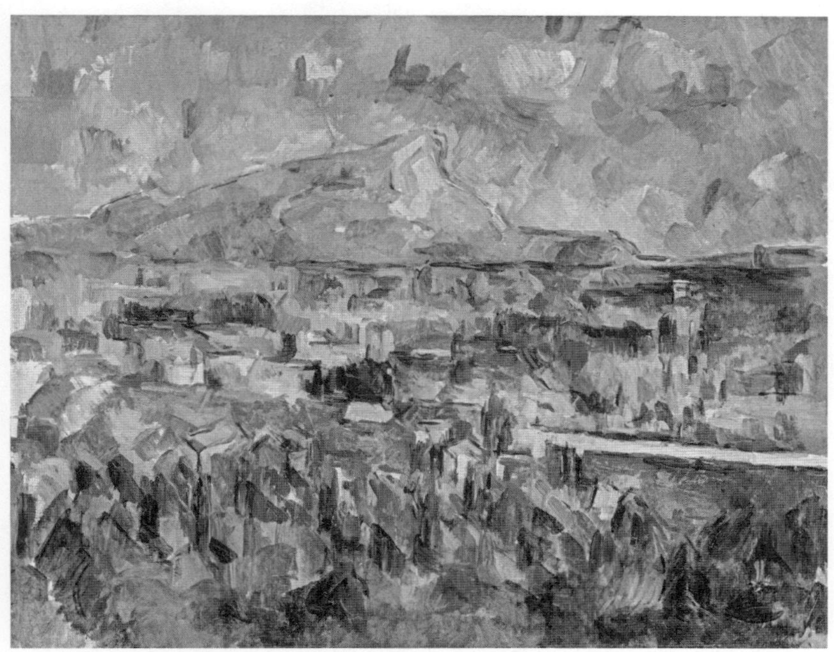

Paul Cézanne, *Mont Sainte-Victoire*, 1902–1906.

perception that were stable, predictable, and supported the notion of a manifest correspondence between the world and what the eye saw. Vision itself may not have changed in the nineteenth century but what did change dramatically was the development of knowledge and theories that foreground very different features of vision: the unreliability, the internal volatility, and the uncertain temporality of visual perception.

This volatility is evident in many places, for example in the late work of Cézanne. Not only does Cézanne disclose the distractions that are inherent in even the most rapt form of attention, but he heralds the dynamization of perception occurring in many different domains by the late 1890s, including those in which someone like Edison was involved. What Cézanne powerfully describes is not a model of contemplative distance, or of perceptual autonomy, but rather an account of a nervous system interfacing with a mobile, continually transforming external environment. Contemporary with early cinema, Cézanne's work in the 1890s and early 1900s involves a sweeping destabilization of what previously had constituted an "image." His work is one of numerous contemporary expressions of the notion that reality can be conceptualized as a dynamic aggregate of sensations. For Cézanne and for the emerging industries of the spectacle, a stable referential model of perception is no longer effective or useful.

Obviously Cézanne's images are static but, like those of Étienne-Jules Marey, they document perceptual experience that is in constant flux and are about the recording of temporal processes, motor responses and rhythms. Part of Cézanne's singularity was the relentlessness with which he was alert to his own perceptual experience. Perhaps as much as any artist, Cézanne disclosed the paradoxes and the malleability of attentiveness—that looking at any one thing intently, rather than leading to a fuller grasp of its very presence, its rich immediacy, finally leads to its perceptual disintegration and loss, its breakdown as intelligible form. Thus, attention and distraction are not distinct but part of a dynamic continuum in which attention was always of limited duration, inevitably disintegrating into a distracted state. For Cézanne, this dissolution inherent in attentiveness not only allowed his radical desymbolization of the world but also produced an interface with a perpetually modulating set of relations between what had been thought of as "external" events and sensations. Paradoxically, it was through his own immersion in the physiological features of vision (for example the distinction between the foveal and peripheral areas of the retina and the disjunct, nonhomogenous visual field that results from that) that he aspired to exceed the corporeal limits of vision in quest of a new mode of inhabiting the material world. Cézanne's late work poses the exhilarating outlines of a new kind of eye that would overcome the monadic nature of embodied human vision and be able to see with an impossible kind of attentiveness, an eye without constraints, cut loose from its physical anchorage.

For example, one key feature of Cézanne's landscapes from the late 1890s is the eradication of any consistent distinction between near and far vision, between what has often been referred to as haptic and optic perception. There is no longer any spatial schema in Cézanne's work which allows those distinctions to retain their coherence; instead, his surfaces are assembled unpredictably out of the enigmatic palpability of distant forms and the evanescence of seemingly near-at-hand objects. This oscillation between close and distant vision, or between focus and out of focus, parallels montage effects in film which bind dramatically different spatial positions into new kinds of syntheses and adjacencies. For all their differences, Cézanne's work and cinema both posed the possibility of what Gilles Deleuze has described as an acentered ensemble of variable elements which act and react on each other. They are products of a moment at the end of the nineteenth century when, according to Deleuze, it was no longer possible to hold or occupy an unambiguous position and when more and more movement was entering psychic life.[5]

It has long been said of Cézanne that he never acquired the *trucs* or gimmicks of the atelier, that he disavowed the readymade schema and traditional solutions for pictorial organization (including, for example, many of the historically accumulated practices associated with linear perspective). But if these accounts of Cézanne as a kind of primitive who avoided any premade interpretations of the world are useful, it is because they suggest his particular sensitivity to perceptual experiences that had been ignored, or marginalized, or that had been incompatible (and hence unarticulated) within older (classical) organizations of knowledge about vision. Cézanne's work, then, is less about a tabula rasa than about repeated and varied attempts to achieve a "presuppositionless" engagement with the visible world, to achieve a liquid, groundless space, filled with forces, events, and intensities rather than objects. But it was just such a malleable and tractable visual space that would become subject to endless forms of external restructuring, manipulation, and colonization throughout the twentieth century. Within modernity the terrain and tools of invention, freedom, and creation are always intertwined with those of domination and control.

One of the most extraordinary evocations of the connection between attentiveness and the changing field of institutional and technological modernity can be found in the work of Fritz Lang. I want to briefly discuss Lang's great Dr. Mabuse trilogy that spans most of his career: the two-part *Dr. Mabuse the Gambler* (1921–22), *The Testament of Dr. Mabuse* (1932), and *The Thousand Eyes of Dr. Mabuse* (1960). These films compellingly chart the mobile characteristics of various perceptual technologies and apparatuses of power, culminating in a precocious meditation in the final film on the status of the television screen. It becomes clear that the name "Mabuse" designates much more than a fictional character central to the narratives of these films (let alone a character that fits Kracauer's "Caligari to Hitler" hypothesis). Rather, Mabuse is the name of a system—a system of spectacular power whose strategies are continually changing but whose aim of producing "docile" subjects remains relatively constant. On a biographical level, the three films together also stand for Lang's own turbulent career itinerary from work in the German theater and silent film industry in the teens, through the era of the big German studios in the early thirties, to two decades in the Hollywood "culture industry," and to his final meditations on the hegemony of television.

In the first of these films, *Dr. Mabuse the Gambler,* Lang explores a panoply of modern practices of control, persuasion, and coercion. In this silent work, Mabuse stands for an array of spectacular techniques of dazzlement, immobilization, and suggestion; that is, for powerful effects generally describable as hypnotic. But unlike Freud, whose essay on "Group Psychology" dates from the same year, 1921, Lang is less interested in the nature of an emotional tie to a charismatic figure than he is in a diverse technology of influence. The protean Mabuse, with his multiple masks and guises, becomes a principle of flexible and versatile power rather than a figuration of totalitarianism. In *Dr. Mabuse the Gambler* control is exerted within volatile cultural and economic spaces, where perception is destabilized, for example, by the rhythmic attractions of the roulette wheel and the shifting quotes on the wall of the stock exchange.

But by the early 1930s, in *The Testament of Dr. Mabuse*, Lang identifies a different arrangement of power effects, and it's in this decade that a modern perceptual regime of reciprocal attentiveness and distraction takes on some of its paradigmatic features. In the extraordinary first five minutes of Lang's 1932 film, which opens in an urban industrial zone, we hear nothing but the deafening and finally numbing noise of the monotonous functioning of heavy factory machinery. (It precedes by nearly forty years a related opening scene in Jean-Luc Godard's *British Sounds* of an automotive assembly line.) The intolerable sensory disorientation of this environment is one marker of what Benjamin described

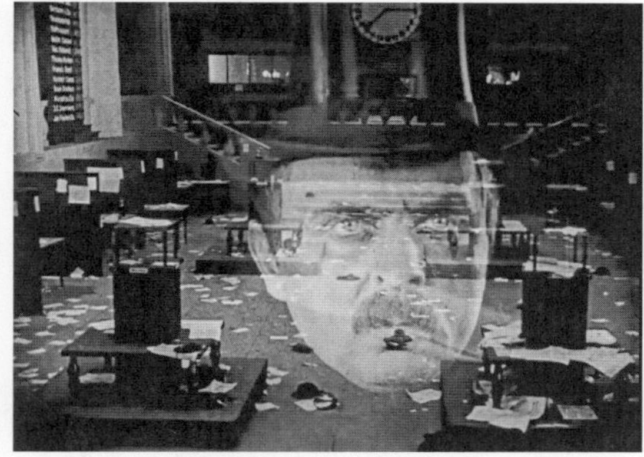

Fritz Lang, *Dr. Mabuse the Gambler,* 1922.

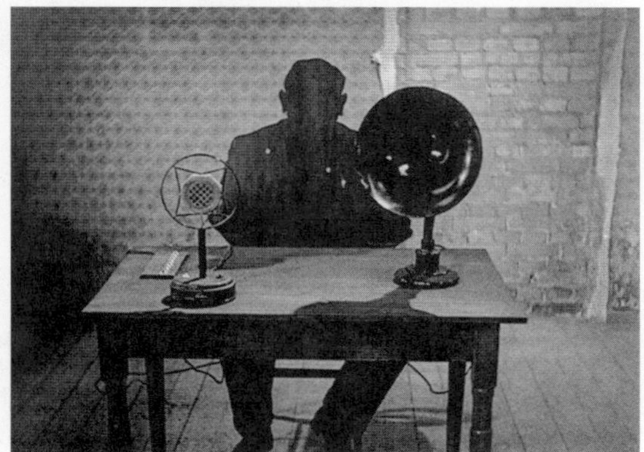

Fritz Lang, *The Testament of Dr. Mabuse,* 1933.

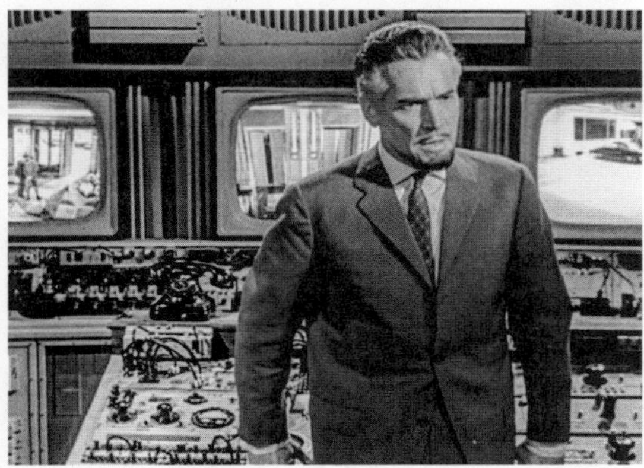

Fritz Lang, *The Thousand Eyes of Dr. Mabuse,* 1960.

as the deterioration of experience—experience reduced to an indifferent sequence of stimuli. Established from the start is a milieu defamiliarized by processes of modernization in which an older model of sensory integration is deranged and fragmented (precisely the opposite of the institutional claims for the sound film). In these circumstances Lang delineates how arrangements of power around forms of ocular domination give way to tactics of simulation, recording, and telecommunication in which auditory experience is primary. In other words, the Mabuse system cannot be reduced to a visual model, for it deploys a broader range of perceptual management. Sound had of course been part of cinema in various additive forms from the beginning, but clearly the introduction of synchronized sound decisively transformed the nature of attention within a spectacular setup. At the same time, this film does away with the figure of Dr. Mabuse completely, further diffusing and delocalizing the operation of power from some center of control and intentionality. One of the key elements in this film is the procedure by which members of the underworld network receive their orders: they are contacted by a voice emanating from a hidden loudspeaker and recording devices. Like the optical modalities in the earlier film, hypnotic forms of influence here proceed by the isolation of a single sense, in this case hearing rather than vision.

By 1960, in *The Thousand Eyes of Dr. Mabuse*, the cathode ray tube emerges as the dominant component of the Mabuse system. Lang hardly presents a homogenous image of television here, specifically differentiating broadcast TV on one hand and the use of closed-circuit video for surveillance on the other. The panopticism of the film's title is not inappropriate in that part of the film's formal structure is built around a network of surveillance cameras feeding video images back to a wall of monitors. Rather than suggest Orwellian models of ubiquitous control, Lang situates the television screens within a larger and chaotic spectacular regime of pseudo-events, disinformation, voyeurism, and scopic desire. Television is the vehicle through which Lang explores the relation between new abstract perceptual spaces that exceed his own accumulated experience of the cultural conditions of cinema. One of the work's most piercing moments is a slow, seamless dissolve from a filmed image of a scene to a video screen of the same image. Lang's particular overlapping of these two kinds of screens is an announcement of a specific historical passage to a new arena of techniques of subjectification, when cinema is supplanted or infiltrated in various ways by television.

It should be noted that themes from the Mabuse films are also evident in other Lang works. Beginning in the 1920s, Lang observed the ways in which different technological networks permeated a densely layered social space, whether in *Spies* (1928), *M* (1931), *Metropolis* (1927), or *Fury* (1936). Well before the advent of television, Lang was attuned to the enigmatic character of a seemingly mundane object such as a typewriter or telephone and how its habitual use incorporated its user within the operations of institutional power. By the mid-1950s Lang was describing a bleaker landscape. In *While the City Sleeps* (1956) he returns to the theme of *M*, the serial killer, but instead of examining a social milieu through diverse investigative and juridical practices, the actuality of the murderer and his crimes is subsumed within a media-saturated regime of information and entertainment. The deviant Peter Lorre figure in *M*, who incited all sectors of society to mobilize in order to eliminate his disruptive presence, gives way here to a murderer who becomes "content" for a media apparatus and is transformed into an object of spectacular consumption via newspapers and television.

Part of what Lang designated by the name Mabuse was a system that produced and depended on subjects who were "open to influence" or, in Michel Foucault's words, who were reduced as a political force. A work that deliriously explored more recent configurations of the Mabuse system was David Cronenberg's 1983 *Videodrome*. This film addresses the addictive and hypnotic effects of electronic media and provides a remarkable account of the ways in which large zones of perceptual experience are being reshaped by an ongoing biotechnic modernization within which the nervous system has less and less of an autonomous identity. Obviously, much attention has been paid to Cronenberg's visceral metaphors for various conjunctions of body and machine, and clearly these exorbitant images of the body's sheer openness are about a maximum condition of interface, about an interpenetration of the subject so thorough that the notion of "interiority" ceases to be relevant. As one shaped intellectually by the Canadian discourse on technology, Cronenberg pushes Marshall McLuhan's famous notion of the "outering" of the senses to a terminal extreme. It is also a vision of Edison's rudimentary system, operating at a more perfected level, in which the brain

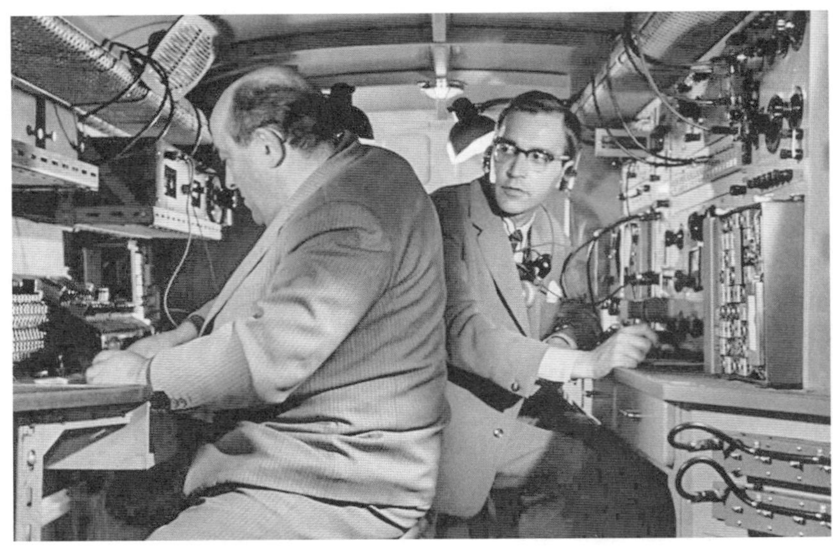

Fritz Lang, *The Thousand Eyes of Dr. Mabuse*, 1960.

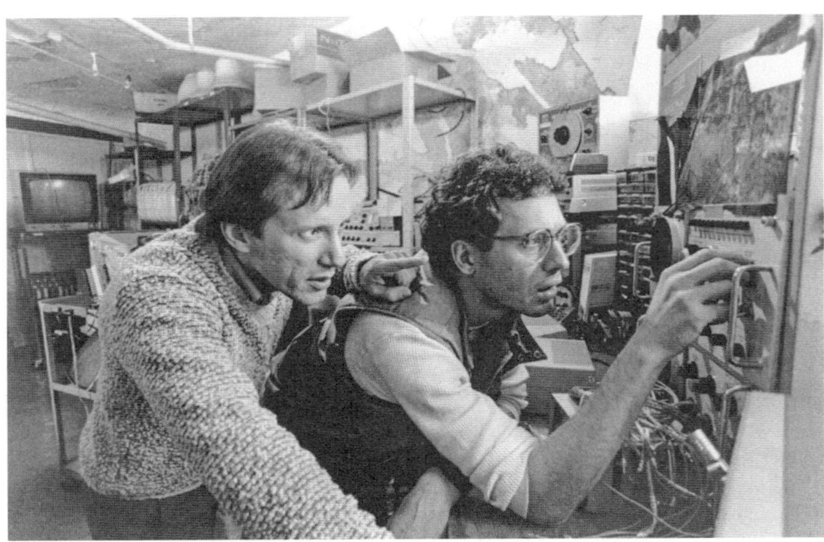

David Cronenberg, *Videodrome*, 1983.

and body are essentially hardware accessible to any powerful external software. The film announces a final break with the last vestiges of a Cartesian tradition of mental images and the eradication of what was once thought of as the imagination. In this sense the film is also an autoreflection on the very transience of cinema as an artifact within the mediated spaces Cronenberg maps out for us. If hypnosis and addiction are central in the film, Cronenberg, like Lang, hardly presents them in terms of a seamless operation of institutional power. The Videodrome system is out of anyone's control, always on the edge of short-circuiting its own effectiveness.

The psychotic disorder of *Videodrome* is part of the crisis of continual adaptation to a mutating technological and image environment. The film details the patchwork nature of contemporary subjective experience: a mix of new and old perceptual modalities, of hybrid zones composed of residual Euclidian space and dimensionless video hallucinations that appear to be seamlessly connected. The substantiality of an objective world is continually undermined by synthetic realities involving the accelerated formation of short-lived microworlds and their equally abrupt breakdown. But this is not unrelated to what Benjamin, Georg Simmel, and others had begun, in relation to a very different set of objects, to describe as shock earlier in this century.

One example of this composite texture is the remarkable moment in the film when the protagonist, now psychically and physically unhinged by electronic images, crosses a city street. As he does so, he encounters two men carrying a large framed window, the glass divided into four panes. For an instant, the center of this horizontal window overlaps with a centralized, axial view of the street and coincides with the vanishing point of classical one-point perspective. Along with a sardonic reference to Leonardo da Vinci and the Medicis, this is a brief reminder of the nominal survival but increasing irrelevance of the Renaissance schema for representing the world in terms of a pyramidal cone of vision and a point to point relation between observing subject and object. *Videodrome* portrays the dissolution of the last remnants of a model of vision which involved distance and a *seeing through*, like the delimited sectional view through a window or even through the viewfinder of a mobile movie camera.[6]

Cronenberg's film provides one particular diagram of the territory which cinema had previously occupied, alluded to in Godard's remarks

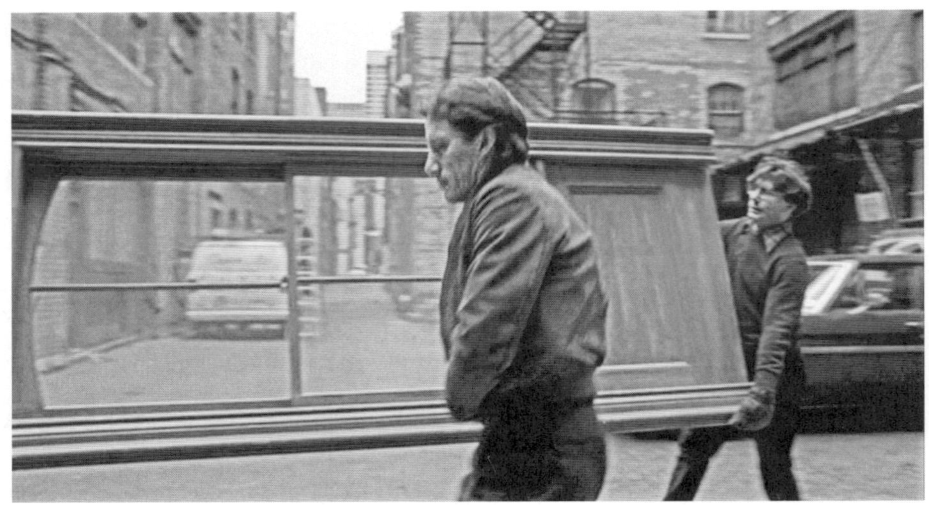

David Cronenberg, *Videodrome*, 1983.

cited earlier. Of course, Godard's notion of the end of cinema must also be read through his own move to video, television, and mixed technical practices, which began in the mid-1970s. It should be remembered too that in 1973 Thomas Pynchon's *Gravity's Rainbow* located cinema as one specific episode within a much broader twentieth-century history of techniques of control, conditioning, and abstract simulation. The 1970s can be historicized as a transitional period in many ways, but they are also important as the time when the status of film and photography as analog media began to shift, slowly at first, into new systems and operations.

Now well into the 1990s, enveloped by superficially diverse but homogenous entertainment products, we have an expanded sense of the consequences and possibilities of that technological realignment begun in the 1970s. From certain critical vantage points this can seem like a major cultural rupture, a rift in the real, the ubiquity of simulacra, a remaking of subjectivity, and so on. But as I have tried to suggest here, whatever age we feel we may have entered, it will, much sooner than we suspect, be rendered obsolete by new technological promises and products, new forms of verisimilitude, reorganizations of social time and of distribution and consumption into a seemingly unprecedented epoch. One of the most persistent features of modernity is the potent seductiveness of the phantasmagoria of progress, and among the ranks of the seduced are those who believe that modernity has somehow been exceeded. But if global capitalism continues to consolidate itself, we will always be in the same historical era in relation to the enduring imperatives of capitalist modernization.

1. "Godard Makes [Hi]stories," in *Jean-Luc Godard: Son + Image* (New York: Museum of Modern Art, 1992), p. 159.
2. Ibid., p. 164.
3. See, for example, Beat Wyss, "Ragnarok of Illusion: Richard Wagner's *Mystical Abyss* at Bayreuth," *October* 54 (Fall 1990), pp. 57–56.
4. Friedrich Nietzsche, *The Case of Wagner* (1888), trans. Walter Kaufmann (New York: Random House, 1967), p. 171.
5. Gilles Deleuze, *Cinema I: The Movement-Image*, trans. Hugh Tomlinson and Barbara Habberjam (Minneapolis: University of Minnesota Press, 1986), p. 61.
6. It should be noted that Cronenberg presents a differentiated global arrangement in which the ideological model for control of the Third World is still that of eyeglasses, produced by the multinational conglomerate, Spectacular Optical.

Originally published in *Art and Film Since 1945: Hall of Mirrors*, ed. Russell Ferguson (New York, Monacelli Press; Los Angeles: MOCA, 1996). This volume accompanied the 1996 Museum of Contemporary Art exhibition of the same name.

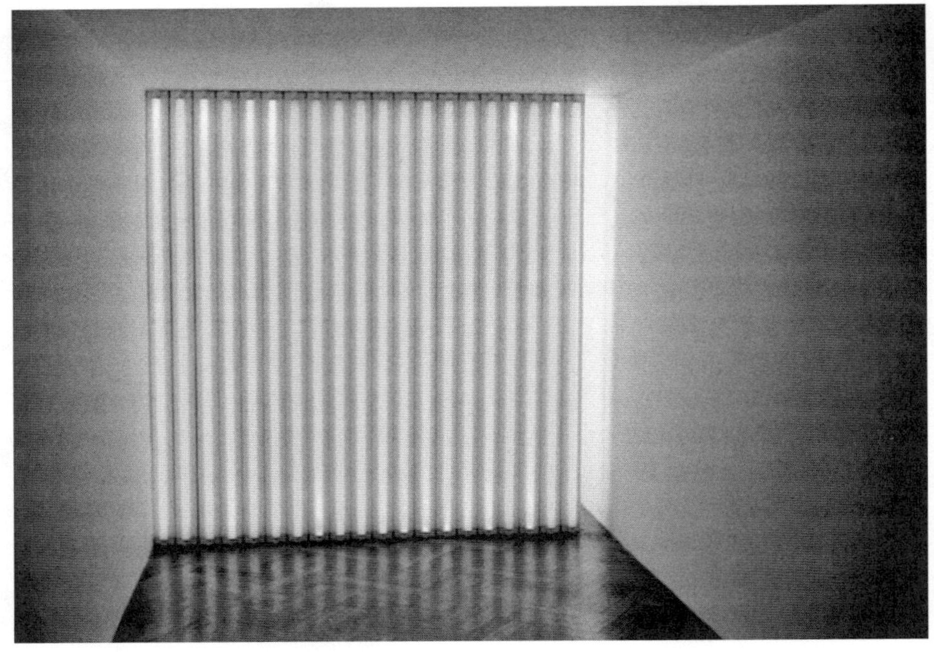

Dan Flavin, *Untitled (to Jan and Ron Greenberg)*, 1972–73.

Dan Flavin and the Desymbolization of Light

Dan Flavin's work, dependent as it is on mural surfaces, has long been understood through its inseparability from the problem of architecture. His art historical significance in large part has turned on how he decisively severed the experience of luminosity from pictorial surfaces and lodged them within the lived, environmental relations amid the architectural givens of his various exhibition spaces. But a piece like *Untitled (to Jan and Ron Greenberg)* from 1972–73 reveals that things are not quite so clear-cut. Flavin here seems aware that, even as his work in the late 1960s disclosed a new unboundedness of color and light, it is not a complete liberation of the viewer from older models of visual and aesthetic experience. We've become so habituated to discussions of Flavin and other minimalists in terms of categorical simplifications that the intellectual complexity and internal paradoxes of the work are often bypassed. The richness of Flavin's thought in this piece derives from its sensitivity to the heterogenous and historically sedimented nature of perception and its constitutive relation to architecture.

Put another way, Flavin's practice vividly breaks with a perspectival conception of how light functions and produces aesthetic effects, but at the same time the doubled, two-sided corridor structure of the work locates us in architectural spaces that can only be described as perspectival. Each of the corridors unavoidably establishes a three-dimensional cubic interior whose defining features, from a subjective point of view, are orthogonals, the lines where the faces of the cube meet. These lines, which are defining elements of Renaissance perspective, allow the apprehension of recessional extended space and, if continued indefinitely, would appear to meet at a vanishing point, a hypothetical point which Flavin of course excludes from the work. But it is within a residual framework of classical representational conditions that Flavin deploys his chromatic effects which disrupt both the subject and object positions of a perspectival system. The tension generated by conflicting, even irreconcilable, expectations and actualities resonates within this and other related corridor pieces. The architectural configuration, in a fundamental way, perpetuates an aesthetics of *distance*, in which the relation of observer to work of art is figured as a conical beam of light rays which correspond to the orthogonals of the exhibition space. Flavin's "barrier" of vertically aligned fluorescent tubes in this sense takes on a pictorial identity as a plane intersecting that visual cone, in the manner that Alberti first described. This relation of distance between observer and object was what Walter Benjamin identified as the basis for "auratic" art, and it is certainly not coincidental that Flavin's radical reimagining of aura engages the paradoxes of subjective distance. It is also important to remember that his work from the early and mid-1970s coincides with the early stages of global technological modernization in which a primary experience of light as illumination is displaced by light as depthless, placeless flows of quantified and financialized information.

Within the long trajectory of visual modernism since the late nineteenth century, Flavin is at least an indirect heir of the optical project of Seurat and neo-impressionism. In his technocratic rationalization of optical processes, Seurat performed a momentous shift: he made the artwork itself into a producer of chromatic and luminous experience. Marshall McLuhan recognized the consequences of Seurat's transformation of painting into a light source. Space could no longer be experienced as neutral, as an empty container to house the discrete, autonomous object. Instead, the viewer and his milieu became active, charged constituent forces in a field of irradiative and vibratory events. It is nonetheless an arrangement in which a traditional set of pictorial expectations provides a background for their eventual nonfulfillment and repudiation.

Flavin's use of light occurs fully outside of a *punctual* model of optical phenomenon in which light is conceived as rays with a directional identity, emanating like a beam from one point and illuminating another point.

This punctuality is inherent in perspectival systems of visual representation, especially for the way in which a point-to-point setup establishes a relatively stable and coherent subject position. It is, however, the directionless quality of Flavin's light that determines the sensory and psychological impact of his work, that is, light as an enveloping, immeasurable, and ubiquitous environment. It is this nonlocalizable saturation which dissolves the possibility of auratic distance. But it also should be obvious why many of the familiar phenomenological readings of Flavin's work are inadequate: phenomenology sought to preserve the rootedness and stability of the individual observer in relation to a primal horizon against which unconditional perceptual meanings could arise. The omnipresence and formlessness of Flavin's luminosity eradicates the coherence of such an orienting horizon.

In this piece the seemingly planar field of fluorescent tubes oscillates between its status as an opaque obstacle which prevents us from seeing or walking beyond it and as a dematerialized pool of light, impalpable and incandescent. It operates in a play of disclosure and concealment, the unmediated presence of light which signifies nothing other than its own heat and energy, the revelation of its own immediacy. But Flavin's crucial gambit in this piece is to disallow that possibility of pure luminous presence by leaving a narrow vertical aperture onto a space and a glimmering radiance *beyond*. The effect of a totalizing monochromatic field is inflected by this indication of transitiveness, of a looking *through*. But the chromatic contamination of this peripheral emanation, of this exterior glow is hardly the indication of a privileged and inaccessible source of light. Rather, within Flavin's architectural schema, the vertical aperture becomes the hinge of the work's logic of exchangeability and duplication. Our own perception of the piece is inseparable from an ambulatory experience of its chromatically distinct but otherwise identical faces which ceaselessly fold in on one another, like a Duchampian model of reversibility. Flavin sustains the nostalgia for a transcendence of merely pictorial space but resolutely keeps us situated in a world of material operations and artifacts.

Originally published in the exhibition catalog for *Dan Flavin: The Architecture of Light*, Deutsche Guggenheim, Berlin, November 6, 1999–February 13, 2000.

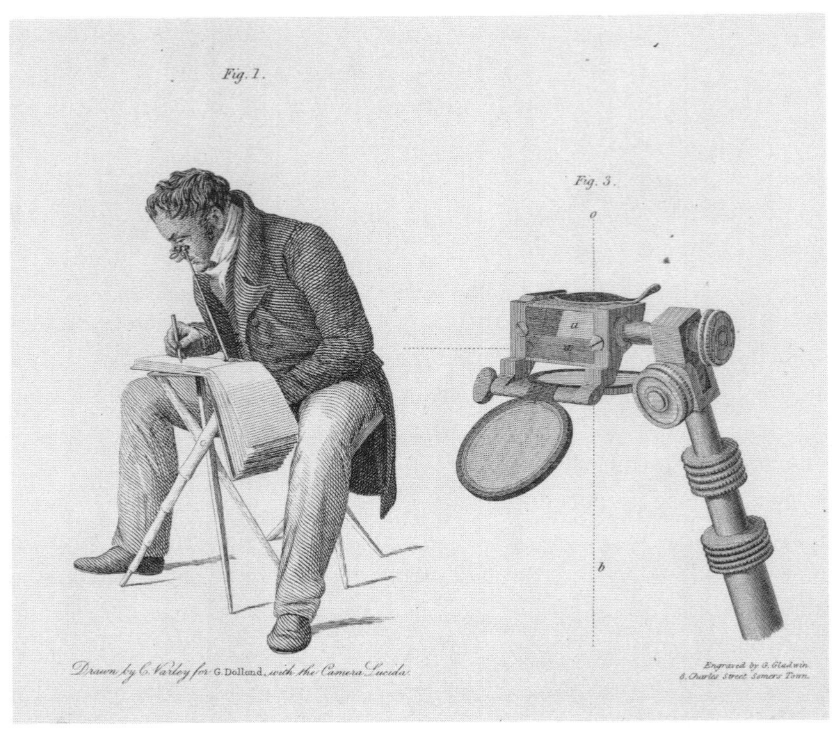

Artist drawing with the camera lucida, 1830.

Fitful Tracings: David Hockney on Art and Optics

Looking through the pages of *Secret Knowledge: Recovering the Lost Techniques of the Old Masters* over the past week, I've been struck by the mix of dogged persistence and sustained perspicacity that led to its conclusions. The book is a demonstration of how an initial intuition, if nourished and pursued, can generate an accumulation of insights, leading toward a new way of looking at very familiar images. One of David Hockney's achievements then is his effectiveness at defamiliarization: regardless of our larger evaluation of the project he allows us to at least try on or test out a fresh viewpoint. Even if he had relied only on the evidence of his own subjective observations, he has foregrounded a binary model of representational practices—optics (the use of optical devices) versus eyeballing (the use of the unaided eye). But, like other systems of ahistorical stylistic categories based on exclusively visual features, this one has significant drawbacks.

It must also be said that for all of the promotional fanfare, Hockney's hypothesis—that between 1400 and 1850 many well-known artists used mechanical aids to make their drawings—is hardly the provocation that some have made it out to be. As someone within the institutional world of art history, I have yet to encounter anyone who is disturbed or thrown off balance by Hockney's claims. Clearly, there are varying levels of agreement or disagreement about the evidence presented, but he has hardly proposed anything earth-shattering, as many journalists eagerly declare. I find the framing of the project as "Hockney standing up to the art historians" to be nonsensical. It wrongly insinuates that this academic field is populated with connoisseurs and aesthetes who revere the inimitable uniqueness of the line and "hand" purportedly evident in Old Master drawings and would be scandalized by the notion that an artist *traced* the outlines of an image with the aid of a camera obscura or camera lucida.

For decades there has been a pervasive critical awareness among most art historians that realist images are complicated plural constructions. They are never unmediated or direct transcriptions, and such images are intelligible only as an accretion of social codes, material practices, and technical procedures, procedures which could of course include a range of optical apparatuses and systems of visualization. Anyone aware of the laborious and nonperceptual calculations and arrangements which produced the illusion of three-dimensional space on a two-dimensional surface beginning in the 1400s certainly is not likely to reject out of hand the possibility that other techniques (lens, mirrors, cameras) may also have been deployed to produce a range of "reality effects." Very recently, when asked by colleagues and graduate students about this well-publicized conference, my tentative outline of Hockney's hypothesis has most often garnered the response: "OK fine, and assuming he's right, what's his point?" At the same time this fabricated controversy has contrived a debate that either sinks or swims in terms of some sort of scientific verifiability, whatever that might consist in. Thus a potentially valuable debate surrounding the project has been sidetracked by a reductive positivist approach that, *a priori*, will never ask very interesting questions. It has been set up, even by some here at this event, as a situation in which Hockney is either right or wrong, in a contest of only winners and losers.

My assessment of Hockney's project is tempered by a wariness of any historical narrative that considers technical devices to be essentially tools or equipment and tools that allowed similar visual effects to be produced over a five-hundred-year period. Instead, I would suggest that the cultural significance of an optical apparatus is always bound up in forces, events, processes that have little or even nothing to do with vision or visuality. In my own historical study of the camera obscura I insisted that an optical apparats is not simply an inert and neutral piece of equipment or a set of technological premises to be tinkered with and improved over the years; but that it was embedded in a much larger social organization of knowledge and the shifting historical makeup of the human observer. In this sense an optical device like the camera obscura always has a mixed or

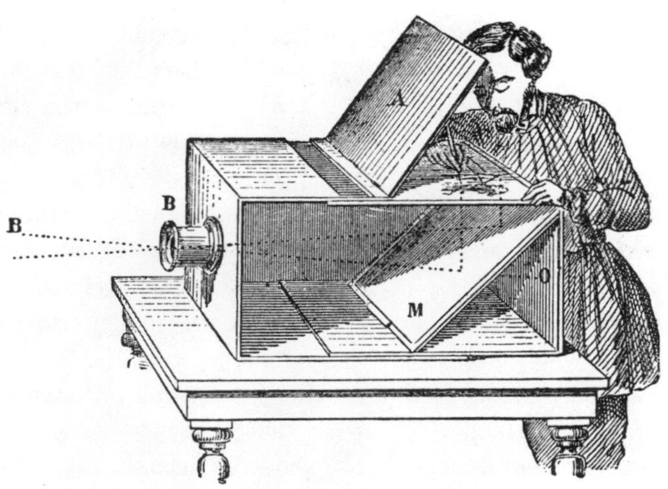

Camera obscura in use as a drawing aid, early nineteenth century.

multiple identity—it is an epistemological figure within a discursive field and at the same time a material object within an arrangement of cultural and technical practices. Any optical device is inseparable from the way in which, at any given period, the relation between seeing and knowing is conceptualized. What is visible and invisible, and what is thinkable and not thinkable in a particular culture or society, is historically mutable, and need I say that these are relations that cannot be explained by quantitative or empirical methods.

In spite of the emphasis implied in the title of this conference, I think it's important to resist an unexamined privileging of a notion of the optical. This would mean moving away from the assumption in *Secret Knowledge* of a homogenous and ahistorical space in which all images are defined by exclusively visual values and where vision is set up as an autonomous and self-justifying problem. I agree with Hockney that his project has been at least partially shaped by the impacts of global media/image culture in the late twentieth century, but it's also important that we be cognizant of the ongoing processes of abstraction, separation, exchangeability, and circulation, including marketplace forces that allow the visual, in so many ways, to have the primacy it has today.

A parallel issue in Hockney's book is the difficult relation between the visual and the field of artifacts that he labels as realism or naturalism. The illusory effect a painting made in the late fifteenth century may, to our image-saturated minds, appear to have striking similarities with an image from the early nineteenth century, but I believe it is more valuable to insist on the very different philosophical, economic, scientific, and material environments in which they were made and on the divergence between the subjective makeup of their respective producers and audiences. To make this more concrete, I would point to Hockney's speculation about the drawings of Ingres. Even if he is right about this artist, my view of Ingres's work will not have been overturned, but it will have been enhanced. The possibility that Ingres may have worked with a camera lucida would supplement what is already known of his practices within a modernizing image economy (even several decades before photography). These included his methods of serial reproduction, of copies without originals, uses of tracing paper, his mirror reversals of motifs, and his recourse to an expanding, multilayered archive of reproductive imagery, evident, for example, in his borrowing, copying or quotation of most of the forty-six portrait heads in his 1827 *Apotheosis of Homer*.

My point is that the realism or naturalism which Hockney sees spanning such a long period is more usefully understood as a discontinuous sequence of very different models of verisimilitude. And as I briefly tried to indicate, realism in whatever period is never primarily an affair of perception. The critic Roland Barthes wrote that "the real is never anything but a meaning, revocable whenever history requires it." Barthes saw that a decisively new model of realism emerges in the nineteenth century, a realism whose main feature was to persuade that whatever it presented had actually taken place or really existed. Its manifestations included "the development of the realistic novel, the private diary, documentary literature, the news item, the historical museum, the exhibition of ancient objects and the massive development of photography."[1] Notable here is that although photography is identified as a reality effect, it is not in any sense a foundation for it. Also, for Barthes, it was the evidentiary status of photography, rather than any purely optical values, that was decisive.

As a way of concluding, I will briefly mention one of the originators of modern realism in the early nineteenth century, the French painter

Géricault. In seeking to depict a shocking contemporary event in his *Raft of the Medusa* with the greatest possible authenticity and immediacy, he chose an approach that reveals the inadequacy of the alternatives of optics or eyeballing. In his quest for what Hockney calls "vividness" and "accuracy," he not only exhaustively studied the live model but also assembled an immense dossier of information. He collected and read huge piles of bureaucratic, journalistic, medical, and legal evidence and documents. He interviewed eyewitnesses, had a scale model of the raft fabricated, and studied decaying corpses from the morgue, all to guarantee the reality of his picture. It was this armature of facts and statements rather than surface appearances that affirmed the truth of his art. Théodore Géricault's work as a whole is a piercing reminder of the limits, vacancies, and disruptions that always stand between the real and the visual, no matter what technical means are used or not used.

1. Roland Barthes, *The Rustle of Language*, trans. Richard Howard (New York: Hill & Wang, 1986), pp. 139–40.

Text of a talk presented at the conference "Art and Optics: Toward an Evaluation of David Hockney's Theories of Opticality in Western Painting," sponsored by the New York Institute for the Humanities, December 1–2, 2001.

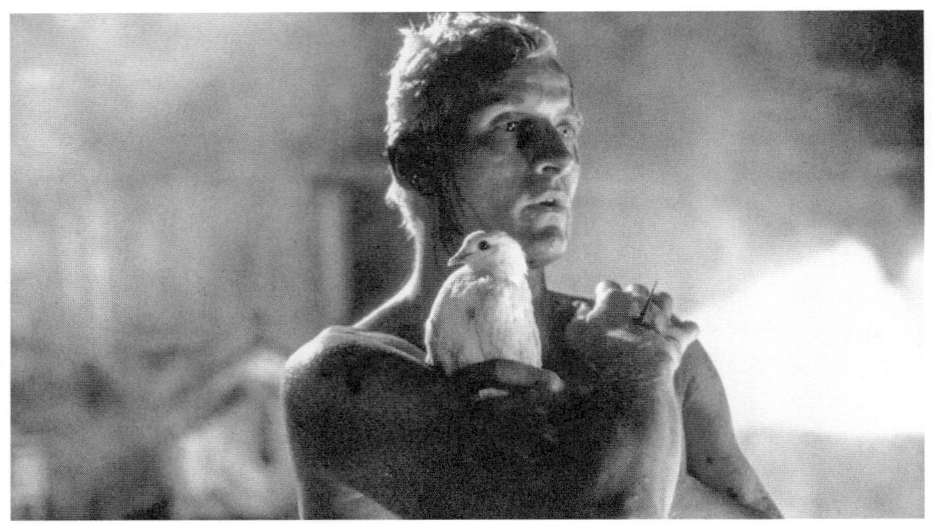

Ridley Scott, *Blade Runner,* 1982.

Blade Runner, Artifact of the 1980s

Blade Runner was a product deeply of its time, but its singularity has sustained its attraction far beyond that moment. Much of the avalanche of commentary that followed it for over a decade is increasingly irrelevant to its status now and in the longer term. Few viewers will be preoccupied with how vividly it supposedly mapped out the "unmappable" shape of the decentered city or of late capitalism in the bipolar days of the Soviet Union and Berlin Wall; likewise, the movie's retrospective links to the now hopelessly elastic category of film noir or its anticipations of 1980s cyberpunk are no longer essential screens through which to view it. *Blade Runner*'s durability may be analogous to that of Fritz Lang's *Metropolis* (1926), which long ago transcended the extravagant surfaces of the 1920s. Both films sustain their immediacy around the blurred distinctions between human life and its manufactured simulations.

In his 1968 novel *Do Androids Dream of Electric Sheep*, Phillip K. Dick portrayed the ubiquity of a reified social world dominated by inanimate things and machines. Dick's remarkable account of the petty ruin of individual experience and hope through the spread of "a peculiar malign abstractness" became something quite different in *Blade Runner*. In the early Reagan/Thatcher era, the novel was remade into a world-weary celebration of the petrifying universe that Dick found so deadening. There are few other recent films with *Blade Runner*'s lyric fatalism: it makes emotionally credible the point at which the technological products of global corporations become the objects of our love, our longings. When Harrison Ford tells the android played by Sean Young to say "kiss me," it discloses a much broader subjective capitulation to the imperatives of technique and instrumental rationality, as if affirming with listless resignation: "Who cares what she is?" This sublimation of engineered otherness is the indifferent 1980s resolution of the alienation which, in Dick's novels of the late 1960s and early 1970s led to psychosis and self-destruction.

Of course, the replicants in *Blade Runner*, especially the Rutger Hauer character, might seem to perpetuate the familiar cliche of allegorizing robots and androids by reading their poignantly human-like behavior as a cautionary index of how machine-like we have become. But the conditions for such a reading do not exist amid the social vacuity of *Blade Runner's* dedifferentiated milieus. What the film did with considerable novelty was to imagine the promiscuous space in which machines and humans were equally rootless, disposable parts of the same derelict pathways. And both, outside of any binary categories, are various patchworks of memories real and false, of media effects, quasi-emotions, and sensory experiences fabricated and programmed externally. Did replicant Roy Batty actually witness the galactic marvels he recalls while "dying" at the end of the film after exclaiming: "I've seen things..." or were they mnemonic implants? Within the logic of the film it doesn't matter. The seductive disorientation of *Blade Runner* is linked to the advent of a fallen world in which there is no longer the historical recollection available to grasp from what it has fallen. The film was a key inaugural model for other '80s cultural artifacts in its creation of free-floating nostalgia with no object. Enhanced by the Vangelis sound track, *Blade Runner's* phantasmagoric operation fraudulently affirms the possibility of retrospective yearning in a world that had made such sentiment effectively impossible.

Originally published in *Artforum*, March 2003, special issue on the 1980s.

Robert Irwin and the Condition of Twilight

Tonight I want to discuss some general problems that are raised by both of the installations, *Prologue*, exhibited last summer, and the currently installed *Excursus*. Basically, I am interested in how this work engages and reconfigures the problem of perception. Of course, this is well-traveled route into Robert Irwin's art, and one of the most persistent responses to it, over several decades, has been a sense that it produces a heightened awareness of the operation of our own perceptual faculties, and that the subject of his art is perceptual experience itself. I have no disagreement with these broad characterizations, but I am more focused on how these issues intersect with major historical and cultural problems. Instead of simply seeing the work as a self-enclosed arena in which novel or complex forms of experience and perception are possible, like some kind of sublime fun house, I believe Irwin's art has to be seen in relation to a contemporary crisis of perception, and that this piece is, in some ways, a meditation on the fate of experience at the end of this century.

I will also say that in very important ways it is a *somber* work in its conception over and above any of its sensory effects. I mean this somewhat in the way Meyer Schapiro referred to Cézanne's later work as "an art of grave attention."[1] To imply that Irwin's work is grave or somber might seem incongruous with much of what we know, at least publicly, about him and his practice. But the apparently unflappable cultural optimism that are manifestly part of Irwin's outlook, especially in some recent public projects, takes on a fuller meaning when considering both the stakes and challenges in maintaining that affirmative position. I see his work as posing a set of counterpractices whose effects become evident only in relation to dominant ways in which perceptual experience is currently being refashioned and regulated. I'm referring to how a pervasive set of social imperatives is increasingly accepted as either desirable or as inevitable, or both. These are the overriding assumptions that productive time, social time, leisure time, essentially all waking time, can or should be usefully spent within the immobilizing interface of a human subject with a luminous screen and keyboard. The exponential increase in the possibilities of accessible information produces a related atrophy and constriction of the range of possible perceptual and sensory experience.

The Dia installation has to be seen as a refusal of contemporary values of speed, storage, uniformity, and exchangeability against which Irwin creates a milieu of singular nonrecordable phenomena for a mobile and spatialized observer. Beyond its ephemeral surfaces and anomalous chromaticism, his project is the provisional making of a clearing in which singular effects of relative slowness and silence are produced within a larger field of sensory dilation. One of the words that immediately came to my mind, and which I subsequently have heard repeated by others, is "muffled," like the experience of the city immediately after a huge snowstorm, implying that there is a latent auditory component to the work as well. I'm convinced that the sense of an auditory modification has more to do with a subjective shift in the ratio of the senses than with any acoustical properties of the materials used and their arrangement in the show. We should be clear, however, that Irwin is not proposing any kind of return or restoration of some more natural or authentic conditions of perception. Perception for him is always a construction, an interpretation, rather than a direct grasp of the world. But his work suggests that there is an immense and unexplored range of possible ways in which it can be constructed. Reality may not be given to us immediately, but we do have choices about the forms of its mediation.

Irwin's work has long been seen as deploying various strategies of defamiliarization, as an effort to detach us from conventional visual expectations and habits. Like William James, who was also responding to what he saw in the late nineteenth century as a depreciation of perception, Irwin redefines the very terms out of which experience is assembled. This means thinking of Irwin less in terms of a language of dematerialization

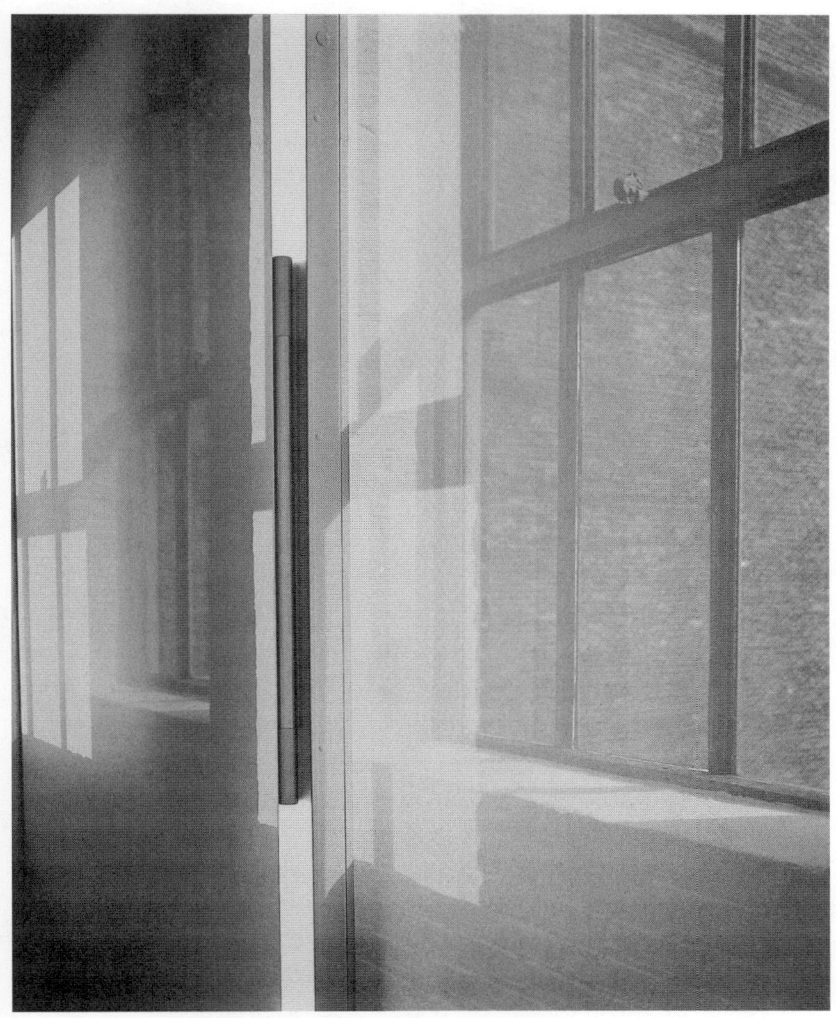

Robert Irwin, *Prologue: x18³*, 1998.

and etherealization and instead seeing his project in its intellectual affiliation with what James called "radical empiricism," that is, a reconceiving of the actual concrete elements of experience, in a sense a sweeping redefinition of what constitutes so-called "facts."[2] Instead of attributing priority to stable objects, discrete forms, individual entities, or instants, James believed that the heart of experience was vague in-between states, transitions, passages, overlappings, a collapsing of figure into ground, intuitions of relatedness and flux. And it in this sense that Irwin's work redirects us to the fringes, the penumbral overtones around transitive processes in both consciousness and in our lived activity in a given milieu. Vagueness here is synonymous with richness of experience, with holding forth the promise of future revelation or discovery. Perception no longer operates in support of a principle of identity. But there are many ways we can associate Irwin's thought with more recent philosophical work. For example, in the work of a thinker with whom Irwin is clearly familiar, philosopher of science Michael Polyani, we see another important project of "reinstating the vague" (to use James's phrase). Polyani, in his book *Personal Knowledge* rehabilitated the word "ineffable" to define crucial components of awareness and perception that most twentieth-century science and philosophy had rejected as meaningful knowledge, and he suggested ways in which Irwin's work can indeed be described as "ineffable" without recourse to a mystical vocabulary.[3] Polyani, in terms that are crucial for understanding Irwin's work, insists on the significance of subsidiary, peripheral awareness in the constitution of experience. But having said this much as a way of approaching what are the most palpable and most seductive effects of Irwin's work, it is important not to overlook the larger organization and impact of the work and the tensions and oppositions that animate it.

Let me start by at least suggesting the dense historical terrain that is embedded in the installation, by the site specificity so central to Irwin's practice. While the layout of the work is derived from the specific structural elements of this converted nineteenth-century warehouse building (the columns and beam arrangement), the third floor is one cubic module in a multistory building that is itself a modular unit within the grid of Manhattan, as all the north–south alignments that Irwin works with effectively coincide with the grid of New York's urban plan from 1811. But perhaps more important are the resonances of this potent historical model, this persistent dream of an urban imaginary, going back to antiquity, of imposing an ideal set of formal relations, on the singularities, the accidents of social and natural life. So any engagement with site here means inhabiting a distillation of the scrambled destiny of this foundational utopian project which had long involved the coincidence of visionary ambitions with techniques of administration and regulation.

But this familiar project of a quantifiable parcellation of space is also bound up in the history of pictorial practices. Clearly the title of the piece suggests some kind of transformational relation between the variables and coordinates of two-dimensional and three-dimensional form, that is between a square and a cube. Whether Irwin is modeling a proposition about a threshold space of creation *in between* painting and architecture is a topic for a whole other lecture and for someone else to do. But in any case, the presence of at least the template of this historical model is a crucial part of the operation of the piece. It subsists as at least the possibility of a legible space that is both unified by its metric relations, and in which distance is abstractly comprehensible. But we should remember Erwin Panofsky's thesis that perspectival construction had no necessary or intrinsic connection to human vision but was rather the artificial imposition of a rationalized and quantifiable system onto the idiosyncrasies of embodied human sight. That is, it was a technique for making visual experience conform to a Euclidean model of external reality and for transcending the limitations and deformations of subjective perceptual experience. Crucial for an artist of Irwin's intellectual interest is how this system coexists in the Dia work with a range of counterpractices. What is at issue here is not some reductive notion about an artist subverting perspective but rather the more difficult problem of work which insists on the inescapably mixed character of contemporary perceptual experience or what we could call its "patchwork" character.

All of us within present-day technological culture inhabit a shifting mix of new and old perceptual modalities, of hybrid zones composed of Euclidean space and dimensionless experiences of electronic networks that often appear to be seamlessly connected. Thus even amid the fluctuating and unstable character of Irwin's work is a human subject who is still at least partially anchored within the enduring remnants of a Newtonian universe, even if these surviving components have been rendered

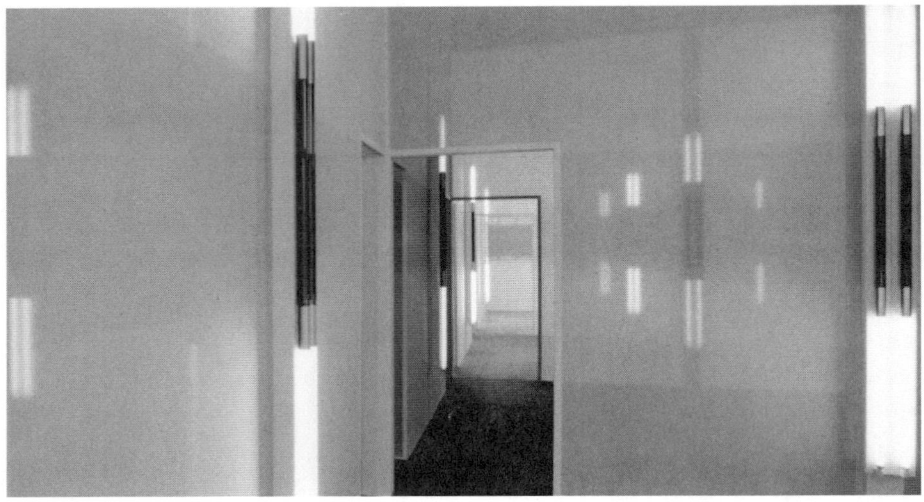

Robert Irwin, *Excursus: Homage to the Square³*, 1998.

contingent and spectral. It recalls how Colin Rowe characterizes some contemporary urban spaces as simultaneously "theaters of memory and theaters of prophecy."[4] One of the canonical definitions of postmodern space was that it transcends the capacity of the individual human body "to locate itself, to organize its immediate surroundings perceptually, and cognitively to map its position in a mappable external world."[5] I believe Irwin's work distances itself from this kind of hypothesis. Certainly he is presenting a complex environment that has even labyrinthine features but, like most of the environments in our lives, it is one to which we are able to bring a toolbox of partial maps and imperfect perceptual skills, which allow the emergence of something more coherent than the postmodern model of incomprehensibility and opacity.

Given how Irwin's work seems more "architectural" than pictorial, it's important to remember how central the problem of architecture was to perspectival practices, whether in the work of painters or architects. But I'm actually more interested here in a third arena in which perspective was articulated one which brings together both the architectural and subjective perceptual dimension of Irwin's work—and that is the history of theatrical scenography. Hubert Damisch and others have indicated the dense intersection of painting, architecture, and theater in the origins of perspective and what is relevant here is how classical theater design was always a mix of three dimensional or quasi-architectural forms and illusory two-dimensional pictorial elements, or flats, that when synthesized together made up an illusory approximation of extensive space, unified by the checkerboard grid of the stage. In Irwin's work we are, at any given position in the piece, embedded in a kind of scenography, although more as actors than audience since we don't have the immobility or distance set up by a proscenium. As we move and turn through the work, there is a kaleidoscopic reconfiguration of orthogonals that defines at least a hypothetical vanishing point around which a given static position might be oriented.

But within these elements, Irwin imposes a very different kind of system and one which has important links with a more recent conception of theatrical experience, and I'm referring to his use of scrims. If you research this word you'll find that it has only a vague etymological history: there is no agreement on what language it derives from but significant is that it was first used in the late 1790s to describe a new durable industrially manufactured fabric. By 1815 this kind of fabric, or variants of it, was being used within a new regime of stage design and this is where the word scrim acquired most of its modern resonances. By 1803 there is the first tentative use of gas in theatrical lighting and fifteen years later it was pervasive in theaters across Europe. The new technology meant that stage illumination could depart from the relative uniform and symmetrical use of candlelight and oil lamps and that lighting could be controlled in terms of both direction and intensity. The scrim took on its full practical meaning with this technological shift for, as we well know, when lit from behind a scrim seems relatively transparent and when lit exclusively from the front it seems completely opaque. The range of illusions that could be created and the spatial and temporal dislocations now possible would take too long to enumerate, but what is still relevant are the ramifications of a technique that simultaneously has the properties of solid and void, of translucence and opacity, of something tactile and dematerialized.

Despite Irwin's remoteness from this historical era, the issues of aesthetic appearance at stake are not completely dissimilar, that is, there is still the double-sided problem, coming out of German Romanticism, of appearance as something fraudulent, as mere illusion and at the same time appearance as a threshold at which the material symbol is transmuted into numinous experience. Perhaps the best known experimenter with the properties of theatrical scrims was one of the most consequential figures in the history of modern visual culture, Louis Daguerre. An unsuccessful academic painter who moved into stage design, he became famous for the lighting effects he created in Paris theaters, which included transparent paintings as part of an overall design. By the early 1820s the optical possibilities inherent in the use of scrims and their illumination led Daguerre to invent one of the important nineteenth-century forms of spectacle, the diorama. It was called that because of the translucent properties of the materials he used for the control and modulation of daylight. This is the sense of the prefix "dia." I note it because it is an instance of a modernized perceptual experience which depends on the expectations of an intelligible apprehension of space and distance, but which simultaneously dismantles the conceptual foundations of that older model of spatial order and rationalization. The diorama basically consisted of transparent paintings but they were presented as a display of stage-type lighting effects which unfolded temporally. That is, spectators would see a slowly changing scene, a sunny day in the Alps turn to a brooding storm, Gothic ruins appear out of mist in a valley, torchlight revealing the throngs in the Temple of Solomon. The spectacle coincided with the breakdown of a homogenous unified conception of theatrical space, and there are numerous accounts of spectators experiencing dizziness and vertigo because of the uncertainty of spatial distance in the illusory effects. It was also not uncommon for audience members to throw coins at Daguerre's scrims as a crude way of figuring out how the illusion was created or how far away it really was. During the 1830s while he managed the diorama, Daguerre was working simultaneously on developing what would become the daguerreotype: like the multiple effects of a painted scrim, it is also an experience that can't be portrayed in a photograph, that is, the image on the metallic surface of the daguerreotype oscillates in and out of visibility, depending on how light strikes it. It does not have a stable optical identity in relation to shifting view of an individual observer. My point is simply to think about the implications of a system or apparatus of variable transparency that is simultaneously designed for both orientation and disorientation.

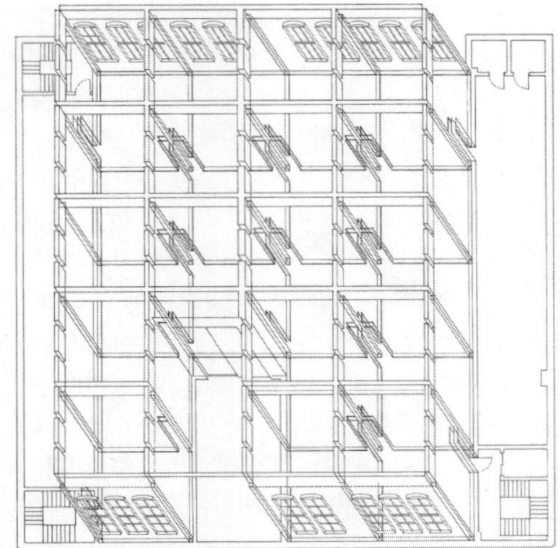

Robert Irwin, study for *Prologue: x18³*, 1998.

Not surprisingly, Irwin's use of scrims has been discussed as a tactile mode of vision, borrowing the term from the Viennese art historian, Alois Riegl. I disagree with this characterization and believe that Irwin is in fact more usefully understood in terms of Riegl's model of an *optical* mode of vision. A tactile art for Riegl (or haptic derived from the Greek word for touch) is one in which the world is made present in an eternal unchanging objective form, and his exemplary model was ancient Egyptian art. The self-evident clarity of tactility was posed against the idea of opticality—optical art in contrast incorporates into it the distortions and concealments of light and shadow, the relativization of distance, and above all the subjective experience of the eye itself. Leonardo's paintings with their effects of *sfumato* would be a decisive example of work that defined an optical mode, that is, they affirm that vision is not about a grasp of stable and discreet forms but is about a dissolution and blurring of identities, about the nebulous intervals between and among objects. This dimension of Leonardo stands behind a long history of perceptual practices which we can trace through Rembrandt, Turner, and Monet. But I think some of the ramifications of Irwin's work become clear in relation to this larger genealogy, which goes back beyond his more obvious affiliations with twentieth-century experiments, including Matisse, Albers, and Rothko.

Thus much of Irwin's work is an affirmation of a heightened *optical* experience in which we are made aware of the operation of our own perceptual capabilities and their limitations. An extreme optical orientation diminishes the ability of the individual to *discriminate* distance, position, contours, substance, it devalues what were John Locke's "primary qualities." Yet simultaneously—and this is part of the extraordinary impact of this installation—Irwin amplifies conditions which enable the eye and the body to make astonishingly subtle and nuanced distinctions between intensities of hue, tone, luster among the delicate, overlapping veils of shadow and soft radiance. This is in part why low-light conditions are essential here, for it is under low light that the human eye demonstrates its remarkable superiority over forms of machine vision, as Joseph Albers noted in his 1963 book on color. It is not a question of night vision, for which all sort of technological sensors exist, but rather conditions of dimness and obscurity in which nothing machinic can match the discriminations of which the human eye is capable. Especially in the inner rooms or units of the piece, the illumination is subdued enough so that we are using *scotopic* vision, basically processing information with the rods of the retina. Thus, there may be essential uncertainty or vagueness about the objective identity of what we are looking at, but we are able to discern the circumstances of that uncertainty with an astonishing clarity and precision. Scotopic vision, that is, the rod-dominated periphery of the retina, is generally believed to be one of the oldest parts of the human eye in evolutionary terms, associated with a range of animal survival mechanisms, but also according to Anton Ehrenzweig and others, linked with unconscious processing and dreaming.[6]

Of course, if this achromatic level of seeing is operative, we must also be using our photopic vision as well, daylight foveal color vision, in order to register the complex binary hues of the fluorescent lighting. In fact most regular indoor experience involves an overlapping of scotopic and photopic vision, but in Irwin's piece what is extraordinary is the particular overall deployment of these two modes of seeing, especially at certain times of the day. There is often sunlight directly striking the floor on the south side of the work and both the north and south windows open directly onto the expanse of sky, city, and daylight. Normally, in such a space, this would involve jarring but very familiar experiences for us as spectators of looking out the windows or at the pools of sunlight on the floor and then an abrupt and extended period of optical accommodation as we turn and move toward the dimmer interior of the space. This kind of adaptation between such varied intensities of light generally goes unnoticed.

But Irwin's "window treatment" is crucial in creating what I think of as the "twilight" conditions of the work. He reduces the amount of light entering the space, yet still preserves the feeling that we are looking at daylight. Whatever filtering he has used simultaneously maintains the sense of the outside everyday world in all its familiarity and strangely produces effects of derealization. Significantly, the brightness is diminished, filtered to the point that when we scan or turn around the space we don't have any noticeable effect of accommodation moving from a bright to a dim point of focus. This "twilight condition" is something with which we're all familiar; for example, after sunset seeing a still bright blue sky and scanning down to below the horizon and distinguishing streetlights or houselights already on among the gathering but detailed pools of shadow. No matter how many times we experience it, there is always something miraculous about that straddling of two different kinds of vision. What Irwin has done is to bring a related kind of twilight uncanniness to an experience that can happen all throughout the day (and the piece itself has specific temporal boundaries that change throughout the year, it always closes at dusk rather than a specific clock time). Daylight, as it was for Daguerre's diorama, then is an integral component of the piece, for it would have been much easier for him to simply cover the windows and create a sealed-off light show inside.

What we get is a redistribution of luminous values that produces a smooth sensory continuum, a kind of equilibrium between daylight and the fluorescent tubes and their multiple effects inside. I certainly don't mean to imply there is any homogeneity of light and its effects, far from it, but what Irwin has achieved is a quietly disruptive scale of disparate intensities and sources. I can't give any scientific or physiological explanation, but my hunch is that these manipulations of light, and the resulting absence of obvious optical adjustments or accommodations, produce the sense of a smooth kinesthetic itinerary through the work, a slower register of movement. I use the word "smooth," borrowing from Pierre Boulez's use of the term, to suggest a vague, amorphous idea of time which overrides the apparent striations or the metric structural distinctions on which the work seems to be based.[7] In ancient churches, the narthex or vestibule was defined as an intermediary space where one made both an optical and spiritual adjustment between the bright profane light of the outside world and the much dimmer but sanctified illumination of the nave. Irwin reverses this principle and constructs a space where that duality is inoperative, where interior and exterior flow into one another, so that transcendence is never an issue for him. In connection with the architectural dimension of the piece, it's worth remembering the premodern sense of the word "contemplation," which meant to go into the space of a temple, to enter a sacred sphere. For a work that is so patently "auratic," it would be a mistake, as Theodor Adorno insists, to ignore in it some of the historical afterimages of the long pre-secular vocation of art.

What I've said so far could be taken to imply that Irwin's work is designed for an individual viewer, for the psychological experience of a private autonomous subject. But one of the most potent features of the work is its insistence on a tension between the private and public character of perception. I've already referred to some of these private aspects, those strategies of the work which produce our sense of intimate absorption in its perceptual enticements and ambiguities—our rapt engagement with its chromatic attractions, its equivocal radiances, the pleasures of its disorientations. In principle, the piece could be viewed by a solitary observer but I believe the institutional conditions determining its use during its exhibitionary existence effectively preclude that from happening. Thus one always inhabits and circulates through this space along with at least a few other people. But the mere presence of other people is not what I mean by its social or public dimension, otherwise we would be talking about the problem of contemplation as it is posed in the context of any traditional gallery or museum space. Part of what I see as the *private* experience of Irwin's work is the apprehension of other people and their movements but seen through the scrims, seen amid what I tried to designate as the optical texture of the work. In fact I don't believe that the scrims and florescent tubes by themselves would have any comparable kind of effect. What activates the piece is the copresence of dimly seen or sensed figures in varying degrees of obscurity, bereft of any specific identity so that they easily, even if temporarily, can become phantasms within the terrain of our own psychic and perceptual economy. With the generality and indistinctness of shadows, they overlap with fleeting, barely remembered movements of those we once knew, of fragments of forgotten scenes, encounters, or reunions yet to occur, or even as murky nonsynchronous mirror images of ourselves. The imprecision with which we can situate them in terms of distance or position suggest some of the operations of condensation and displacement in what Gaston Bachelard describes as reverie, a waking suspension of the reality function.

But the modularity of the work, the cube as the figuration of a monadic isolation is also defined by portals opening onto passages, onto routes of circulation which disrupt the possibility of reverie or of self-absorption. In other words, the entrance of other people, in all their vivid concreteness, their prosaic intrusiveness, into one's unobstructed field of vision, cancels one's private immersion in a proprietary perceptual event. I don't mean to imply any sort of Sartrean reversal in which the observer (or the voyeur) suddenly becomes the object of another's gaze. Rather I'm suggesting something very different—Irwin is simply insisting that the fragile intimation of a shared collective space is inseparable from but not easily consonant with the recognition of our own solitude and separateness. And the reconciliation of collective and individual, of obscurity and clarity, of structure and dematerialization, of rationalization and illegibility are left deferred and unachieved.

In the framework of these issues, I want return to the late nineteenth century and Riegl's articulation of tactility and opticality as part of his anxiety about the fate of European culture. It must be emphasized that these were not just formal or analytical categories but were charged with significant cultural and even political valuations. One of the artists crucial for him was Rembrandt, whose chiaroscuro seemed to pose a rare and precious balance between the cognitive clarity of tactility, its affirmation of a solid tangible reality and the subjectivity, relativity, and insubstantiality of opticality. It was out of his study of seventeenth-century Dutch painting that Riegl postulated a subject whose integrity depended on a reciprocal relation between an unwavering subjective contemplation and a coherent objective world. In his book *The Dutch Group Portrait* he made clear that his privileged model of the individual observer presupposed an ideal of meditative *intersubjectivity* as opposed to modern forms of interiority, absorption, and psychic isolation, or to the dissolution of this communal world which he saw figured within the general cultural

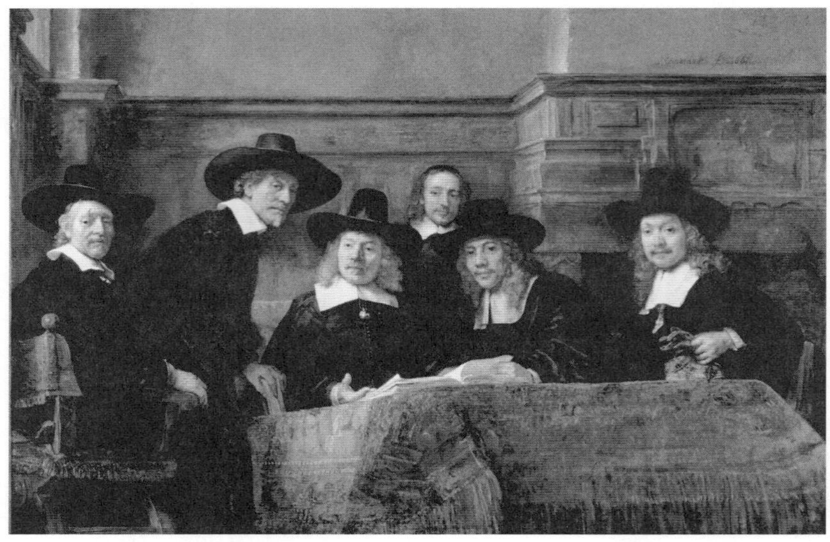

Rembrandt, *The Syndics of the Clothmakers' Guild*, 1662.

phenomenon of "impressionism." Thus the group portraits of seventeenth-century Holland, and above all the group portraits of Rembrandt, provided, at the very start of the twentieth, a utopian figuration of a world of mutual communication (a secular equivalent of religious experience) and a world in which art would be inseparable from an imaginary harmony of individual and community, of a meditative solitude and social collectivity. For Riegl the goal of these paintings was the "representation of a self-less psychological element by means of which the individual psyches were forged together as a whole in the consciousness of the beholding subject."[8] Modern distraction or self-absorption in this context could only erode the possibilities of democracy. But for Riegl, the dream of community, of a hushed moment of psychic communion, as figured, say, in Rembrandt's *Syndics,* existed as an aesthetic construction to be apprehended by a solitary individual observer. In one sense, this can be understood as an elitist and regressive fantasy of a pre-modern, ethically charged visuality.

But if we can, in a qualified way, speak of chiaroscuro in Irwin's work, it is in the service of something very different from an imaginary realm of social and aesthetic harmony. Instead there is a disquieting restlessness in the oscillation between the private and public poles of the work. Within that oscillation is a sense of what Geoffrey Hartman has recently called "phantomization," by which he means those effects within modernity in which in a feeling of individual wonderment is inseparable from an unsettling sense of nonpresence or self-estrangement.[9] An acute sense of homelessness can occur amid an intuition of art's *promesse du bonheur*. Everything today, he says, tends toward a condition of placelessness even as our desire for authentic or auratic experience is artificially stimulated. But at the core of Hartman's argument is the insistence that to take seriously the very possibility of culture is to keep hope in embodiment alive, to maintain hope for a living and functioning milieu. It is possible to identify aspects of Irwin's work as utopian, but it is not a self-enclosed compensatory utopian practice, using Ernst Bloch's categories, but rather a concrete anticipatory utopian imagination which operates on the basis of an ameliorative relationship to an actual collective future.

In many ways utopian thought today coincides with debate over the nature of the "virtual." Now at the end of our own century, the idea of virtual reality, in electronic and digital forms, is indifferently associated with new possibilities of invention and innovation. Irwin's work is much closer to an idea of virtuality that designates that which is not yet seeable, explainable, representable in terms of existing concepts or expectations. Thus the actualization of the virtual must involve the creation of the unforeseen, the emergence of an event that is not deducible from conditions which preceded it. The American philosopher John Rajchman writes that "a virtual construction is one that frees forms, figures and activities from *a priori* determination or grounding of the sort they have, for example, in classical Albertian perspective, allowing them to function or operate in other unanticipated ways—the virtuality of space is what gives such freedom in form or movement."[10]

When William James wrote, in 1890, his concise proposition, "My experience is what I agree to attend to," he meant it as an affirmation of an autonomous self-choosing, world-creating subject, liberated from the *receptive* status of a subject for whom experience was "the mere presence to the senses of an outward order."[11] He probably did not suspect that this equation might be an indication of a historical crisis in the nature of experience itself. That is, perception, as an indispensable part of an expanding terrain of modern spectacle, becomes both a simulation of and compensation for a chimerical "real" experience. As perception is posed as fundamentally constitutive of subjectivity, "experience" is increasingly resituated outside of collective, lived historical time. In a way the problem for Irwin is not fundamentally different from what it was for James, how can a reflective individual absorption in the fringes, transitions, pulses of one's own particular "pure experience" be effectively reconciled with "experience" as immersion in the tangled confusion of a shared, mutually inhabited world. In its overwhelmingly pervasive forms within contemporary technological culture, perception coincides with an individual evasion of both history and memory. In its myriad commodified modes, it becomes an imaginary deletion of all that is unbearable or intolerable in collective and individual experience. But for the ways in which perceptual selectivity is indispensable to the functioning of normative society, where it is about usefulness and efficiency, perception can also be, as Irwin shows us, an opening onto a heterogenous world of nonproductiveness, of decomposition: in itself, it leads to the ruin of certainties and stabilities. It produces the conditions in which the apparent necessity and self-sufficiency of the present could be dissolved, allowing the tentative formation of a clearing in which its forgetfulness can be the basis for a reclaiming of the derelict objects of memory.

1. Meyer Schapiro, *Cézanne* (New York: Abrams, 1963), p. 9.
2. See William James, *Radical Empiricism* (New York: Longmans, 1912).
3. Michael Polyani, *Personal Knowledge: Towards A Post-critical Philosophy* (Chicago: University of Chicago Press, 1958), pp. 87–91.
4. Colin Rowe and Fred Koetter, *Collage City* (Cambridge, MA: MIT Press, 1978), p. 49.
5. Fredric Jameson, *Postmodernism, or the Logic of Late Capitalism* (Durham, NC: Duke University Press, 1991), p. 44.
6. See Anton Ehrenzweig, *The Hidden Order of Art: A Study in the Psychology of Artistic Imagination* (Berkeley: University of California Press, 1971), pp. 273–74.
7. See Pierre Boulez, *Orientations: Collected Writings*, trans. Martin Cooper (Cambridge, MA: Harvard University Press, 1986), pp. 84–89.

8. Alois Riegl, "The Dutch Group Portrait (excerpts)," trans. Benjamin Binstock, *October* 74 (Fall 1995), p. 11.
9. Geoffrey Hartman, *The Fateful Question of Culture* (New York: Columbia University Press, 1997), pp. 21–27.
10. John Rajchman, *Constructions* (Cambridge, MA: MIT Press, 1998), p. 119.
11. William James, *Principles of Psychology* (1890) (New York: Dover, 1950), vol. 1, p. 402.

Text of a lecture given at the Dia Art Foundation, New York City on April 9, 1999. First published in *Robert Lehman Lectures on Contemporary Art*, eds. Lynne Cooke and Karen Kelly (New York: Dia Art Foundation, 2004).

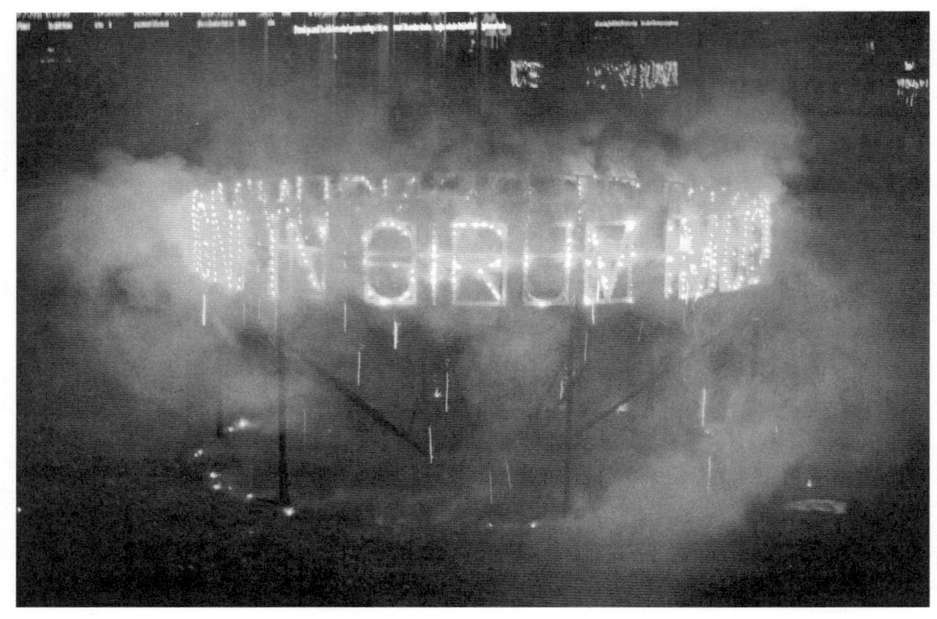

Cerith Wyn Evans, *In girum imus nocte et consumimur igni,* 2009.

Cerith Wyn Evans's Luminous Stagings

> The screen is a dim page spread before us, white and silent. The film has broken, or a projector bulb has burned out. It was difficult even for us, old fans who've always been at the movies (haven't we?) to tell which before the darkness swept in. —THOMAS PYNCHON, *GRAVITY'S RAINBOW*

The merging of screen and page, the virtual whiteness within film and text, the exhaustion (not purification) of their possibilities, the dilapidation and silence at the heart of any play of images or words. Scattered in this fragment from the annihilating last page of Pynchon's 1973 novel are some provisional terms for engaging Cerith Wyn Evans's deeply challenging art: his is work richly shaped by its critical and historical relation to the accumulated and interrelated possibilities of film and writing and by its effective renunciation of them both as contemporary aesthetic strategies. It would be misguided to say that Evans operates in a space between these practices; rather, his work draws on some of their dwindling affects in its dazzling and unsettling invention of unfamiliar relations between space, light, language, and objects. Each of his pieces (which draw on an insistently broad range of genres, media, and discourses, high and low) is a demarcated clearing in which new modes of visibility, readability, sensation, and presentation are enigmatically materialized.

One of Evans's well-known pieces that elaborates its postcinematic context is *In girum imus nocte et consumimur igni* (2006). This suspended circular construction with letters made of neon, spelling out its title allows one to see the words both frontally and in reverse. *In girum* is also the name of both a text and a film by Guy Debord, the former published in 1978 and the latter first screened publicly in 1981. Like many of the proper names referenced in Evans's titles and in the works themselves, Debord's *In girum* is a work made up of citations of other projects, films, and texts. Equally relevant is that *In girum* was a film that disavowed its own status as "film," attacked the essential presumptions of film spectatorship, and demanded to be evaluated from standpoints other than the cinematic. So many of Evans's pieces disclose a related refusal to provide his spectators (if that designation is even appropriate) with familiar or preestablished openings onto his work. If any particular category of aesthetic experience or schema of media seems initially relevant, sustained attention to the intricacy of the work inevitably displaces that apparent connection. The fact that the Latin phrase is a palindrome may have been especially important for Evans. A palindrome in its redundancy, its tautological excess, contains a disruptive reversibility that destabilizes both syntax and letter. It is a specialized instance of the kind of supplementary system of signification that so fascinated and troubled Ferdinand de Saussure in his study of Latin anagrams. These issues are certainly prominent in Evans's work, given the many ways in which his various syntactical operations are overcoded or conjoined with countersyntactical processes and effects, often luminous in nature. The Möbius strip, which features in a recent work, is another form in which continuity or extension necessarily doubles back, dissolving the possibility of a start or finish, setting up multiple events of reversibility and repetition. But the cylindrical structure of Evans's *In girum* also literalizes the circularity of the reel of film, as well as film's intrinsic independence from narrative conventions. The cylinder or drum-like architecture of the piece recalls forms of precinematic devices in the nineteenth century, especially the Zoetrope, in which looped imagery often had a palindromic character; for example, little pictures of dancers, acrobats, or clowns whose simulated movements could be viewed veristically regardless of whether the drum was spun forward or backward. At the same time, the rotational potential of the work incarnates the turning in the title, "We turn in the night and are consumed by fire," but the bleak admonitory tone of the medieval epigram is reinscribed as a glittery element of contemporary spectacle, like a neon advertising sign one might see in a shopping mall.

Often Evans's work combines an evocative plenitude with a willfully

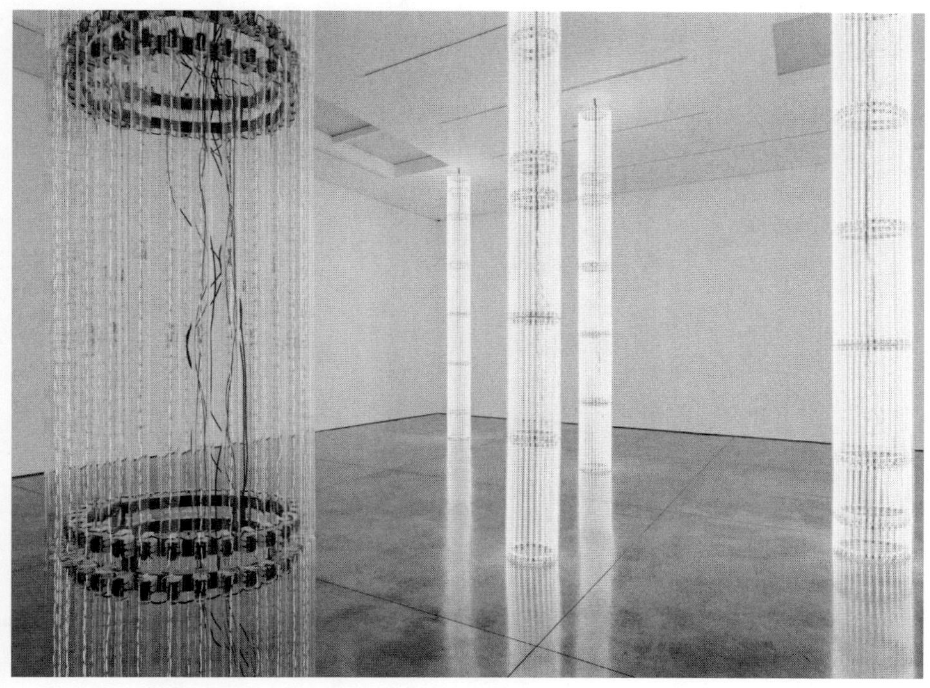

Cerith Wyn Evans, *S=U=P=E=R=S=T=R=U=C=T=U=R=E (Trace Me Back to Some Loud Shallow Chill Underlying Motive's Overspill),* 2010.

elliptical organization. This mix creates the sense of an insufficiency, not as an incompleteness, but of the incommensurability between the contingency of his mise-en-scène and the ideas and effects it generates. One's visual relation to the work becomes deflected, deferred, and rendered suspect, giving it what might be termed its melancholic cast. Melancholy as an intellectual position, of course, has nothing to do with individual sadness but rather with a particular sensitivity to the dislocating consequences of modernity. It is a privileged vantage point from which the disappearance of stable meanings from the world can be most acutely apprehended. At the same time it is an acknowledgment of the dissolution of a link between authenticity and meaning, and of the insurmountable limits of representation. Melancholy, in this sense, is an unsparing acceptance of the impossibility of immediacy, of recovering the origins of things, or of creating order and coherence in the world of appearances.

But it would be misguided to push this characterization of Evans's work too far, because his work seems equally driven, in an affirmative sense, to invent new machinic possibilities, new ways in which experience, including remembrance and loss, can be made part of physical relations and transformative processes. There is a principle of convertibility, distinct from translation, in which languages, sounds, information can be provisionally transmuted into new rhythms, materialities, or signs within reversible or oscillating networks. At work here is a Nietzschean understanding of metaphor as central to creative thought, as a *carrying over* of something from one sphere into another. It should also be stressed that Evans has no particular commitment to current technological paradigms. His toolbox is intricately sedimented in a historical sense, mixing the obsolete (e.g., the World War II searchlight in *Cleave 03*) and the cutting edge (e.g., the digital BIX facade used in *The Sky Is Thin As Paper Here…*). But the transitivity between apparatuses, objects, words, and images is hardly seamless or based on relations of exchangeability. There is a play of imperceptible gaps and disjunctions within all the visible linkages and adjacencies, where there occur faint disturbances or perturbations of what can't be converted or circulated, as, for example, when a text or poem is refigured into Morse code or an old photograph is digitally reproduced. In this way there is an intimation of spectrality in many of Evans's pieces, when visual or semantic clarity is undermined by the proximity of something untimely. The spectral here is the disruption of the present by the unexpected intrusion of something out of time, from another time. In Evans, it is the persistence of voices, forms, of unfulfilled hopes (both collective and personal) that interrupts the amnesiac and homogenous time of the contemporary world.

At times Evans can seem a twenty-first century Joseph Wright of Derby. However anachronistic this comparison, their works are both luminous baroque stagings, enigmatically suspended between alchemical, visionary operations and the harsh instrumentality of a modernizing present. For Evans, the investigation and deployment of light (or any photo emissive phenomena) generates a plurality of effects and meanings, never fully drained of auratic possibilities. No doubt he is aware of one of the contextual parsings of the *In girum* palindrome, which concludes that the "turning in the night" is a figure of the doomed flight of moths circling around a flame. What better vantage point than from within Evans's revelatory milieus to ponder a global present in which millions become ever more drawn and captive, like moths, to the seductive flickerings of the glowing screens, monitors, and displays that illumine our 24/7 day/night world.

Originally published in the exhibition catalog *Cerith Wyn Evans: Bubble Peddler* (Graz: Kunsthaus Graz, 2007).

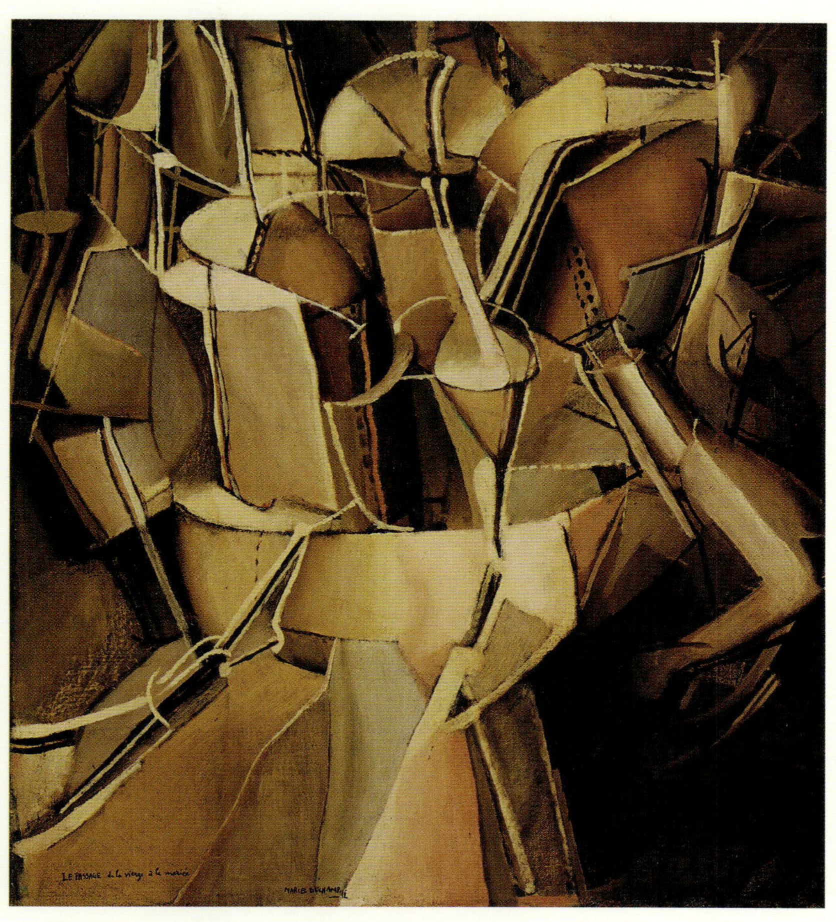

Marcel Duchamp, *The Passage from Virgin to Bride*, 1912.

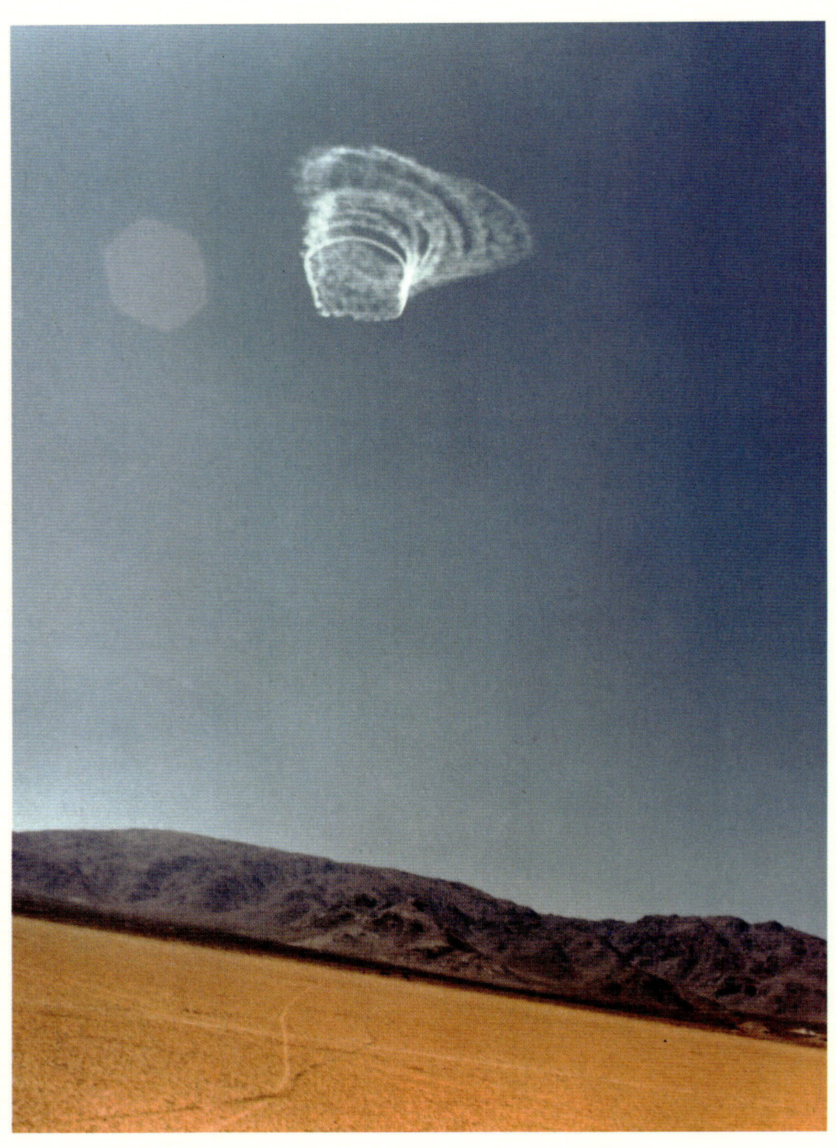

Dennis Oppenheim, *Whirlpool: Eye of the Storm*, 1973, El Mirage dry lake, southern California, ¾- × 4-mile schemata of a vortex (whirlpool), traced in the sky using standard white smoke discharged by an aircraft.

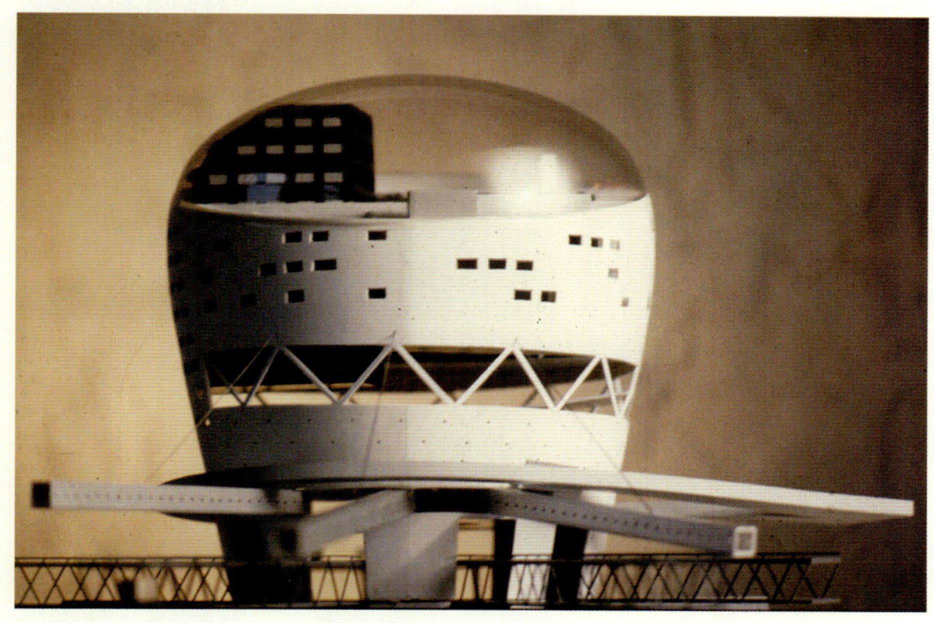

Rem Koolhaas, *Zeebrugge Sea Terminal*, 1989, project proposal.

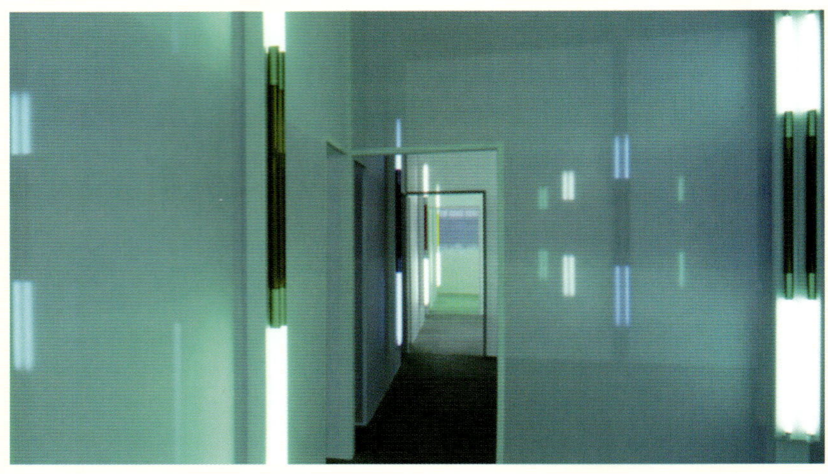

Robert Irwin, *Excursus: Homage to the Square*^{3}, 1998.

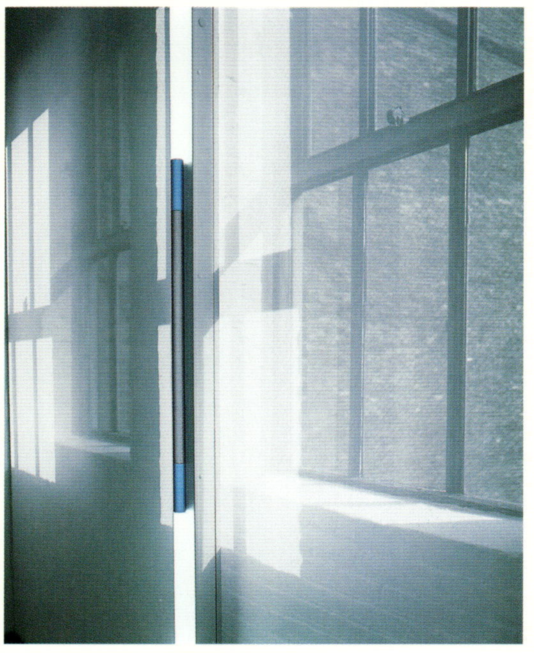

Robert Irwin, *Prologue: x18*^{3}, 1998.

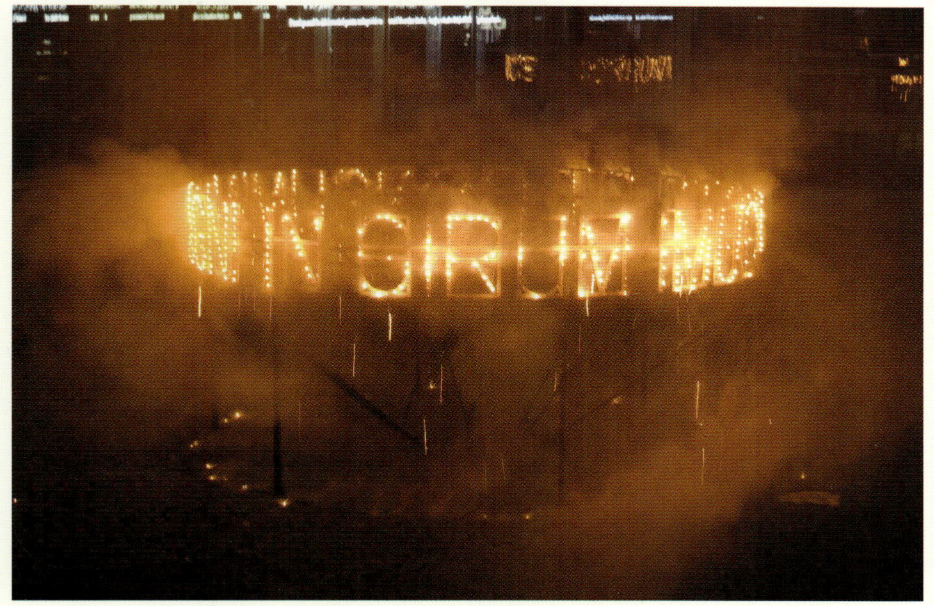

Cerith Wyn Evans, *In girum imus nocte et consumimur igni,* 2009.

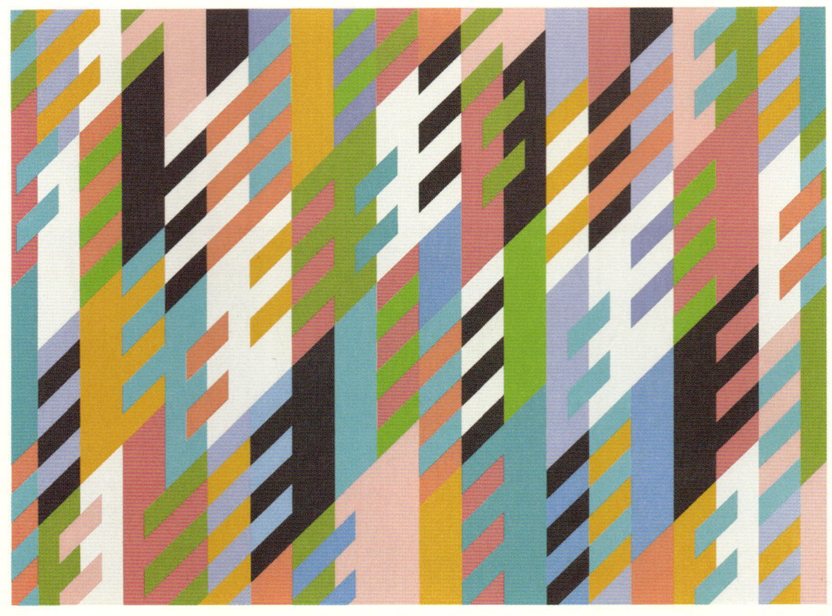

Bridget Riley, *New Day,* 1988, oil on linen, 63 × 89 in.

Bridget Riley, *Song of Orpheus 5,* 1978, acrylic on linen, 77 × 102 1/4.in.

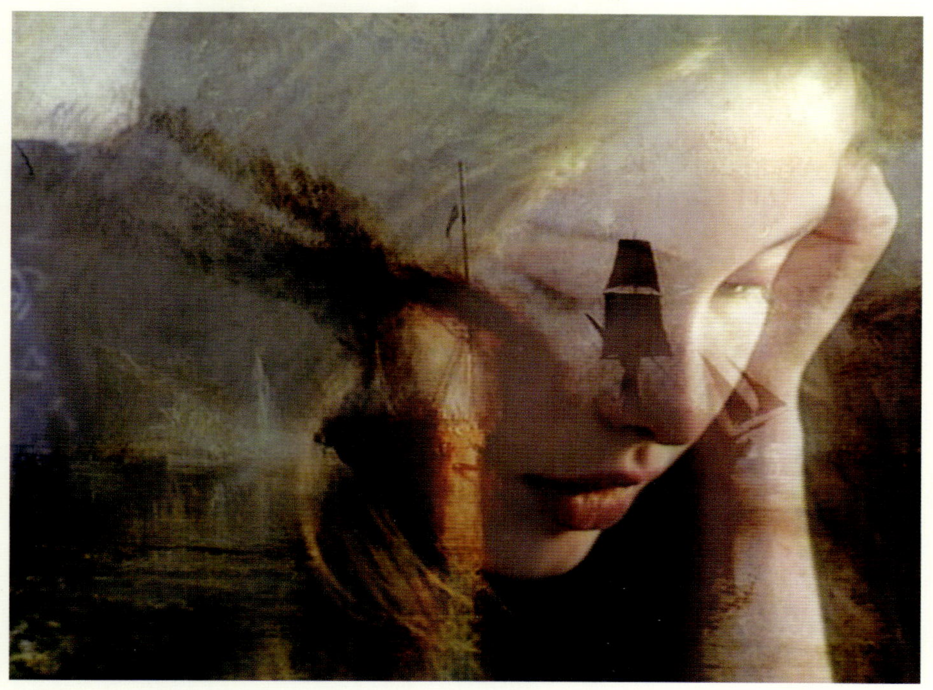

Jean-Luc Godard, *Histoire(s) du cinéma*, 1988–98.

Uta Barth, *Untitled (aot 4)*, 2000.

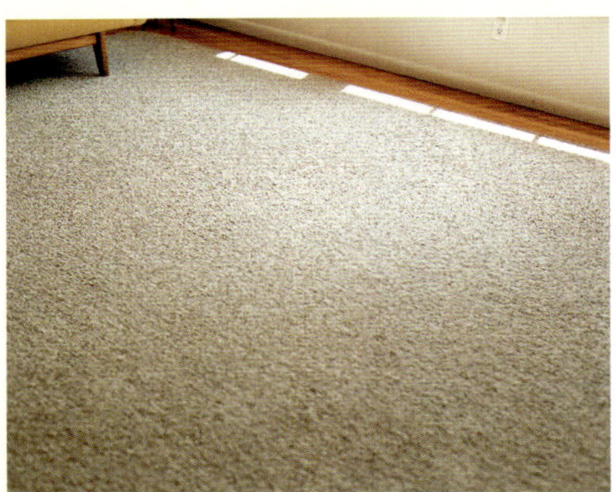

Uta Barth, *Untitled (aot 1)*, 2000.

Spinning Histories at the Sydney Biennial

One of the prevailing truisms of the past two decades of neoliberal hegemony is that the notion of revolution has been discredited, that it is a nostalgic and obsolete dream which events have shown to be based on delusional promises and hopes. Of course, these platitudes are inseparable from larger ideological positions, such as the "end of history" thesis which began circulating in various guises in the early 1990s following the collapse of the Soviet Union and Eastern bloc. The core premise of this pseudo-Hegelian fantasy was that all of the imperial, national, and dynastic conflicts that had been the driving engine of historical change for several thousand years had come to an end, or at least to the recognizable beginning of an end, culminating in the apparent success of a global economic/political system that would henceforth expand and flourish without any significant challenges to its triumphant inevitability. When the events of September 11, 2001, and afterward highlighted the preposterousness of the posthistory narrative, the aggressive advocates of corporate-led globalization made a slight modification in their essentially unchanged end-of-history fiction: a world dominated by ever-expanding free markets and consumerism would coexist in perpetual conflict with minorities of irredeemable groups and individuals bent on irrational evil and violence. As in Orwell's *1984*, the end of history is imaginable in terms of atavistic antagonisms that persist outside of any historically intelligible framework, exempt from any other resolution than the ever-deferred annihilation of one side or the other. Nonetheless, in all the celebratory accounts of a globalized *post-histoire*, even the possibility of political revolution is rendered unspeakable.

Yet at the same time the developed zones of our increasingly interconnected planet are repeatedly experiencing a wide range of other forms of "revolution." Innovations in technology, science, and other areas are readily promoted as "revolutions" with sweeping and categorical claims, such as "the Internet changes everything," "the mapping of the human genome changes everything," or "nanotechnology is the new industrial revolution." Political regime changes viewed as favorable to capitalist development are deemed "velvet" or "color" revolutions. The situation, as numerous critics and historians have noted, is the ceaseless appearance of novelty within a regulated cultural environment in which proposals for fundamental social or political change are effectively prohibited. One of the challenges for artists working today is how to engage and contest the manufactured and dehistoricized temporalities of contemporary global culture.

Walter Benjamin was one of a number of twentieth-century thinkers who understood that politically effective art needed to be an assault on the complacent regularity or predictability of historical time as it functioned in bourgeois society. Much of the abiding interest in Benjamin's work is due to his evocations of how art (as well as other perceptual experiences) could sabotage a comforting belief in notions of material improvement, and how this disruption could be achieved in the name of what had been forgotten or obliterated by compulsory fantasies of progress. But the relevance of these formulations to contemporary practices is obviously problematic, in part because the ideological priority of inevitable historical advancement has been superseded by other temporalizing imperatives. There is no longer any "official" history for counterdiscourses to challenge, and the calamitous antagonisms of Benjamin's 1930s Europe are remote from the spectral dissimulation of current global struggles. The generalized narcosis of today's megalopolis consumer societies sustains a collective obliviousness to the savage inequities of affluence and poverty on a global scale. The only "states of emergency" to which we respond are those fraudulently manufactured to consolidate existing regimes and institutions, and to neutralize opposition.

Nonetheless, the disparate images or figures with which Benjamin chose to convey the mixed possibilities for the human experience of historical time continue to resonate and engage us. He pointed to the shared redundancies and rhythms of machines and procedures defined by turning, looped, or circular motions: the revolving motor elements of factory machinery, the roulette wheel in the gambling hall, and the reel of film turning in the movie projector. They were all indicators of the routinization of time that did not simply accompany modernization but which became constitutive of modernity itself by the early to mid-twentieth century. For Benjamin, these were some of the automated or rote processes to which the senses become habituated but to which the individual returns again and again out of varying kinds of compulsion, economic necessity, pleasure, addiction, or boredom. The turning, rotating functions that Benjamin discerned are contradictory and multiple. They flatten out duration, draining it of singular events, but they simultaneously produce the breaks or jolts (as in the moment when the gambler either wins or loses, in a startlingly unexpected effect in cinematic montage, or in the abrupt malfunctioning of factory machinery) to which the individual adapts as one of the requirements of modernized social reality. But the decisive part of Benjamin's argument was that perceptual redundancy might contain the possibility of unforeseen illuminations and understandings, that both the technologies of the workplace or the distractions of the cinema could generate at least a momentary superseding of the standardization of the senses. Although in the last years before his death, Benjamin became increasingly pessimistic about the revelatory and transformative capacities of film and saw it becoming honed into an instrument for fascist mobilization.

Benjamin's notion of the "dialectical image," remains an idiosyncratic model of how insurgent insights flare up in an instant of collapsed, imbricated time, but his experience of cinema clearly contributed to its articulation. One of the many filmmakers whose work Benjamin knew was Dziga Vertov. His best-known film, *Man with a Movie Camera* (1929), opens up a field of kinetic and temporal explorations that had enormous ramifications for subsequent artists working in many media. It is no coincidence that the pseudonym chosen by the filmmaker (born Denis Kaufman) was a collision of Ukrainian and Russian that means "spinning top," with its suggestions of dynamic, unregulated rotational energies, as well as a sense of perpetual motion. *Man with a Movie Camera* elaborated approaches for understanding the modernization of perception within an explicitly "revolutionary" context. So much has been said about this remarkable work,

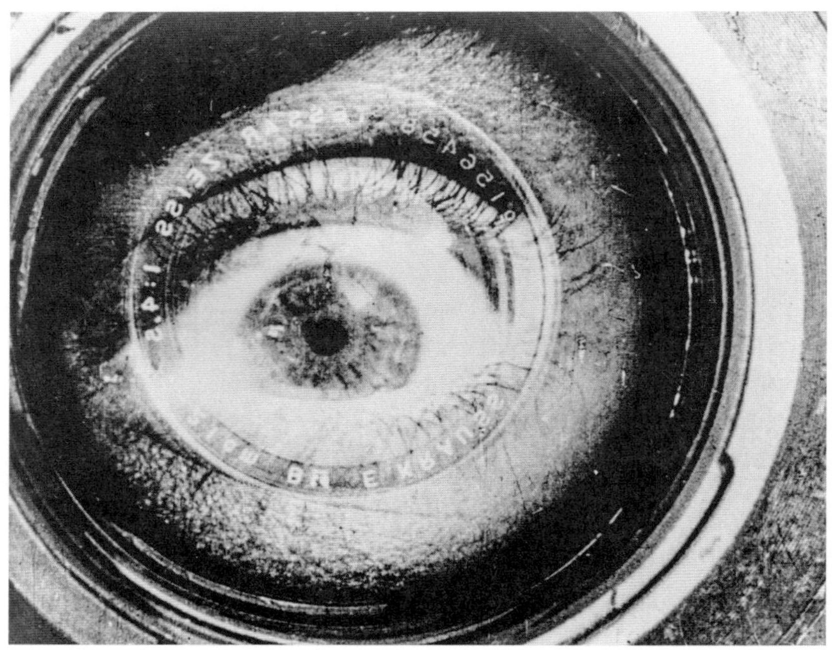

Dziga Vertov, *Man with a Movie Camera*, 1929.

but it still can be stressed how Vertov succeeded in developing multiple images and affects to affirm the inseparability of individual human experience from the reverberations of historical change and technological modernization. In one sense, *Man with a Movie Camera* is a meditation on how older epic forms of imagination could be recreated afresh with the unprecedented resources of cinema.

As some recent critics have shown, *Man with a Movie Camera* is not simply a celebratory manifesto of machine vision, but rather a more problematic account of the persistence and reconfiguring of biological human life in a milieu in which technology has increasing suppleness, potency, and implacability.[1] Thus, *Man with a Movie Camera* is a visualization of a single day in the life of a (composite) human being, for whom individual and social identity are not separate but yet never harmoniously integrated. The film encompasses the markers of an archetypal human existence, bringing birth, work, marriage, play, misfortune, childhood, old age, and death into a world of speed, machinic productivity, and disruptions of linear, sequential temporalities. For Vertov, political revolution required a rethinking of how historical time moves and produces effects at different thresholds and durations. Revolution, in his film, intersects with the diurnal, solar revolution which defines both the social and cosmological reality of a twenty-four-hour day. But Vertov also makes clear that revolution was a set of fractured and incomplete processes in which the past and survival of the obsolete interpenetrated with the making and anticipation of a future not yet realized. The film-work was a crucial part of the volatile figuration of that future, a future that was less a goal ever to be finally achieved than a regulative principle for praxis in the present. Part of the formal innovation of *Man with a Movie Camera* was its insistence on the historically sedimented reality of a post-revolutionary society in which remnants of class hierarchies, bourgeois individualism, and quasi-magical forms of illusion survived alongside emerging forms of class struggle, collective solidarity, and aesthetic defamiliarization.

A few years before *Man with a Movie Camera*, a very different artist made use of more literally revolutionary innovations. Marcel Duchamp's *Anemic Cinema* (1925) has long been positioned within an avant-garde tradition at odds with the "political" one in which Vertov and other Soviet artists participated. But such distinctions are frequently based more on extraneous contextualizations than on actual formal achievements. In any case, experimental filmmaking in the 1920s was still historically close to the very beginnings of cinema and to the many nineteenth-century antecedents of the movies. Both Vertov and Duchamp were, for unique reasons, well aware of the mechanical and social genealogies of cinema, in particular its origins in popular techniques of magic and illusion. For Duchamp, the rotating structure of *Anemic Cinema* is bound up in crucial features of his work and are obviously linked to projects such as his *Precision Optics* (1925–29) and the *Rotoreliefs* (1935). *Anemic Cinema*, with its alternation between forms and words on spiraling, circling abstract disks, directly recalls some of the earliest productions of proto-cinematic movement in the nineteenth century, specifically the phenakistoscope, invented around 1830. An apparatus which allowed a viewer glimpses of a rotating disk, it

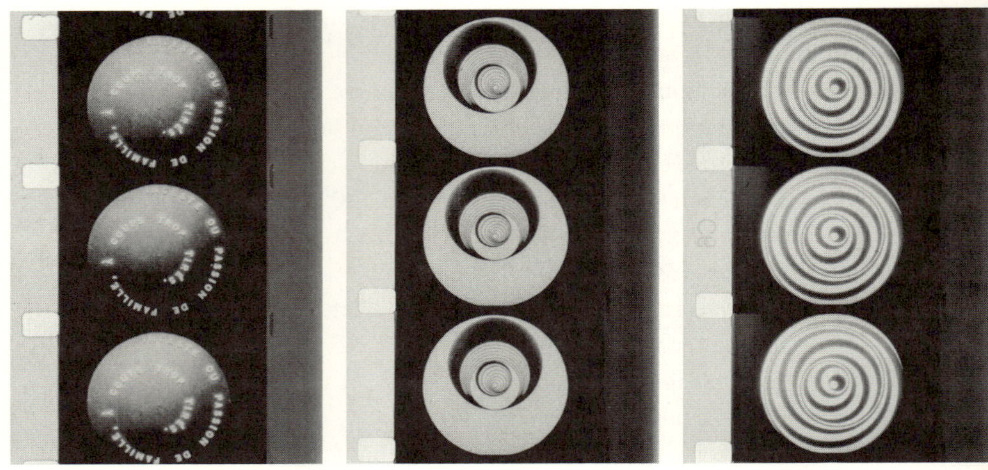

Marcel Duchamp (with Man Ray and Marc Allégret), *Anemic Cinema*, 1926.

was one of the earliest demonstrations of how the eye could be exposed to a rapid sequence of static positions and yet perceive them as part of a seemingly unbroken flow of movement. Momentous epistemological and practical consequences ensued from the discovery that there never was a simultaneous or one to one correspondence between individual experience and a stimulus presented to the individual at any given moment. The conceptualization of even a minute desynchronization between subjective perception and external reality was the basis for a broad range of techniques for mass-produced visual commodities.

Duchamp recuperates how these early devices created the appearance of continuous movement without using the illusionistic capacities of photography. *Anemic Cinema* retains something essential about those older spinning apparatuses that were rendered outdated by later "advances" in verisimilitude. Both repetitive and fascinating, a device like the phenakistoscope was an attraction that had little to do with specific pictorial content. It was a fascination with the illusion of movement itself, with the pulsing, expanding, and contracting forms in their endless (and reversible) loops of motion. It constituted a kinematics rather than a semantics. The fundamentally antinarrative structure of these older apparatuses no doubt stood behind some of Duchamp's formulations, for *Anemic Cinema* is one of various repudiations in the 1920s of the normative syntactical possibilities that film had seemed to legitimize in the previous decade. Its uneasy oscillations and shallow suggestions of depth and relief prevent the film from establishing any developmental or unidirectional temporal flow. The other rhythmic movement in the film is the fluctuation between the rotations of abstract spiral patterns and of involuted sequences of words. The anti-diegetic force of the film is heightened not only by the derangement of a left-to-right reading and the difficulty of reading a rotating string of words but also through the internal destabilization of language with puns and double entendres. As many critics have insisted, these visual/verbal derangements include an erotic component in their operations, even if it is an erotics of frustration and displacement.

Anemic Cinema, the *Rotoreliefs*, and other mobile works point back to the fabled *Bicycle Wheel* (first executed in 1913). In all of these, Duchamp introduces a delinking of function from any purposive end. He sought to situate his art outside of developmental or linear temporalities. Severed from usefulness or instrumentality, these objects are consistent with the larger economy of his work which continually challenged the productive functionalism of bourgeois society. It's ironic that Duchamp was harshly attacked in the 1970s by artists such as Robert Smithson and Carl Andre for what they saw, in pseudo-Marxist terms, as his frivolous and elitist denial of use-value and labor.[2] They were unable to grasp the radical implications of Duchamp's attempt to align his art with something close to Georges Bataille's notion of a "general economy," in which human energy, erotic or otherwise, was diverted from the utilitarian and accumulative values of a "restricted economy." The *Bicycle Wheel* can stand for Duchamp's multiple figurations of movement and time as intensive events, discontinuous with a past or future. Crucial for Duchamp was the exploration of these concepts beyond the confines of a single medium or of notions of multimedia. The affects he produced were more important than the various material supports between which they migrated. That is why the idea of "kinetic art" in the century of cinema has had such a dubious legacy. Once the movement-image (to use Gilles Deleuze's term) became a constitutive part of the consciousness of anyone who went to the movies, it required Procrustean measures to sustain older aesthetic boundaries and categories.

In 1925 (the same year as Eisenstein's *Battleship Potemkin*), while Duchamp was engaged on *Anemic Cinema*, Lászlő Moholy-Nagy was in the middle of the extended creation of his *Light-Space Modulator* (1921–30). This widely misunderstood work has also been inappropriately endowed with the "kinetic art" label. Unfortunately, for decades, the work was known by many only through still photographs, which allowed it to be hypostatized as a work of sculpture (albeit with moving parts). But clearly what concerned Moholy-Nagy was not its machine-tooled appearance but rather how its steel and glass disks, reflectors, and latticed screens, when set in motion by its gyrating mechanism, could generate mobile multilayered luminous effects in an interior space. The *Light-Space Modulator*, in spite of having been endlessly celebrated as announcing a machine art of the near future, is also recapitulation of a long and seemingly antiquated heritage of light and shadow shows going back hundreds of years. Moholy-Nagy's writings disclose his awareness of the long history of "painting with light." His various and constantly shifting concepts for light display coincide with but also exceed the contemporary capabilities of cinema. His broad sense of the utopian possibilities of luminosity required an expanded range of how *projection* could be imagined, without ever rejecting its dense history and magical premodern origins.

Recapitulating these modernist practices provides a window onto the work of some of the most adventurous contemporary artists. One frequently noted feature of current work are explorations in the dense history of abandoned or marginalized visual techniques. A recourse to the "outmoded" is hardly nostalgic or antiquarian. Rather, it is a refusal of the neoliberal ideologies of endless technological progress and the related patterns of accelerated obsolescence. More important, the collision of outdated perceptual practices with a whole panoply of contemporary digital tools is capable of revealing the ruin and dereliction that always accompanies processes of modernization. For example, some of the work of William Kentridge, featured in this biennial, depends on a seemingly incompatible mix of antiquated procedures with various forms of new media, in which all of them are equally derealized or denaturalized. Specifically, his work foregrounds a reliance on hand-based craft in the production of animated

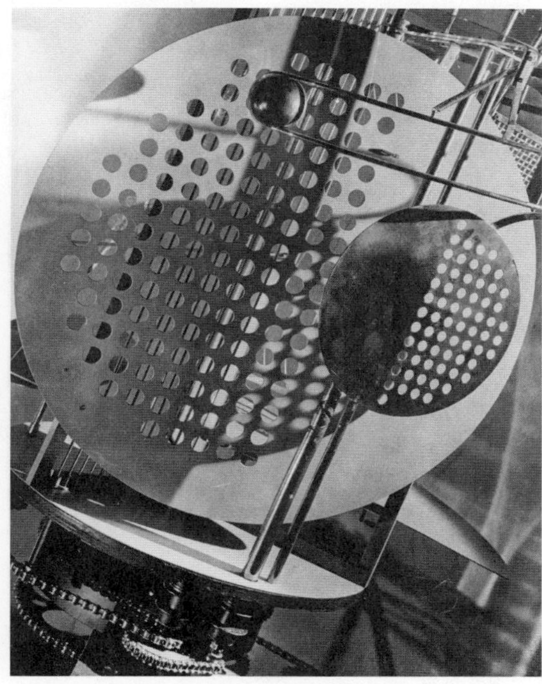

László Moholy-Nagy, *Light-Space Modulator*, 1922–30.

films in digital formats (what he calls "stone-age filmmaking"). His obsessive erasure and reworking of individual drawings convey a halting and broken sense of the actual time of fabrication. In a larger sense, his art explores ways of engaging the disruptions and disasters of contemporary global history, including the sweeping social and political transformations in South Africa.

Kentridge is one of many artists today whose work challenges or evades the homogenous, instantaneous temporalities required by corporate media culture. Along with others, his use of a flexible assemblage of old and new tools, media, and effects aligns itself with an understanding that history (if it is to be a meaningful concept) is not a matter of chronological succession. Rather, it is the unrepresentable experience of human beings, in large and small aggregates, living, competing, working, struggling with each other in myriad ways. Most important, as the materiality of his work makes clear, human history is meaningful only as a fragile,

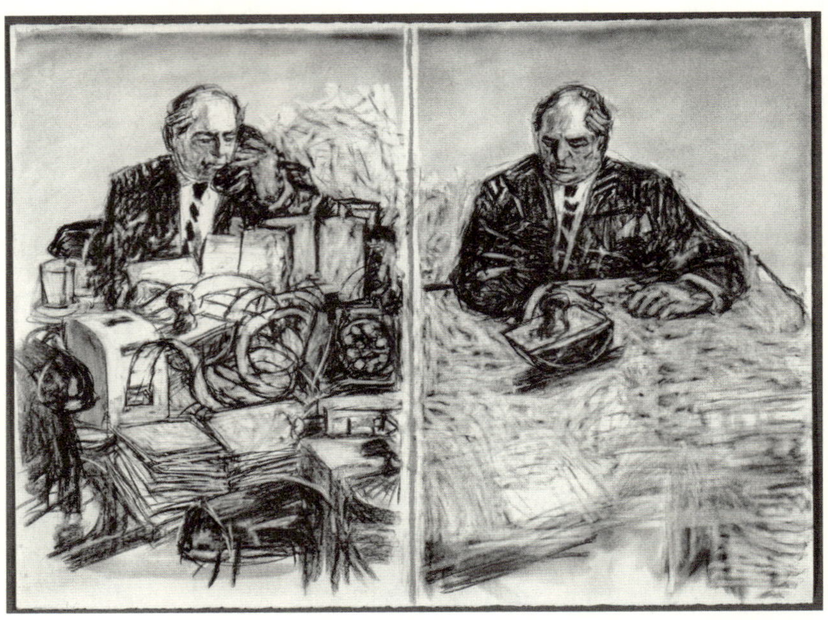

William Kentridge, drawing from animated film *Stereoscope*, 1998–99.

imperiled, and deeply marred striving for justice and equality. Like Vertov and many others, Kentridge understands that political and cultural change is always a prolonged and contested process of metamorphosis in which many intractable structures, habits, and forms endure, with unpredictable consequences. They persist, not identically, but powerfully enough to produce new kinds of psychic and social dislocations and previously unforeseen ethical crises and choices. Amid this broken terrain, his art moves backward and forward on digressive pathways through collective memories, repressed horrors, and individual self-deceptions, to pose its fleeting truths and revelatory flashes. Along with many of his international peers, there is a shared recognition that art does not produce social change nor can art directly agitate effectively on its behalf. What it *can* do is to provide unfamiliar vantage points from which the apparent necessity of dominant perceptual and cognitive habits can be unsettled or dismantled.

1. See, for example, Malcolm Turvey, "Vertov: Between the Organism and the Machine," *October* 121 (2007), pp. 5–18.
2. See Carl Andre, "Against Duchamp," *Praxis*, Spring 1976, and Moira Roth, "Robert Smithson on Duchamp: An Interview," *Artforum* 12.2 (October 1973), p. 47.

Originally published in the catalog of the 2008 Sydney Biennale, *Revolutions: Forms That Turn*.

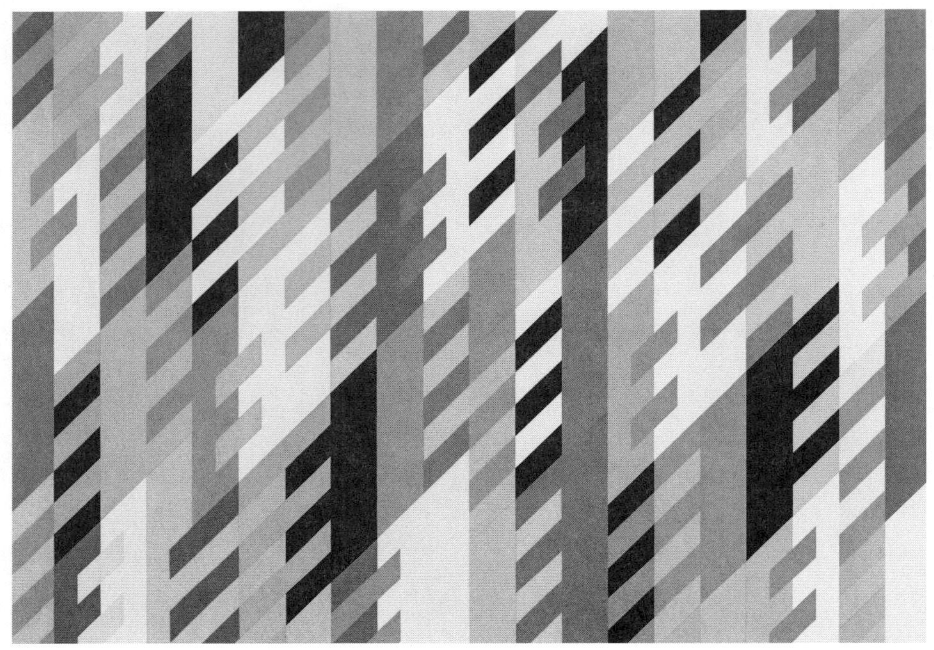

Bridget Riley, *New Day,* 1988, oil on linen, 63 × 89 in.

Bridget Riley's Activations of the Eye

Over the last two decades, criticism and commentary on Bridget Riley has frequently claimed for her work an impressive position within mainstream genealogies of twentieth-century painting. The affinities of her work with important features of Matisse, Pollock, Klee, late Mondrian, and numerous others have been variously and sometimes convincingly demonstrated. However, many of the affiliations (e.g., School of Paris) that have been posed as interpretive entryways into her work have tended to bypass or domesticate some of the defining features of her painting. Numerous accounts are based on the assumption that Riley's extraordinary work of the 1960s was widely misunderstood amid the popular response to her innovations and through the cultural milieu with which she was uncritically associated. But perhaps by so fully distancing her from the extravagance and wrongheadedness of what was written about her initial aesthetic and cultural impact, some singular elements of her work have been lost to view. In this brief essay I propose a few openings onto Riley's work along less discussed lines of affiliation and association in the interest of recovering some sense of its intrinsic alterity.

My estimation of Riley as a groundbreaking artist, an incomparable creator of perceptual experience, stems in part from her alignment with the axis in English art defined by Blake and Turner. The discipline of art history, born on the European continent, has never quite known what to do with these immense, idiosyncratic figures from the British Isles. Their importance and originality are duly acknowledged, but they have been effectively exterior to the most influential explanatory accounts of nineteenth- and twentieth-century art. Different as they are from each other, Blake and Turner can stand for certain understandings or assumptions about vision and perception to which Riley is linked as much as she is to any continental ideas and practices. These artists share a conviction that only an unmediated subjective vision can engage the primal forces that shape and color the physical world. The visionary autonomy that each sought required the abandonment or reimagination of existing pictorial codes and conventions. Most relevant for Riley's work in this context is the decisive renunciation by Blake and Turner (in his work after 1835) of the fundamental place of chiaroscuro in painting. Over several centuries the conceptualization of a painting as an organized distribution of lights and darks established one of the dominant models for the exercise of intellectual control over the indwelling disorder of perception. It was also a system through which an implied pictorial syntax could operate and which postulated a spectator competent to "read" it.

Blake and Turner extrapolated from their own experiences that one perceives not a world structured around binary oppositions but a single continuous field of illumination, however it might be articulated. Crucial for Blake was the primacy of the indivisible light of one's "emanation" over the divisions and falseness of one's "specter." Important in Turner, is his refusal of Descartes's prohibition of perceptual dazzlement, most evident in his numerous later paintings of unmediated, unprotected encounters with solar radiance. These lead not to madness, as Descartes and others insisted, but to revelatory insights into nature and history. The overturning of the presuppositions of chiaroscuro obviously is part of a larger history in which the phenomenon of luminosity begins to be privileged as an autonomous term, extracted from its *relational* position in an older set of codes, from its *reciprocal* pairing with shadow or darkness. In this history, additional elements of English art play a significant role as well, including some of the Pre-Raphaelites, Whistler, and the broad emergence of watercolor practitioners in the late eighteenth century.

To reiterate, I am simply suggesting a tentative way of considering Riley's work in relation to historical precedents that have not been central to evaluations of her work. It's tempting to elaborate her autobiographical accounts of her youth and rural upbringing in terms of existing English archetypes and narratives: the childhood in a natural, often austere, environment, uncluttered by the distracting products and reified images of urban culture, where there is born a heightened sensitivity to the subtleties and refined modulations occurring within a variegated, living milieu. But regardless of what contexts with which it is affiliated, her painting, in all its major phases, affirms the pictorial surface as a continuous network of luminous events that are irreducible to an underlying dualistic structure. It implies that the conceptual equivalent of shadow does not effectively exist for her. Rather, in Michael Baxandall's terms, there are only variations or discontinuities in brightness. To what extent this predilection is a conceptual choice or is actually derived from experiences accumulated from childhood, or a mixture of both is something finally not demonstrable. Even in her work of the 1960s, which might seem superficially compatible with binary models of various kinds, Riley produced fields in which black and white, light and dark are bereft of any intrinsic values and are subservient to the larger dynamic forces at play in the work. As has often been noted, there is no opposition of black and white for Riley; instead, she works with them as extremes of the single indivisible phenomenon of color. It is her particular distributions of color that produce, not the drama of "internal relations" which defined much midcentury abstract painting, but a range of events that occur in the exchanges between painted surface and embodied spectator. The specific character of these transactions has modulated along with shifts in her style and formats, but some core ambitions of her project have remained relatively constant.

Riley's work solicits from its viewer a particular mode of engagement, which she herself has referred to as "receptive attentiveness." As Wittgenstein and some other modern philosophers have argued, attention is not necessarily synonymous with either consciousness or perception: one can choose to attend to various aspects of individual experience, but never all at the same time. Attention is not only concentration, in terms of a kind of willed effort, but it is perhaps more importantly an act of selection. Most often it functions involuntarily and unconsciously: one selects a limited range of potentially relevant stimuli in order to avoid being overwhelmed by too much information or sensation. As both artists and scientists have discovered in different ways, human attention is an imperfect and capricious capability with inherent limits. We all know in our own experience of what happens if we look at some unchanging object or form for too long: our visual hold on it begins to dissolve in a series of perceptual modulations. As the eye fatigues, the constancy of colors and shapes undergoes various transformations. Rather than prompt a suspended exchange between a rapt spectator and an inert object, Riley allows viewers to become aware of the volatility of their own attentiveness. Her paintings produce a dynamic continuum in which the optical identity of the individual work is always in the midst of a process of self-differentiation. Early on, Riley must have sensed the impossibility of assuming the unmediated givenness of sense-data and at the same time understood that she could not make visual art predicated on notions of perceptual constancy.

In the mid- to late 1970s she developed a stunning series of ribbon or wavelike fields. In this work Riley tapped into an enormously potent vocabulary of dynamic form, drawing on a variety of specific interactions of light and matter. One can look back to the notebooks of Leonardo for a related kind of exploration, to his studies of streams of water in which he attempted to identify some fundamental regularities within ceaseless movement and activity. Thus, in a painting like *Orpheus* (Boston Museum of Fine Arts) Riley produces a unique space of autonomous sensory events but which nonetheless are parallel to the effects generated in the natural world, such as the reflections of sunlight off a moderately calm ocean surface or the undulations of a large expanse of tall grass moving in a steady wind. Our attention to *Orpheus* then begins amid a vivid sense of perceptual instability, and one of Riley's remarkable achievements is to provide the conditions for an attenuated and continually reactivated engagement.

The specific texture of one's encounter with the work depends to some degree on one's physical distance from it. Unless one is quite close to the painting, the experience of looking both fixedly and panning across its width, involves unusual interactions between the central and peripheral parts of the eye. Whatever we see with the fovea (or the small central area of the retina which registers the clearest detail or the sharpest color discriminations) can simultaneously be in competition with our retinal periphery (which is highly sensitive to the least sensation of movement, whether real or illusory). Thus, any sustained regard of Riley's iridescent and torquing ribbons of color is unsettled by the subdued intrusion of perturbations and flickerings at the edges of our visual field. Any

Bridget Riley, *Song of Orpheus 5*, 1978, acrylic on linen, 77 × 102 1/4 in.

significant change in distance, either closer or away, from the work allows a noticeably different but related network of effects to occur: The pulsating routes through which we are led at some point poses the question of where these events are taking place.

One can also observe Riley's painted surface up quite close and plainly examine the patterned sequence of marks out of which *Orpheus* is made. However, none of the previously mentioned shimmerings and undulations will be detectable. Similarly, a very near view of a Seurat discloses the systematic microstructure of painted touches out of which his images are constructed. For example, one can observe an area made up exclusively of dots of orange, blue, and yellow-orange. Yet when seen from a distance of approximately fifteen feet, that same area appears to be a hazy glimmering violet. As is well known, Seurat was working with considerable knowledge about the physiological capacities of the human eye. Specifically, he understood how the retina could synthesize several adjacent color sensations into the impression of a color that existed only subjectively. In a related sense, much of what is fundamental to our experience of a Riley painting has an *atopic* or placeless character. The stunning perceptual events which in various ways define her work provoke us to ask not only *what* exactly we are seeing but *where* in fact it is "taking place." And Riley makes clear that the answer to latter question will never be clear cut or categorical. There is always an indissoluble and active play between eye, mind, and the artwork itself.

Riley has had an abiding interest in many aspects of Seurat's painting and drawing, but her own work could never be said to have any programmatic ambitions. In spite of her expansive awareness of the science, psychology, and philosophy of both mind and vision, such knowledge is never allowed to intrude on the beauty and mysterious life of the work and how we encounter it. The ideas of various philosophers have been productively enlisted to elucidate Riley's art. My own sense that there are affinities between Riley's own evident rejection of a subject/object bifurcation and the vitalism and anti-dualism in the later work of Alfred North Whitehead. Criticizing the belief in the possibility of "simple location" or in the notion of inert, enduring entities, Whitehead defined our relation to the world as a "structure of activity" in which we are always a constitutive part of continually developing occurrences. The vibratory interweaving of vision, consciousness, art object which Riley brings into being with work after work, privileges the reality of process and flow over the idea of independently existing minds or matter. This is something she probably did not learn from books but more likely from those initiatory and youthful immersions in natural environments.

Riley's concerns, though, are hardly just philosophical. What seems to matter to her in the end is the vocation of the artist and the accompanying responsibilities. In this connection I want to conclude by again positioning Riley in an English context by invoking the writing of John Ruskin, an essential thinker on the relations between vision, art, nature, and the responsibility of the artist. For this much-misunderstood writer, vision was always an open-ended process without a final goal or object. If there was a "truth" of vision for Ruskin it was to be grasped through its inexhaustible capacity for refining and extending its own limits and sensitivity. But it was also in understanding the inexhaustibility of visible reality, which for Ruskin meant great art or the natural world. To look at nature, for Ruskin, whether a leaf, a rock formation or even a cloud, was to inhabit a process of formation that had no closure, no finality. And for Ruskin the artworks of the greatest value were those which were similarly indeterminate and unfinalizable. Riley, in her own fashion, has transferred her intuitions about nature into a conviction that the artwork too, as it interacts with the human sensorium, can be a source of unprecedented occurrences that challenge any habituation or standardization of perception.

Originally published in the catalog of the Bridget Riley retrospective, Musee d'Art moderne de la Ville de Paris, June 12 – September 14, 2008.

Paul Virilio's *Aesthetics of Disappearance*

Nearly three decades have passed since the publication of *Esthētique de la disparition* in 1980. The immediate context in which it was written was the late 1970s, now to all of us like a foreign country. This was still the bipolar world of the Cold War; globalization (though very much occurring at the time) was not on everyone's mind; most people still used typewriters, not yet word processors; even the VCR had not yet become a pervasive consumer item; the internet was years away from widespread implantation; and the late twentieth-century catastrophes of the Balkans, Rwanda, the Persian Gulf, and elsewhere were hardly foreseeable from within the 1970s balance-of-terror management system.

So how now, in the early twenty-first century, does this remarkable Paul Virilio text resonate? Perhaps, at the least, its rereading can help correct some of the wrongheaded characterizations of his work that have accumulated in these intervening years. This text in particular clearly affirms what has been obvious to any careful reader of Virilio all along: he never was or is a critic/historian of media or a philosopher of technology in the way these labels might apply to figures as disparate as Ellul, McLuhan, Kittler, or Stiegler. Of course, his work has been uniquely valuable to anyone interested in these areas, but Virilio's guiding preoccupations lie elsewhere. To use quasi-Kantian terms, it is more useful to see his work as a relentless examination of the conditions which make experience possible. But it is hard to imagine a more sweeping abandonment of the universalizing presumptions of Kant's critique than the arguments of *The Aesthetics of Disappearance* (the irony of the title is notable in this respect). For Kant, the essential role of time was to coherently unite all the elements of knowledge by establishing a relation between thought and perception. That is, time was the necessary condition of any particular experience we have; time is what makes perception possible and intelligible. Virilio's project is to relentlessly survey the role of time in the multiple and abyssal delinkages between perception and its possible objects.

But Virilio is not outlining a new philosophical account of time, in the footsteps of Bergson, Husserl, Heidegger, or others. His stance is more Nietzschean in his insistence that time is irreducibly plural, discontinuous, nonhomogenous, and reversible. As they were for Foucault in the 1970s, questions of time for Virilio are of interest primarily as the consequences of a given field of forces and effects. Thus, both Foucault and Virilio were aligned, at least for a time, in their related concern with how individual and collective experience is shaped territorially by strategic relations of power.

It should also be stressed that Virilio is not suggesting that prior to the industrial revolution, humans had some more "natural" relation to temporality. At the heart of *Aesthetics of Disappearance* is his insistence that experience as duration has always been constituted as desynchronized and fractured. This is the importance of his thematic of "picnolepsy," his depathologizing of the epileptic "petit mal." Perhaps he could have chosen another, equally effective illustration to make his point, for he is writing not from the standpoint of medical physiology but from that of the phenomenology of perception, even if his project diverges from most of the work done within the framework of the latter (including by Merleau-Ponty). Virilio's "phenomenology" (for which he would substitute the term "logistics") discovers perception to be made of breaks, absences, dislocations as well as by the capacity to produce patchworks of various contingent worlds.

Historically, there has been a wide range of ways in which societies have responded to the vagaries and inconsistencies of perception, for example, the many premodern privilegings of states of trance, possession, or daydream and the ways these states were creatively integrated into collective life. But Virilio implies that wherever forms of logical or rational thought have dominated, especially in the West, the vacancies and absences in perception are assimilated and desingularized into a homogenized and potentially controllable texture of events. The goal of reason, he says, is "to redistribute methodically the occasional eliminations of picnoloepsy...to deny to particular absences any active value."

Thus, Virilio is proposing that an individual is never organically situated in some *a priori* river of time but rather that history has always been a matter of shifting arrangements and techniques through which provisional effects and strategies of time are produced. The problem of speed, for example, with which Virilio's thought is popularly identified, is hardly something specific to recent modernity. Every historical epoch, whether the Roman Empire or the Napoleonic, is understandable in terms of speeds, forms of motion and stasis, and their possibilities of modification, of acceleration. The last 150 years are different only in the rate of change and the intensified accumulation of overlapping technologies and networks. Surely this much broader historical vision of speed and territory was part of what appealed to Deleuze and Guattari in their use of Virilio's ideas in *Mille plateaux* (also published in 1980). At the same time, the *Aesthetics of Disappearance* makes clear that speeds are produced not just by what are commonly thought of as technologies, but by vectors and itineraries of many kinds.

One of the decisive elements of the present text (and in much of Virilio's writing) is cinema and the cinematic. In these pages, cinema is important as one of the most pervasive ways in which the absences in human perceptions are both supplemented and redeployed by an external production of speed, displacement, and luminosity. Virilio certainly does not underestimate the consequential significance of the invention of the cinematograph in the 1890s, but his sense of the cinematic is far more expansive and suggestive than most perspectives on film history. Components of a cinematic machine have been in use over many centuries: forms of projection, moving images, immobile voyages, and visionary illuminations. No doubt the extraordinary fascination on the part of artists and filmmakers with Joan of Arc in the first half of the twentieth century was a dim recognition of a kindred picnoleptic in the fifteenth century who watched and listened to her own "home movies" as a girl in the countryside. But the various cinemas of the long precinematic are in no sense anticipating their teleological assembly and unification at the hands of the Lumière brothers. As is clear from our twenty-first-century vantage point,

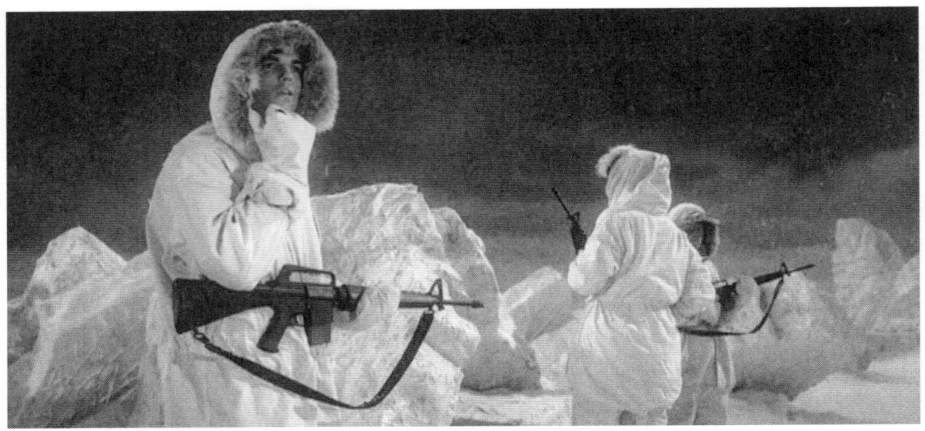

John Sturges, *Ice Station Zebra*, 1968.

the cinematograph was itself only a temporary aggregate of parts that have been discarded or subsequently recombined into other proliferating "vision machines."

As Virilio wrote in the late 1970s, psychoanalytic film theory was exploring the similarities between the movie spectator and the sleeper/dreamer. But unlike Christian Metz and others, Virilio saw cinema as part of a much wider breakdown of the boundaries between sleeping and waking, between the real and dreaming. Like Deleuze, Virilio understood cinema as part of crisis of belief, in which we no longer believe in the world. This loss of faith is inseparable from an ongoing incapacitation and neutralization of vision. Over the last century vision has increasingly been denied any hierarchy of objects within which the important could be distinguished from the trivial, as figure might be isolated from ground. Without these distinctions vision becomes a derelict and uninflected mode of reception and inertia, incapable of seeing. Along with its motorized speeds, cinema and an array of other luminous screens announce the installation of a permanent day that by now has become the 24/7 globalized present we all inhabit. Virilio in the late 1970s was already noting the broad inscription of human life into a homogenous global time without downtime, a milieu of continuous functioning, of countless operations that effectively are ceaseless. 24/7 is a time that no longer passes, beyond clock time, beyond any measure of lived human duration.

This is why Virilio's epiphanic account of Howard Hughes remains so compelling. Hughes is a personification of the overlapping effects of speed (his obsession with flight) and light (his efforts to dominate the movie industry). The claustrophobic debacle of his later life is bleak evidence of the unintended consequences of these new configurations. Hughes's atemporal isolation as he obsessively watched and rewatched screenings of *Ice Station Zebra* in his Las Vegas penthouse prefigures most of the forms of timelessness and nonstop digital management of our now micro-programmed and placeless lives. In Virilio's remarkably prescient words, "the internment of bodies is no longer in the cinematic cell of travel but in a cell outside of time, which would be an electronic terminal where we'd leave it up to the instruments to organize our most intimate vital rhythms, without ever changing position ourselves, the authority of electronic automatism reducing our will to zero."

Originally published as the introduction to Paul Virilio, *The Aesthetics of Disappearance*, trans. Philip Beitchman (Los Angeles: Semiotext(e), 2009).

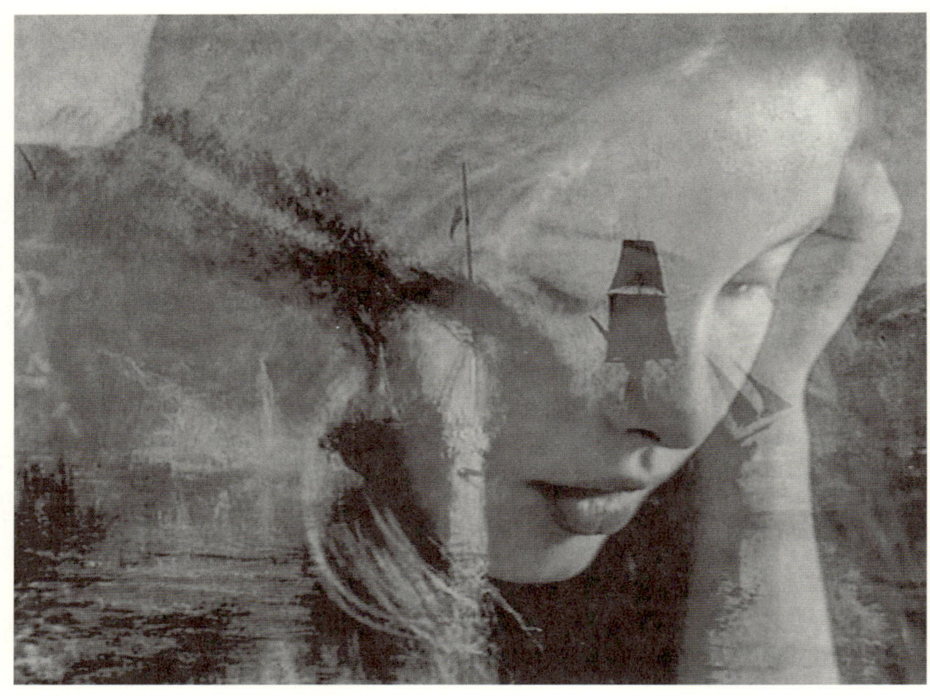

Jean-Luc Godard, *Histoire(s) du cinéma*, 1988–98.

On Jean-Luc Godard's *Histoire(s) du cinéma*

In a segment of Jean-Luc Godard's 2003 film *Notre musique*, the filmmaker is meeting with students in post–civil war Sarajevo. When Godard pauses in his ruminations on language and image, an audience member asks him: "Do you think the new little digital cameras will save the cinema?" The film cuts to Godard's face, holding it, almost invisible in deep shadow; the audience waits but he makes no reply. Godard's silence is of course his self-dramatized response to a wrongly conceived question. Certainly he has nothing against mini-DV equipment, which he has used creatively in numerous projects. He would also have been acutely aware of the many possible uses of such digital tools, for witnessing, for documentation in the immediate social context of Bosnia. But as his monumental *Histoire(s) du cinéma* makes clear, the fate of cinema for him has never primarily turned on questions of technology or media. Godard's concern now is also not about "saving" cinema, but to invent a form through which it can be remembered, and in remembering it, to locate what in it might yet be redeemable.

Godard worked for over a decade on *Histoire(s)* but spent many more years, beginning in the 1970s, pondering and planning for it. He began showing sections of it in the early 1990s and even before its first completed exhibition in 1998, it was already an object of intense critical attention. Its initial reception coincided with widespread discussions in the 1990s around notions of the death of cinema, the end of film, the obsolescence of the analog film image and its material support. At the time, Godard's work was frequently associated with the melancholic obituaries of film in the writings of Susan Sontag, Serge Daney, Peter Greenaway, and many others. But now, a decade and more since those hyperbolic debates of the 1990s, Godard's film has proved to be enduringly relevant for very different reasons, above all for its exemplary demonstration of alternate narrative and historical practices, and for its innovative experiments with word, sound, and image. Although Godard has said many times that one of his goals was to tell the history of cinema through cinema itself, the obvious fact is that *Histoire(s) du cinéma* is a video work that relies on an array of technologies that postdate the time-frame of cinema which he purports to survey. While much of its visual texture comprises extracts of more than five hundred films, the work is fundamentally unlike any existing "compilation" movie. Obviously the rich history of the film-essay, (which includes Godard himself), stands behind *Histoire(s)*, and in fashioning his film-based historical practice he would no doubt have been mindful of the work of Chris Marker, Alexander Kluge, Syberberg's *Our Hitler*, and the elegiac *In girum imus nocte* of Guy Debord, to mention a few.

Godard's work, ever since the 1960s, has depended on a range of "citational" practices, but he rarely makes a quotation, whether of text or image, without modifying it in some substantive fashion. Thus almost all the cinematic fragments in *Histoire(s)* are never shown as film-clip segments, but as images (still or moving) that have been subjected to a variety of metamorphoses and processings. The fleeting shards of films are often second- or third-generation images, treated with effects of flickering, oversaturation, repetitive oscillations, flashings, extreme slow motion, and many more. However, Godard never allows his manipulations to obscure or override the legibility or indexicality of a given image. His operations are achieved deliberately without the appearance of refinement or technical finesse even though many of his dissolves in fact have been painstakingly crafted with the digital and other means that were at his disposal.

The vast and intricate fabric of the work led many critics to associate its scope with earlier twentieth-century works, such as Pound's *Cantos*, Musil's *Man Without Qualities*, Joyce's *Finnegans Wake*, and Benjamin's *Arcades Project*. Clearly Godard has drawn deeply on the accumulated experiments of twentieth-century avant-gardes and modernisms (whether as collage, montage, stream of consciousness, surrealist automatism) in the creation of an unprecedented syntactical organization of spoken word, graphic text, music, and image (as artwork, film, or photograph), of what Jacques Rancière has discussed as Godard's "image-sentence."[1] But if these are reference points for Godard, they are not simply a medley of various formal strategies (as they might have been for him in the 1960s). Rather, they are embedded in the histories he is attempting to relate. His particular account of cinema is heavily weighted to the 1920s and 1930s and much of the spoken textual content of *Histoire(s)* is also from these two decades: for example, Virginia Woolf's *The Waves*, Denis de Rougemont's *Penser avec les mains*, Hermann Broch's *The Death of Virgil* (begun in 1938), and many other works which pose various counterstrategies to traditional narrative or historiography.

Godard and Gilles Deleuze share a related sense of the historical importance of the early to mid-1920s as a moment when silent cinema seemed to have opened a stunning and revelatory field of possibilities in which thought itself might be reinvented and endowed with unprecedented, unbounded capacities. But, in this view, the tentative experiments of Gance, Epstein, Vertov, Eisenstein, and others were never fully taken up and the moving image, burdened with sound, became, in Deleuze's words, "linked to the organization of war, state propaganda, ordinary fascism, historically and essentially."[2] Thus the fortunes of cinema in the 1920s and 1930s, when its very best and worst prospects were realized, is in part what led Godard to his conflation of the history of cinema with the history of the twentieth century. No other medium or art form ever had the capacity to fabricate images and myths which subsequently became social and political reality. If Walter Benjamin sought to disclose the images and spaces which constituted a dream-world of emerging capitalism in the nineteenth century, Godard has attempted to account for some the cataclysmic consequences that were inseparable from the dream-worlds created by cinema in the twentieth century.

As many have noted, the French word "histoire" does not translate easily into English and the plural sense of this word is crucial to Godard's aims: its overlapping of the English notions of history, story or tale, the matter, affair or business of something, and even the sense of a lie or fib. Thus there is a mobility and a contingency to the threads that are the building blocks of Godard's particular storytelling. If taken at face value, his account lacks nuance, it is often rhetorically exaggerated, it presumes a universality when in fact it treats a limited European and American framework. But as they are developed in the larger audiovisual layering of the work his themes all acquire far more complicated shadings and associations: the immense loss that occurred with the introduction of sound, the dominance of the Hollywood dream factory, the destruction or colonization of the national cinemas, the failure of film with regard to the Holocaust, and the final devastation of cinema by television and Spielbergism. Primary are his mobile constellations of sound, image, and text that shatter any linear development of ideas, that unfold in a quasi-musical structure, composed rhythmically out of disparate speeds and temporalities. Godard's ambition, which he has insisted on, was not a project of thinking about images but a project in which images themselves would operate like thought, would become, in his words, "a form that thinks."

In interviews, Godard has mentioned how art history was of little value in providing models or starting points for his history of cinema project. He stressed, however, that there were two exceptions: the works of Elie Faure and André Malraux, and both of them figure in crucial ways in *Histoire(s)*. Malraux in particular provided Godard with the example of a historical project with important parallels to his own undertaking. Many people forget or choose to ignore the fact that the text which finally took shape in the 1950s as *Les voix de silence* had its intellectual genesis in the antifascist struggles of the 1930s. Like Benjamin, Malraux meditated on the consequences of both the modern museum and the effects of photographic reproduction on our relation to artworks. Malraux, with even less nostalgia than Benjamin, saw the deracination of art from its original meanings and uses as irrevocable and unlamentable. At the same time, he refused to accept that artifacts of the past thus became only mute, inert traces of lost and alien cultures. In the 1930s the idea of discovering new and unforeseen commonalities and resonances between historically disparate objects was a means of opposing pervasive Spenglerian notions which saw civilizations as inescapably insular and non-communicating with each other. Thus, the guiding impetus of Malraux's art history was to counter the reactionary and racist implications of Spengler's hierarchies and segregations, and also to repudiate the ominous cultural prohibitions he saw expanding in the Soviet Union. Even as he made one of the greatest of all political films,

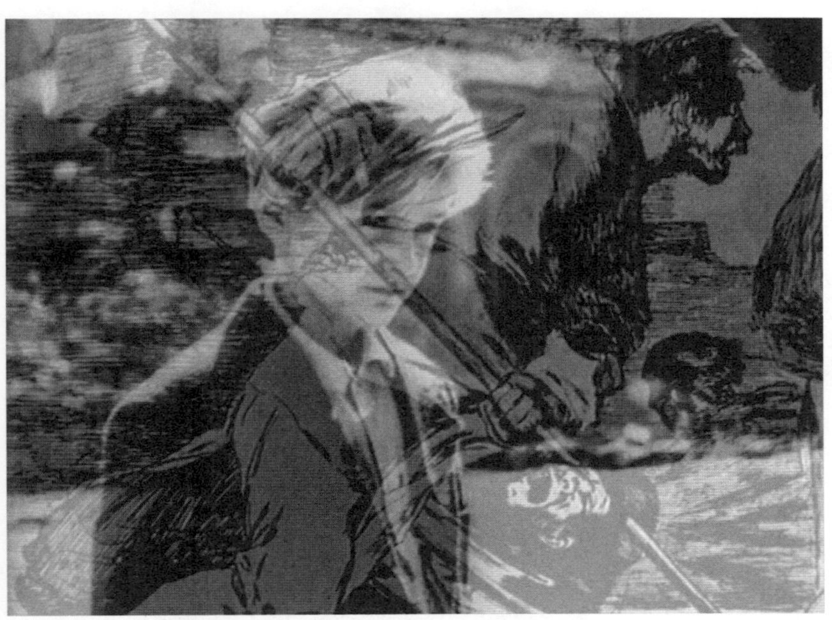

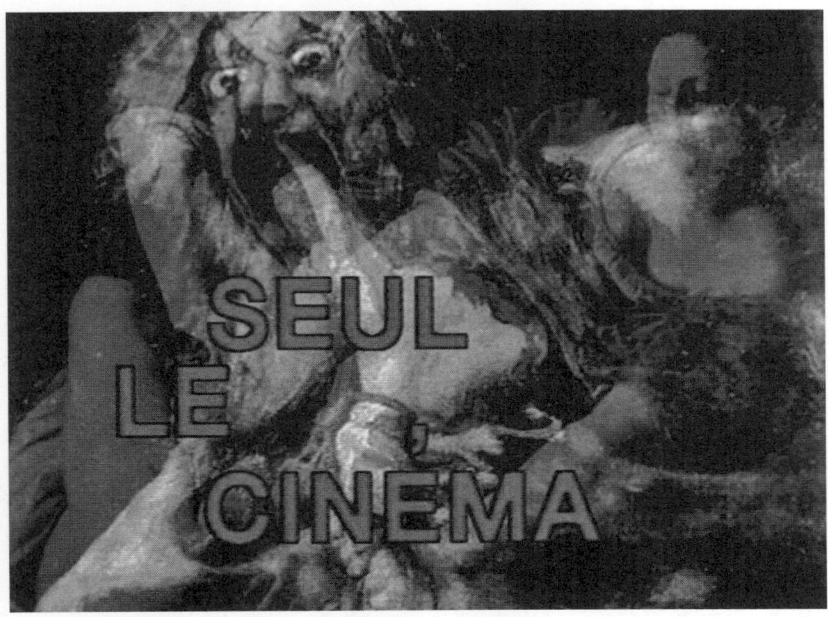

Jean-Luc Godard, *Histoire(s) du cinéma*, 1988–98.

L'espoir (1937) in the midst of the Spanish Civil War, he was insistent on the comparable political importance of his notion of the imaginary museum and the cultural affirmations that were possible because of it.

Obviously, there are enormous differences between these projects, and Godard is hardly uncritically affiliating his own work with Malraux's. But Godard is cognizant that cinema, within a far briefer time span, has undergone an irreversible loss of its origins and conditions of possibility. Just as artworks were uprooted and recreated as photographic images, the entire universe of cinema is either chemically disintegrating or has been transubstantiated into digital formats of various kinds. As Malraux believed that there could be no recovery of an originary relationship to artworks, Godard also refused the possibility of recuperating an innocent relationship to historical cinema.

Godard places Malraux within a critical/historical genealogy on which his own project is founded and with which it is in many ways continuous. He maps out a sequence of names, leading from Diderot, Baudelaire, and Eugène Fromentin to Elie Faure, Malraux, and then to Truffaut, Serge Daney, and implicitly Godard himself. Within the larger French tradition of criticism, he thus foregrounds a subcategory of writers for whom the visual arts are at least as important as literature, and whose representatives include poets, novelists, painters, and filmmakers. For Godard, each of these figures is linked to his history of cinema in essential ways, and each shares a preoccupation with the boundary lines at which one art form overlaps with or dissolves into another.

Baudelaire's work, in particular, marks the beginning of a shift in which existing pictorial art is reimagined and rediscovered to become the basis for an unprecedented set of perceptual and creative possibilities, which Godard locates within his expanded model of the cinematograph. Of the numerous texts that have an auditory presence in *Histoire(s) du cinéma*, the most striking is Baudelaire's "Le Voyage" from 1859, of which long sections are recited within a densely layered sound/image montage. Written in a pivotal year of Baudelaire's career, this masterpiece of romantic disillusionment discloses the futility and disappointment of actual voyages. Its words reverberate in the film against the terminal stasis of J. M. W. Turner's funereal ship at anchor from 1842. Godard has insisted that Baudelaire's poem contains not just an anticipation of cinema but a partial invention of it. Its general evocation of the boredom and bitterness of experience in a flattened, disenchanted world describes the conditions for new kinds of journeys or dislocations that can occur without movement in space, in its figuration of an apparitional screen on which images and memories are projected:

Nous voulons voyager sans vapeur et sans voile!
Faites, pour égayer l'ennui de nos prisons
Passer sur nos esprits, tendus commes une toile
Vos souvenirs avecs leurs cadres d'horizon

We would fain travel without steam or sail
To enliven the tedium of our prisons,
project onto our minds which are stretched tight like canvas,
your horizon-framed memories.
(Francis Scarfe, prose translation, 1961)

And in the extraordinary change of tone at its conclusion, "Le Voyage" extends the possibility of encountering a previously unseen world of experience with the wonderment of youth, although not its innocence.

Turner's painting is important for its materialization of Baudelaire's "toile," the ship's blank and darkened sail, stretched tight, a virtual surface for projection, ready to be struck by the flashes of light shining elsewhere in the painting. Godard has commented on this section of film: "Having that poem read aloud gave me a lot of thoughts, that perhaps others had had already, but that came to me suddenly. I understood that Baudelaire, in fact, did not write that poem at that time by chance, and that it described cinema."[3] Godard was likely aware that another poet, also in 1859, imagined a screenlike surface on which one could witness a luminous and living representation of history. In the opening pages of Victor Hugo's *La lĕgende des siècles*, the poet announces how "the wall of the centuries" appeared to him, with vision after vision unfolding in flickering light and shadow before his eyes. Of all the centuries that Hugo surveys in this sprawling work, the longest century is, of course, his own, the nineteenth.

Godard's larger suggestion here is that the material basis for cinema, including projection, owes as much to the imaginative labor of poets and writers such as Baudelaire, Hugo, Zola, and Charles Cros as it does to any nineteenth-century traditions of applied science or mechanical bricolage. One of the many pronouncements that he works with repetitively throughout his film is, referring to cinema: "Not an art, not a technique, a mystery." The aphoristic force of these words disperses and multiplies their meanings, and Godard is indicating the insufficiency of either of these categories for understanding the experience of the cinematic image. Nor can cinema be explained as a hybrid of the two, with a catch phrase like "the industrial art." Rather, he is proposing that we are only at the beginning of figuring out what cinema was.

Given his preoccupation with "Le Voyage," Godard no doubt would have engaged with what seems to be Baudelaire's manifest disavowal of any collective political hopes in the reference to the visionary socialist Étienne Cabet and his popular utopian novel *Voyage en Icarie* from the early 1840s. This reference in the poem has long been seen as Baudelaire's ironic repudiation of any remnants of his brief socialist/republican identifications from 1848. However, in Godard's dialectical reading of the poem, the dream of an egalitarian and collective social world is not so easily erased or deleted as one of the determinations of this voyage, whose point of departure is the deathly estrangement and heartlessness of a Second Empire life-world. Godard plainly understands that a key aim of utopian imagery is to produce problems, not to solve them. Evocations of voyages have remained crucial for him in the years since making *Histoire(s)*, both in his problematic Pompidou Center exhibition in 2006, *Voyage(s) en utopie*, and, in the same year, *Film socialisme*. In the latter, an allegorical sea voyage is part of a single long European century that seems to be begin on the night of August 4, 1789, and whose resolution still hangs in the balance in the fractured Europe of 2010. It's a film that makes clear the ways in which the political history of this long period is inseparable from a parallel or intertwining history of the camera arts.

Godard's *Histoire(s)* asks whether the ghostly remains of what had been cinema could become pieces of new creative or critical practices, or even new models of thought itself. His assumption is that the spectral persistence of film, in whatever ruined forms of afterlife, can still be deployed in ways that unsettle the amnesias and evasions of the present. If cinema is to be rescued from oblivion, it can only be to ensure the remembrance of catastrophe and of unfulfilled emancipation. *Histoire(s)* foregrounds the specific historical circumstances that surround its making with pointed references to civil conflict and genocide in Rwanda and the Balkans, reverberating back through the preceding disasters of the twentieth century. Godard is not interested in the maintenance of a merely documentary or archival memory, except as a resource for contemporary experimentation. His response to historical forgetting is not a project of recovery or preservation but of invention and transformation. Godard has often been faulted for sustaining a naive faith in the power of images to transmit revelatory meanings and affects, but nothing could be further from his practice than a notion that an image, whether painting, film, or photograph, can retain any intrinsic affectivity or essential meaning over time. In *Éloge de l'amour* (2001), which recapitulated some of the themes of *Histoire(s)*, Godard implies that each generation must wage its own battle against historical amnesia from the lived conditions of its unique historical vantage point, and that this struggle necessitates a remaking of the techniques and languages available to it. The only way an image/artifact escapes the ossification of veneration or repetition is through a collision with unforeseen materialities which open onto the ethical and political exigencies of the present.

1. Jacques Rancière, *The Future of the Image*, trans. Gregory Elliott (London: Verso, 2007), p. 45.
2. Gilles Deleuze, *Cinema 2: The Time-Image*, trans. Hugh Tomlinson and Robert Galeta (Minneapolis: University of Minnesota Press, 1989), p. 165.
3. Jean-Luc Godard and Youssef Ishaghpour, *Cinema: The Archaeology of Film and the Memory of a Century*, trans. John Howe (Oxford: Berg, 2005), p. 56.

This is an expanded version of a text originally published in Meg McLagan and Yates McKee, eds., *Sensible Politics: The Visual Culture of Nongovernmental Politics* (New York: Zone Books, 2012).

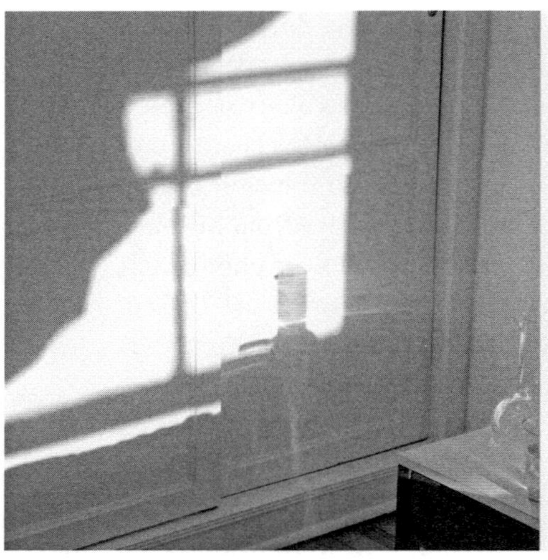

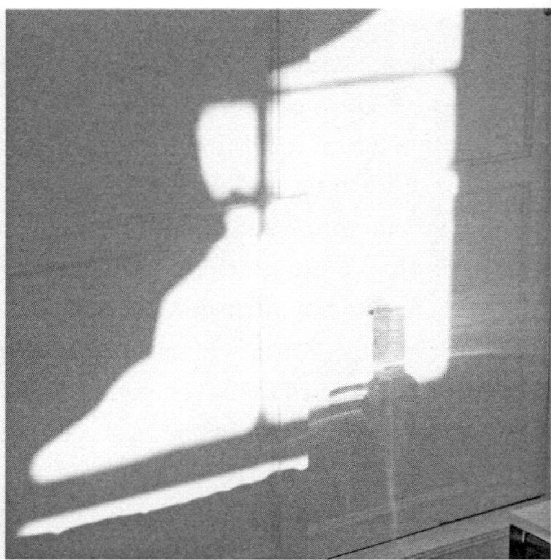

Uta Barth, *Sundial (07.5)*, 2007.

Uta Barth: The Singularity of the Everyday

The 1990s, when Uta Barth staked out many of the defining concerns of her work, were a crucial historical threshold for visual practices of many kinds and whose consequences continue to reverberate in the present. During this decade, a cultural awareness emerged, on many different levels, of the far-reaching impact of new forms of digital media. The displacement of older, long-standing understandings of photography and film generated a flood of critical attempts to address this shift, along with many obituaries and laments for the loss of these systems of reference, meaning, and technique. The 1970s, in contrast, seem a different era when it was still possible to approach film and photography as though they were media for which essential and enduring features could be defined, in spite of their changing historical forms. However, efforts to articulate some core identity of photography (whether by Susan Sontag, Roland Barthes, or others) inevitably foundered by being based on a restricted view of what defines it, usually privileging camera-made images resulting from a very limited range of lens openings and shutter speeds. From its beginnings, photography encompassed a far wider set of luminous possibilities that were never compatible with the normative models of objectivity and verisimilitude which long dominated critical accounts of its history.

Although I will not pursue the larger cultural context of Barth's work in this essay, it is no doubt likely that the breakdown and abandonment of enduring assumptions about the meanings of photography have allowed her images to be seen and read in ways that might not have been possible a decade or more earlier. For one aspect of her practice, whether a central one or not, is a determined enlargement of what can constitute the vocabulary of a photographer. Her disavowal of many of the familiar expectations of the "photographic" is not simply in the service of a polemical exploration of expanded formal or technical possibilities. Many of the prominent features of her work derive from goals that are more elusive and reflective in nature. Numerous critics have observed that photography and its resources, whether digital or analog, are a means for Barth to explore the operation of perception and the ambiguous access it allows to the world. Perhaps this could be said of various other photographers as well, but here I will attempt to suggest some of the unique ambitions of her work.

If the nuances of human vision are an enduring concern of Barth's, this is ultimately part of a meditation on the nature of experience itself. One layer of her work could be tentatively termed "phenomenological" in that she explores the specific ways in which we are actually aware of the visual world. That is to say, she is preoccupied with the raw experience of perception as it occurs before or behind our habitual recourse to the seeming unity and coherence of appearances. Equally important, it is a viewpoint that privileges what is immediately perceivable, in contrast to a hermeneutical (or interpretive) position which searches in depth for meanings to be discovered beneath or behind the surface of what we take to be reality. But the primary data of perception for her are not isolable or discrete forms and sensations, which would be the building blocks of a stable visual field. Instead, Barth gives priority to other kinds of phenomena. The contents of perception, as revealed in her images, are transitions, overlappings, indistinct limits, inconstancies, depositionings, and vacancies. She singles out those conditions of vision which make perception nonidentical with itself, which refute the commonsense conviction that the eye provides a seamless mirror image of whatever it encounters.

Of course, these conditions have physiological determinations which are inseparable from the effects of her images. They would include (1) the fact that the human eye has a blind spot; (2) that because of binocular disparity, each individual eye sees a slightly different image; (3) that only a small area of the retina is capable of optical clarity and that most of what we see at any given moment is indistinct, spatially uncertain, and chromatically vague; (4) that the luminous sensitivity of the eye produces afterimages that effectively prolong past perceptions into our experience of the present; (5) that our visual field comes into being, not through the instantaneous intake of a complete image but through a complex aggregate of eye movements that provisionally assemble a homogenous, in-focus appearance of reality. This list could be expanded substantially, but it already suggests examples of the specific ways in which Barth understands that the familiarity of the world is dependent on a forgetting or repression of how we actually see. But the scientific basis (whether physiological or neurological) of perceptual operations is hardly a central concern for her, nor is any of her work, in any sense, a demonstration of "how vision works."

To put it another way, Barth is primarily interested in what can be discovered through her own attentiveness to how we perceive, and this entails, among other things, being acutely aware of the experience of attention itself. She understands how looking intently at anything will redirect our focus toward the actual operations of vision. This positions her within a long genealogy of artists whose creative priorities manifest a related concern with the lived ambiguities of visual perception, including Turner, Cézanne, Rothko, James Turrell, and many more. Common to these otherwise very different artists are practices derived from their discernment of the subjective elements that are always part of any perceptual access to the world. Barth, for her part, is particularly attuned to the instabilities and absences within vision which disrupt the linearity of time and deflect the easy knowability of what seems most immediate. She has learned firsthand how the act of looking at any object or area of interest can lead, not to a fixing or clarifying of what is seen, but to a disturbance of its solidity and legibility.

Thus central to her work is the making of images, or series of images, that uncover something revelatory about the ambivalences of our perceptual relation to the world. Clearly, in pursuit of these goals, she has thought deeply about the capacities and limits of the camera, a form of nonhuman machine vision. But it is crucial to understand that her photographs are not meant to provide a transcription or simulation of her own sensory intuitions. An enactment of subjective vision is not her aim, in the way this might said, for example, of some of the work of Stan Brakhage. The latter sought to reclaim the visionary and creative possibilities of the

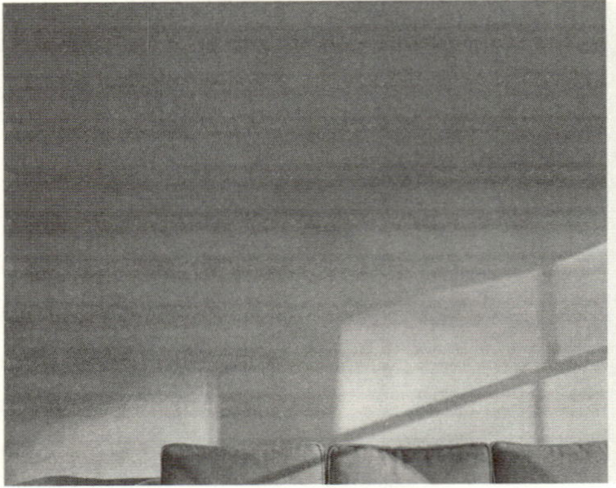
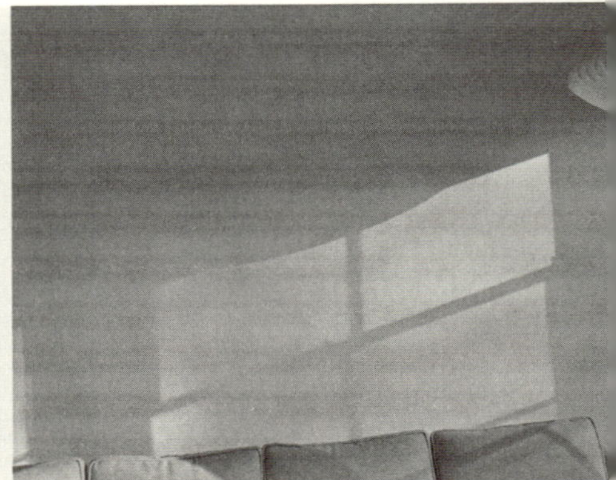

Uta Barth, *Untitled (aot 4)*, 2000.

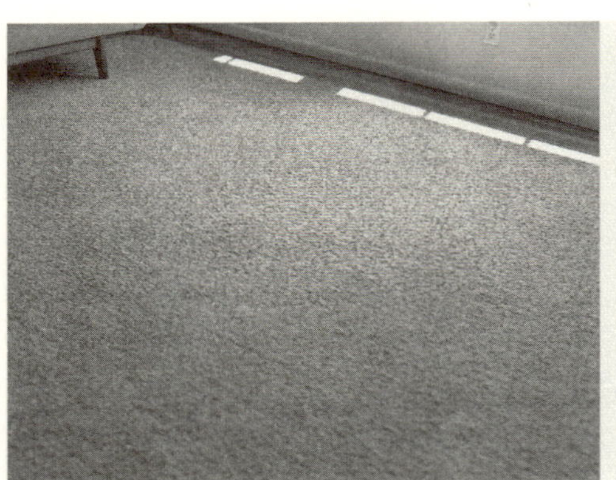
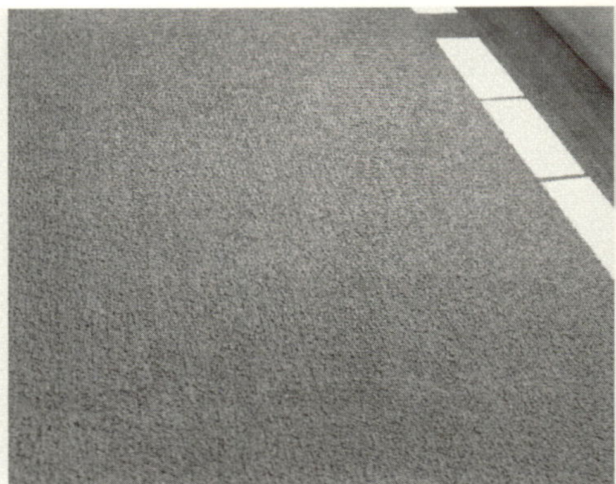

Uta Barth, *Untitled (aot 1)*, 2000.

eye by affirming the richness of a subjective vision over the automatic and unthinking habits of looking which dominate most of our lives. Barth, in contrast, is concerned with the dispossession of self that a sustained visual attentiveness can produce. And it is within the most routine and familiar patterns that sight becomes something deindividualized, cut loose from both intentionality and mastery.

Barth's is one of the few bodies of work in contemporary art in which we can see the ongoing articulation of a mode of *anonymous* seeing. Not anonymous in the sense of concealment, but rather the older connotation of having no name or identity. It is a seeing that labors to free itself from the limitations or confines of subjectivity or personality. A seeing that renounces the aim of holding on to its objects, of extracting from them a confirmation of the depth or distinctiveness of the self. It must be emphasized that the anonymity in question is unrelated to the unmotivated or mechanical "objectivity" of the camera. Barth, even though working with the camera, is seeking something fundamentally different, and much harder won. It is an abstaining from a perspicacity which comprehendingly absorbs and recognizes what it perceives. It is anonymous in its reticence about positivity and affirmation, and it is marked by its deflection of attention to what is not seen, or is seen only as that which escapes seeing, as the invisibility of the visible. Much of Barth's work is an acquiescence to the indeterminacy of phenomena and to the dispersion of what might be thought of as the present. Yet she simultaneously conveys the unsettling intimacy and proximity of this experience of the fugitive and ungraspable.

In a closely related way, Barth's work is inseparable from its embeddedness in the temporality of the everyday. Countless photographers, especially in the last half century, have been characterized as chroniclers of the everyday, but few have ever examined this mercurial category as rigorously or as uniquely as Barth. In an obvious way, the "content" of her images is the unremarkable, the already known milieu of what is close at hand, for example a tree or telephone pole that one sees outside one's window every morning. But it is within this sphere of what is familiar beyond notice that her photographs contain something unprecedented, in the way they address the very heart of the quotidian. These notions—the everyday and the quotidian—are remarkably interchangeable in their accumulated meanings: the notion of recurrence on a daily basis but also something that is ordinary, commonplace, or unexceptional. But the latter word (with its Latin roots) has a particular and longstanding sense of time as that which is marked or counted, in its recurring diurnal form.

Barth's installation *Sundial* (2007) is of special relevance here for its sequence of images that record the (apparent) passage of late afternoon sunlight on the walls, furniture, and floors of a home. Each image in this stunning work exposes an ephemeral interlacing of surfaces, reflections, and luminous refractions which Barth also presents in reversals and inversions. Light and shadow are removed from a logic of figure/ground and sunlight is both illuminated surface and the black sun of an optical afterimage. A clock, seen on the wall in several images, with its specification of different instants, seems oddly unsynchronized with the temporality of the setting sun's radiance. Clearly the evocation of the sundial, with its direct relation to solar position, evokes a form of measurement radically distinct from the abstract and metric composition of clock time. Its tracking of a moving shadow long exemplified a model of time made visible as a smooth and ceaseless flow, as unbroken as the turning of the earth.

But Barth's *Sundial* affords no access to anything like a stream of time. Rather, the structure of her installation reveals time to be a succession of contiguous but not continuous arrangements. The incessant activity of the eye in its focusing and refocusing, its constant oscillation between fixation and movement, and in its continual adjustments to luminous and chromatic modulations—it discloses intermittently and haltingly, an irreducibly plural world, a world made up of spacings and interruptions. These are not conditions supportive of a subject who requires the illusion of homogenous time as the medium for action and self-recognition. In contrast, the everyday is the milieu of the impersonal, of that which escapes both individual and social particularity. The philosopher Jean-Luc Nancy has portrayed the "undifferentiated singularity of the everyday" in a way that seems close to Barth's project. Within the quotidian he sees "its constantly renewed rupture, its polymorphy and its polyphony, its relief and its variety. A 'day' is not simply a unit for counting; it is the turning of the world—each time singular. And days, indeed every day, could not be similar if they were not first different, difference itself."[1]

In a present in which the impoverishment and routinization of human perception is only intensifying, the urgency and importance of Barth's art is incontestable. If her photography is deemed "difficult" it is a measure of the lucidity with which she explores the often inexpressible texture of lived experience. She solicits from the viewer a patience, a suspension of the pervasive habits and speeds of visual consumption. To spend time with Barth's work is to enter, even haltingly, into a self-effacing vision freed up from the imperative to produce meaning. Hers is a wayward seeing, in that it functions without seeking points of focus, climax, or attraction. It is a vision whose fragile exercise occurs only by resisting a congealing of its objects into images. She offers us both the immediacy and the otherness of a visual world that is beyond certainty and sameness, situated somewhere between opacity and clarity.

1. Jean-Luc Nancy, *Being Singular Plural*, trans. Robert D. Richardson (Stanford: Stanford University Press, 2000), p. 9.

Originally published in *Uta Barth: The Long Now*, eds. Russell Ferguson and Holly Myers (New York: Gregory R. Miller and Co., 2010).

John Berger, Art Critic in Dark Times

I'm going to begin with an observation that I believe would have been of particular interest for John Berger. Some of you from Columbia and elsewhere may know that we are not gathered here in a generic and anonymous classroom building on a North American university campus but in a place of catastrophic historical significance. When students pass through its main entrance, few if any take notice of a tarnished metal plaque on the wall that officially declares Pupin Hall to be a Registered National Historic Landmark. Notably, the plaque gives no indication as to why this site has been so designated. For three years from 1939 to 1941, several floors below where we're now sitting, crucial research on nuclear fission by Enrico Fermi and his team provided the scientific foundations of the Manhattan Project. The isolation of the isotope U-235 in Columbia's laboratories culminated in the making and detonation of the first atomic weapons on human populations.

I want to use the location of this conference in this ghostly Manhattan Project site to recall one of John Berger's most piercing essays, written in the spring of 2002, "War Against Terrorism or a Terrorist War?" In it he juxtaposes the aerial bombings by the United States of Hiroshima and Nagasaki with the airliner attacks on September 11, 2001 and poses the question of what actions merit being designated as terrorism. It was courageously written during a fearful time when there was a broad intolerance, even an effective prohibition, on any attempts to assess the September 11 events in a historical context. In this essay Berger foregrounds two themes that run through much his later writing, beginning in the

1990s: (1) the massive erasures and disablings of historical memory and (2) the parallel corruption and falsification of language and public forms of communication. For Berger, the mendacity with which language is used by institutional power is hardly something recent, as he quotes from President Truman's message to the American people days after the destruction of Hiroshima, when he announced that "a new kind of bomb had been dropped on a Japanese army base." He also cites the grotesque claim by General Leslie Groves, head of the Manhattan Project, that "radiation poisoning was a painless, even a very pleasant way to die."

But Berger directs most of his anger at the lying and hypocrisy that permeated the aftermath of September 11 in this country. He points to a widely circulated document signed by sixty US academics and intellectuals in February 2002 titled "What We're Fighting For: A Letter from America." The signatories cynically cite Saint Augustine, Martin Luther King Jr., and others to fabricate a preposterous and fatuous argument for the morality of mass murder. The letter was a chilling endorsement of Operation Enduring Freedom, in which tens of thousands of Afghan civilians died in US bombings in the last months of 2001 and beginning of 2002 (not to mention the much larger death toll over the following decade). Berger's characterization of these "just war" advocates (who included Michael Walzer, Amitai Etzioni, and Francis Fukuyama) might be his single most scathing piece of writing. But this letter was merely one manifestation of a much wider capitulation to an agenda of American exceptionalism. In both 1945 and 2002, the pernicious and opportunistic misuse of language was, for Berger, directly complicit in the perpetuation of violence on an enormous scale, in which non-Western peoples were destroyed without remorse. The identity of the victims was irrelevant to the perpetrators or to Americans insulated from the horror of technological killing. And as we know, it's a question of violence and terror continuous with the horrific US bombings of civilian targets now ongoing in Syria, Yemen, Iraq, and elsewhere.

Berger's most important work of the 1990s and into the 2000s is found in the extraordinary collections *Hold Everything Dear* and *The Shape of a Pocket*. Driving many of these essays is less a response to the collapse of the USSR and the fall of the Berlin Wall than a witnessing of the emergence and spread of a new, more virulent form of global capitalism. Berger concurs with the overview of the Zapatista leader Marcos that the end of the Cold War signaled the start of the Fourth World War (the Third was the Cold War). The aim of the hegemonic powers is now the conquest of the entire world through the market and the financialization of all aspects of living. Berger's key essay here is "Against the Great Defeat of the World" (1997) with its extraordinary recuperation of Bosch's *Garden of Earthly Delights*. Through this painting, he draws a map of our shattered present: concentration of wealth in fewer and fewer hands, the collapsing of distinctions between the billionaire class and global crime networks, systemic violence that produces the forced migration and homelessness of vast populations. He shows how neoliberalism is facilitated by the degradation of language, the rise of technologies dedicated to misinformation, the crisis of work and of the expropriation of the senses. In another text, he writes, "it is not only animal and plant species which are being destroyed or made extinct today but also set after set of our human priorities. These are systematically sprayed not with pesticides but with 'ethicides,' agents that kill ethics and therefore any notion of history and justice.... And the ethicides are sprayed day and night by the mass news media."[1]

Berger's post-1990 writing and activism is a vibrant refutation of the label left-melancholy, which came out of elite academic circles in the 1990s. Using Freudian terminology, the reactionary left-melancholy analysis pathologized anyone committed to socialism or revolution as backward-looking, paralyzed by loss, and self-punishing. It's hard to think of another writer on the left in recent decades who is less nostalgic, who deploys the words "hope" and "future" so insistently, and who refuses a diminished agenda of identity politics, legislative reforms, and single-issue activism as the limit of the possible. Obviously, there is memory and fidelity to the struggles and defeats of the past, whether of the Commune, Che Guevara, Allende, the Black Panthers, Tupamaros, or the ongoing strivings and setbacks of the Palestinians and many others. But from a *longue durée* vantage point, he insists that "the whole of history is about hopes being sustained, lost, and renewed."

When asked in 2005 if he is still a Marxist, his unapologetic reply is the following: "Never before has the devastation caused by the pursuit of profit, as defined by capitalism, been more extensive than it is today.... How then is it possible not to heed Marx who prophesied and analyzed the devastation?"[2] He was acutely aware of the unbearable levels of despair and immiseration among the global poor, and in one essay after another he evokes the long history of survival and resistance of the poor to shifting regimes of domination and dispossession. The question he continues to pose for all of us: how to sustain or restore the social fabric that capitalism fragments or destroys. Survival, he shows, is aided by forms of local culture in which patterns of sharing and mutual support still persist. But he saw clearly how forced urbanization and rapacious resource extraction were destroying and local and Indigenous culture around the planet, and he persistently honored the ingenuity of survivors and outcasts and their sheer endurance amid desolation, deprivation, and war.

Unlike many others after 1991, he continued to insist that the overriding antagonism of our time is still one of class. He pointedly retains the image of a wall to refute the triumphalist inanities that followed the fall of the Berlin Wall. In 2004, he wrote:

> The essential activity of the rich today is the building of walls. Concrete, bureaucratic, surveillance, security, racist, zone walls. Everywhere the walls separate the desperate poor from those who hope to stay relatively rich... The Wall is the front line of what, long ago, was called class war. On the one side: every armament conceivable, the dream of no-body-bag wars, the media, luxury, hygiene, many passwords to glamour. On the other, stones, short supplies, feuds, the violence of revenge, rampant illness, an acceptance of death and an on-going preoccupation with surviving one more night—perhaps one more week—together. The choice of meaning in the world today is here between the two sides of the wall. The wall is also inside each one of us. Whatever our circumstances, we can choose within ourselves which side of the wall we are attuned to.

Parenthetically, it should be noted that the preceding citation is from an essay ostensibly on the paintings of Francis Bacon.[3]

One can imagine what must have been Berger's impatience or irritation with postmodern notions of a borderless rhizomatic global surface of flows and seamless circuits that somehow had leveled established hierarchies and redistributed power to the multitude. The wall, for him, is a figure for the increasingly harsh forms of exclusion and segregation being imposed across the planet, along with more predatory and lethal forms of repression and neglect. Perhaps most important is Berger's refusal of the enforced invisibility of the immense global underclass, its desperation, and its hopes.

As some have noted, Berger's own work was never an application of Marxist theory, but rather his own experiences and intuitions found confirmation in Marx and others writing in a Marxist tradition. One repeatedly encounters the consonance between Berger's thinking and crucial sections in the *German Ideology* and the *1844 Manuscripts*. Some of the core ideas of his art writing reverberate with Marx on the estrangement of the human senses under capitalism, and his hostility to the influence of Louis Althusser in the 1980s is palpable. For both Marx and Berger, the omnipresence of private property is inseparable from the impoverishment of perception. Looking becomes entangled with ownership, vision becomes the corroboration of possession and having, or looking becomes what incites envy and the bitterness of not having. One of Marx's conclusions here was, "The transcendence of private property is therefore the emancipation of all human senses." We can affiliate this with Berger's declaration that "there is an absolute incompatibility between art and private property..." and he continues with an echo of William Blake—"property must be destroyed before imagination can develop any further."[4] But for Berger perhaps the worst consequence of the reduction of art to commodity status is that "it eliminates art as a potential model of freedom."

Especially for European art after 1850, he shows how social and economic realities make it inevitable that every serious artist comes to be understood in terms of both successes and failures. His remarkable analyses of individual artists detail the difficulty of working and creating between a zone of autonomy on one hand and the often crushing constraints of systemic pressures and inducements on the other. He judges artists on their relation to the shared, lived reality of the world. Either their work points toward a revelatory engagement of this reality or it is an evasion or indifference to it. In his book *Permanent Red* we find this challenging and often cited formulation: "Imagination is the capacity to disclose that which exists." Like the German artist and writer Peter Weiss, Berger believed in the capacity for resistance that can be rooted in art and in other material forms of human labor. He worked from the premise that some artworks are embedded with latent creative powers which, under certain circumstances, can be transformed into living energies. His writing demonstrated how the meaning and force of artworks from the past could be recovered and rechanneled into the exigencies of the present.

I'll conclude with one of the many instances in which Berger reclaims a work from the past for its value as an opening onto the crisis of our own time. The essay in question was written on the occasion of the 1991 bicentenary Géricault exhibition in Paris.[5] But instead of commenting on the art displayed in the halls of the Grand Palais, he responds to an image reproduced on the poster advertising the exhibition which he saw displayed on the streets and subways of Paris. On the poster was one of Géricault's *Portraits of the Insane*, specifically the one often identified as *the Kleptomaniac*, though Berger refers to him as the "Man with Tousled Hair." His essay bypasses all the art historical, medical, psychological, sociohistorical speculation about the work in order to pinpoint what is crucial for him about the painting: it is simply the empathy and pity with which Géricault has looked so unwaveringly at a damaged human being, crushed by burdens we will never learn, and whose links to a world of shared experience and communication have been broken. Whether we deem him mad or not, we are faced in our own time with far vaster numbers of broken and bereft individuals to whom the world is indifferent. Berger here turns to Simone Weil for her avowal that the one of hardest tasks we face is the recognition of affliction, the recognition that the sufferer exists. This is what she calls the highest form of attention. For Berger, what Géricault's portrait retains for us in the present is simply a trace of the fragile human faculty of compassion. "Compassion," he writes, "has no place in the natural order of the world which operates on the basis of necessity...compassion opposes this order and is therefore best thought of as being in some way supernatural." Typically, his conclusion is charged with threads of hope—"The poster looked down on Paris as might a ghost. Not the ghost of the man with tousled hair, nor Géricault's, but the ghost of a special form of attention, which for two centuries had been marginalized but which every day now was becoming less obsolete."

1. John Berger, *Hold Everything Dear: Dispatches on Survival and Resistance* (New York: Vintage, 2008), p. 89.
2. John Berger, "Ten Dispatches About Place," in *Hold Everything Dear*, p. 119.
3. John Berger, "Prophet of a Pitiless World," *The Guardian*, May 28, 2004.
4. John Berger, *Permanent Red: Essays in Seeing* (London: Methuen, 1960), p. 7.
5. John Berger, *Portraits: John Berger on Artists*, ed. Tom Overton (London: Verso, 2015), pp. 209–14.

Text of a lecture presented at the symposium *A Tribute to John Berger*, March 30–31, 2017, Columbia University. It also appeared in *Politics/Letters* 8 (2017).

Terminal Radiance

Among the many billion diversions accessible on YouTube is a video of film footage taken through the window of a Soviet bomber on October 30, 1961, moments after dropping the so-called Tsar Bomba on the island of Novaya Zemlya above the Arctic Circle. The film records what is by far the largest human-caused explosion ever on the planet, a fifty-eight-megaton hydrogen bomb, four times more powerful than any prior or subsequent blast. When set against the hundreds of films of other nuclear explosions, its singularity isn't visually obvious. One listens to the narration of stupefying statistics: the mushroom cloud is over forty miles high, the fireball five miles in diameter; it is 3,800 times the destructiveness of a Hiroshima-size weapon, ensuring the annihilation of anything living within a sixty-mile radius of its impact. But to watch this film and gape at the colossal radial symmetries of the detonation and its ghostly luminosities is to succumb to an aestheticization of this extreme limit of nuclear terror.

Ever since the 1950s, film clips of US nuclear tests were woven into the kitsch of Cold War consumer culture but also into the work of artists such as Bruce Conner. Images of the South Pacific blasts were part of an iconography of scientific mastery that partly domesticated nuclear savagery and aligned it with fantasies of material progress and middle-class affluence. In his explorations of the links between kitsch and death, Saul Friedlander remarks that kitsch produces "the neutralization of extreme situations" by making death into something ritualized or stylized that effaces the actual horror.[1] He identifies in Nazi kitsch a consistent presentation of death as "paroxysm" or "explosion." The atomic test films obviously are the product different historical factors, but their fascination can clearly be traced to some of the same psychic processes. The video of an atomic-bomb explosion replicates a pornographic image in its endlessly repeatable display of a convulsive discharge of energy on an unimaginable scale, and the Tsar Bomba film is the ultimate, unsurpassable "money shot" of a potency and expenditure beyond measure.

Steven Shaviro has noted the interconnection between pornography and horror as crucial to understanding the attraction of the cinematic image.[2] His association of film spectatorship with "the extinction of sight" is extravagantly demonstrated by film of an event that is, from a human vantage point, literally unseeable: even distant viewers of a nuclear blast will be blinded by third-degree burns on an unshielded retina. Part of the obscenity of the test films, made solely for analysis in the development and enhancement of future weapons, is the making visible of the unwatchable. A viewer occupies the vantage point of the recording device, the mechanical eye of the perpetrator, of the weapons designers. Using the formulation of Rey Chow, these films position the world itself as a target, and thus an object to be destroyed.[3] The formal properties of the spheroidal fireball or the swirling undulations of the mushroom cloud lodge the event within the confines of the image and spectacle. The unthinkable, unutterable violence of this outer limit of the real is deleted.

It's perhaps understandable, if not justifiable, that Alain Badiou chose to omit any reference to the leveling of Hiroshima and Nagasaki (or to the nuclear arms race) in his book *The Century* on the implacable violence that he sees as the defining heart of the twentieth century.[4] Badiou postulates a pervasive and quasi-heroic "passion for the real" which sanctioned remorseless violence in the name of various emancipatory dreams, militant programs, or aesthetic experimentations. But his imagined history of "an absolute politics" of purification and antagonism is hopelessly irreconcilable with the visionless, futureless, biocidal madness of nuclear war. The Tsar Bomba, built by a team led by Andrei Sakharov, is the culmination of a "project" that points only to the annihilation of historical time and the vaporization of any space of social or political relations.

The filmic representation of a nuclear explosion is an erasure of its invisible lethality. The physics of the bomb are inseparable from the scientific investigations of the nonvisible wavelengths of the electromagnetic spectrum beginning in the late nineteenth century. During the years 1886–1914 there is a cascading accumulation of research discoveries that spawned nuclear weapons and many other features of the techno-political-social world we inhabit more than a century later. A very cursory outline of these years would include the names Hertz (radio waves), Roentgen (x-rays), Becquerel and the Curies (radioactivity), Villard and then Rutherford and Bohr (gamma rays). Of course these discoveries and their irrevocable remaking of visibility did not occur fortuitously or as part of some inevitable advancement of objective scientific knowledge. Rather, the devaluation of human sight happened within powerful institutional complexes specific to the nation-states that were, during the same years, competing for military and economic domination on a global scale.

One of the most important developments of that 1886–1914 period was the research on the radioactive properties of uranium which culminated over two decades later with the discovery of nuclear fission and the making of an atomic bomb. The use of these weapons brought into being, for the first time, conditions in which both visible and invisible wavelengths of the spectrum were directed against human life. In the initial microseconds after a nuclear blast, invisible gamma radiation is the first to hit the human body, destroying it at a cellular level, ripping apart DNA molecules. Following the gamma-ray burst are intense and blinding levels of visible light accompanied by the thermal flash of heat that sets clothes and hair on fire and melts eyeballs. Human vision becomes irreversibly exiled from a world in which in which this threshold of technological terror has been crossed, in which forms of radiant energy are manipulated to produce harmfulness on an unimaginable scale. This is the energy that Akira Lippit refers to as "the catastrophic light of atoms."[5]

When the Tsar Bomba detonated, the temperature of the five-mile-wide fireball reached 150 million degrees Fahrenheit, hotter than the sun. That human enterprise was able to rival, even briefly, the heat of the sun on earth might tempt some to invoke the "technological sublime." But there is no possible standpoint from which a ruinous demonstration of malevolent scientific tinkering can be framed by aesthetic categories. The supposed disabling of the imagination by the sublime and the accompanying inadequacy of representation become irrelevant, preposterous problems. Referring to the accumulated consequences of Hiroshima, Auschwitz, and

Fukushima, Jean-Luc Nancy writes that human life, in its capacity to think and to create, "is precipitated into a condition worse than misery itself: a stupor, a distractedness, a horror, a hopeless torpor."[6] It's amid such a pervasive collective stupor that Barack Obama's 2016 authorization of a trillion-dollar program to "modernize" America's nuclear weapons arsenal elicited not even a whisper of protest from his admirers.

1. Saul Friedlander, *Reflections on Nazism: An Essay on Kitsch and Death* (New York: Harper & Row, 1984), pp. 42–43.
2. Steven Shaviro, *The Cinematic Body* (Minneapolis: University of Minnesota Press, 1991), p. 54.
3. See Rey Chow, *The Age of the World Target: Self-Referentiality in War, Theory, and Comparative Work* (Durham, NC: Duke University Press, 2006).
4. Alain Badiou, *The Century,* trans. Alberto Toscano (Cambridge: Polity Press, 2007).
5. Akira Mizuta Lippit, *Atomic Light (Shadow Optics)* (Minneapolis: University of Minnesota Press, 2005), pp. 81–84.
6. Jean-Luc Nancy, *After Fukushima: The Equivalence of Catastrophes*, trans. Charlotte Mandell (New York: Fordham University Press, 2015), p. 11.

Originally published in the anthology *Unwatchable*, eds. Nicholas Baer, Maggie Hennefeld, Laura Horak, and Gunnar Iversen (New Brunswick, NJ: Rutgers University Press, 2019).

ACKNOWLEDGMENTS

Much of the writing in this collection parallels my long involvement with Zone Books. It would be hard to overestimate how my own thinking has been nourished by the critical and creative milieu that has collectively been sustained at the press. I'm fortunate to have collaborated on so many consequential projects with Michel Feher, Ramona Naddaff, Meighan Gale, and Hal Foster. In particular, I want to thank Michel for all that I've learned from him and, most importantly, for his loyalty and generosity as a friend. I'm also appreciative of Kyra Simone's contribution to the book's production and of Julie Fry's superb design. Lisa Peck, Stefaan van Liefferinge, Gabriel Rodriguez, and Tim Trombley of the Media Center for Art History at Columbia provided much needed assistance. Special thanks to my family for their love and support

Regrettably, it would be an impossible task to name all of the many friends, colleagues, students, artists, curators, and editors who, over several decades and in countless ways, contributed to the making of the essays in this book and to whom I'm enduringly grateful. I've chosen to use this retrospective project as an occasion to thank some of the extraordinary teachers and mentors who were an immeasurable part of my intellectual and aesthetic formation. These include my high school teachers Robin Campbell, George Carow, Ray Goodlatte, and Ed Shore; my teachers at the San Francisco Art Institute: James Broughton, Jerry Burchard, John Collier Jr., Linda Connor, Ralph Gibson, Larry Jordan, George Kuchar, Gary Metz, Gunvor Nelson, and Tom Zimmerman; my professors at Columbia during my undergraduate and graduate school years: Dilip Balamore, F. W. Dupee, George Holoch, Bert M-P. Leefmans, Sylvère Lotringer, Joseph Masheck, David Rosand, John D. Rosenberg, Edward Said, Jean Sareil, Meyer Schapiro, Karl-Ludwig Selig, and John Toews.

INDEX

Locators in italic type indicate figures.

IMAGE CREDITS

13. Alvin Comiter. © Allan Kaprow Estate, courtesy Hauser & Wirth.
16. Framart Studio, Naples. © Allan Kaprow Estate, courtesy Hauser & Wirth.
22. © The Museum of Modern Art/Licensed by SCALA/Art Resource, NY, © ARS, NY.
27. Philadelphia Museum of Art: The Louise and Walter Arensberg Collection, 1950, 1950-134-51. © Artists Rights Society (ARS), New York/ADAGP, Paris/Association Marcel Duchamp.
34, 37, 40. Courtesy of the artist and Ronald Feldman Gallery, New York.
44, 46, 47, 49, 52. © Ed Ruscha.
54, 57, 59, 60, 62, 63, 65, 66. © Dennis Oppenheim, courtesy Dennis Oppenheim Estate.
68, 71, 72. Courtesy of the artist and Ocean Earth Construction and Development Corp.
80. PictureLux/The Hollywood Archive/Alamy Stock Photo.
85. Ronald Grant Archive/Alamy Stock Photo.
87. Collection Christophel/Alamy Stock Photo.
96. © Gretchen Bender Estate, courtesy Sprüth Magers.
98. Gravure française/Alamy Stock Photo.
99. Courtesy Roughneck Kennels.
105. *Top:* Mary Ann Moorman (Mary Krahmer), Niday Picture Library/Alamy Stock Photo. *Bottom:* John F. Turner. Courtesy of Chip Lord and SFMOMA Collection. © Ant Farm.
114. Grove Press/Photofest. © Grove Press.
116. Collection MoMA, New York. © Archigram.
118. Erwin Reichman, courtesy of Coop Himmelb(l)au Archives.
122. Andreas Rossetti, 2015. © Gretchen Bender Estate, courtesy Sprüth Magers.
125. FXP Photography, 2017. © Gretchen Bender Estate, courtesy Sprüth Magers.
131. Philo T. Farnsworth Photograph Collection, Special Collections, J. Willard Marriott Library, The University of Utah.
135. Alamy Stock Photo.

140, 144. Courtesy of OMA.

151. Library of Congress.

153. Philadelphia Museum of Art: Gift of Helen Tyson Madeira, 1977.

160. Photofest.

164. The Solomon R. Guggenheim Foundation, New York Panza Collection/© ARS, NY.

168. Beinecke Rare Book and Manuscript Library, Yale University.

171. World History Archive/Alamy Stock Photo.

174. THA, PictureLux/The Hollywood Archive/Alamy Stock Photo.

179, 182. Thibault Jeanson, courtesy Dia Art Foundation, New York. © 2022 Robert Irwin/ Artists Rights Society (ARS), New York.

185. © 2022 Robert Irwin/Artists Rights Society (ARS), New York.

190. Rembrandt van Rijn, *The Syndics of the Clothmakers' Guild*, 1662. Rijksmuseum, Amsterdam, Netherlands.

194. © Cerith Wyn Evans. Photo © Rudi Wilderjans. Courtesy White Cube.

197. © Cerith Wyn Evans. Photo © White Cube (Todd-White Art Photography).

206. Wikimedia Commons.

208. Herve Veronese. Digital Image © CNAC/MNAM, Dist. RMN-Grand Palais/ Art Resource, NY. Location: Musée National d'Art Moderne/Centre Georges Pompidou/Paris/France.

211. © Estate of László Moholy-Nagy/ARS, New York.

212. © William Kentridge. Courtesy of the artist and Marian Goodman Gallery.

214. © Bridget Riley 2021. All rights reserved.

219. Museum of Fine Arts Boston, purchased with funds donated by the Catherine and Paul Buttenwieser Fund, Mr. and Mrs. Martin M. Hale, gift of the Linde Family Foundation, and Eloise and Arthur Hodges 2000.978. Photo © 1978 Museum of Fine Arts Boston.

238, 242. Courtesy of the artist and Tanya Bonakdar Gallery, New York/Los Angeles.

Series design by Julie Fry
Typesetting by Meighan Gale
Image placement and production by Julie Fry
Printed and bound by Maple Press